What Every Manager Needs to Know About MARKETING

What Every Manager Needs to Know About MARKETING

David J. Freiman, Editor

Excerpted from the
AMA Management Handbook, Second Edition,
William K. Fallon, General Editor

American Management Association

This book is available at a special
discount when ordered in bulk quantities.
For information, contact Special Sales Department,
AMACOM, a division of American Management Association,
135 West 50th Street, New York, NY 10020.

Library of Congress Cataloging-in-Publication Data

What every manager needs to know about marketing.

   "Excerpted from the AMA management handbook, second
edition, William K. Fallon, general edition."
   Includes index.
   1. Marketing.   I. Freiman, David J.   II. AMA management handbook.   2nd ed.
HF5415.W48 1986   658.8   86-47625
ISBN 0-8144-7666-X

Printing number

10 9 8 7 6 5 4 3 2

Publisher's Note

The revised and expanded second edition of the *AMA Management Handbook,* originally published in 1983, is the single most comprehensive source of information on management available today. Over 1,600 pages long, the handbook contains 163 chapters, which are divided into fourteen major sections. Every conceivable management and business topic is covered.

Now, in response to numerous requests to make discrete sections of the handbook available to managers and executives with interests in specific fields, AMACOM Books takes great pleasure in publishing this excerpt, the complete section on marketing, as it originally appeared in the *AMA Management Handbook.*

This comprehensive volume provides indispensable information on every aspect of marketing—from the basics of defining the market and positioning the product to the complexities of market research, multinational marketing, and much more. It is our hope that this volume will prove as valuable as the original handbook has been to its thousands of readers.

Robert A. Kaplan
Publisher
AMACOM Books

Contents

Multinational Marketing   **224**

Measuring the Performance of Marketing Operations   **262**

Index   **269**

MARKETING AND ECONOMIC PROSPERITY

Marketing is the execution of the total business activity that directs the flow of goods and services from the producer to the end user. The condition of a nation's economy is usually indicative of the sophistication of its marketing infrastructure and activities. Some futurists suggest that the period from 1800 to 2200 will be regarded as "the great transition" from the poverty of the past to a world society of affluence and leisure. This transition results in major changes in technology, centers of power, and society, as well as in moral and other social values. The futurists see four basic periods of change in the twentieth century. They are described as follows:

La Première Epoque: 1886–1913. The Industrial Revolution and its aftermath caused the creation of the enormous gap between the advanced capitalist nations and the rest of the world.

La Mauvaise Epoque: 1913–1947. The period of the two world wars, the Great Depression, the rise and fall of fascism, the growth of communism and the communist sphere of influence, and the emergence of the superpowers.

La Deuxième Belle Epoque: 1947–1974. Period marked by cold war, decolonization, and emergence of the middle-income nations. Japan became an economic power. This period was one of great prosperity for the United States, but the end of the period saw the start of great economic trouble for the country. There were great social unrest, loss of foreign markets, loss of prestige throughout the world, the decline of the dollar in world markets, energy shortages, and the abdication of control of many of our domestic markets. During this period, we were concerned with effecting a better quality of life quickly, without recognizing that it comes only from an evolutionary process that includes such things as increasing productivity and a national effort of people, business, and government working together toward a common goal.

L'Epoque de Malaise: 1974–2000+. This final period of transition in the twentieth century saw and will see the further emergence of middle-income nations, great potential for violence and disorder, and vulnerable national and world economic systems. This is also a period of slowing economic growth in the developed nations.

The average economic growth rate of advanced capitalist nations during the four periods of transition is: La Première Epoque—3.3 percent; La Mauvaise Epoque—1.8 percent; La Deuxième Belle Epoque—4.9 percent; and L'Epoque de Malaise—3.5 percent (estimated).

The 1980s could turn into a period of great economic sickness for the United States. We are losing our domestic markets to foreign competition. We are losing our leadership in foreign markets. We are not against free trade, but we must be against foreign domination of our domestic markets. If we lose dominance in our domestic markets, we cannot maintain dominance in foreign markets, which adversely affects our balance of trade and the world value of the dollar.

Marketing is the catalyst that transforms technology into the tangible elements that support and establish our standard of living. By being "better" marketers, we can change the course of history and make the coming decades a period of economic prosperity.

Meeting the Challenge: A Crisis Strategy

While marketing strategies can take many forms, a unique opportunity exists to take quick marketing action to counter the negative business effects that occur during periods of economic downturn. These economic crises occur with increasing frequency in our present sophisticated economy. We will lead off this marketing section with a discussion of how to establish a strategy to cope with short-term downturns. To establish your crisis strategy, the following action steps should be taken:

■ Know your market—establish tracking systems to uncover sudden trends and changes. GNP, housing starts, overall retail sales, automobile production, and other commonly used economic indicators may have little significance to your business. Instead, a simple regular audit of key retail outlets may constitute a valid tracking system that will provide your business with an early-warning system of market trends that can be used to produce business downturn counter-strategies. (Parenthetically, it is just as important to track for the upturn trends when they occur since opportunistic strategies can be implemented in this time period.)

While we all think we know our market, we often find our information on market size and segmentation is several years old. While growth can often be projected on an average percent basis, the major dynamic market changes occur in segmentation. Price and subsegments of demand are the most frequent areas of changes in market segmentation. In crisis markets, inflation shrinks disposable income and causes rapid changes in life style. It thus behooves us to maintain our market research efforts to identify changes and then adapt strategies to take advantage of the opportunities presented by them.

We must also recognize that every business has measurable factors that are critical to the success of that business. These factors should be monitored closely. We call these critical success factors. Some typical critical success factors for most businesses are shown in Table 6-1.

■ Plan for changes in the market and identify opportunities. After clarification of our market and the identification of long- and short-term trends, we should reevaluate our present business plans and develop strategies to counter short-term threats. An important part of this evaluation is the identification of future business opportunities from trend analysis. From personal experience, I have found that pricing opportunities are often uncovered that permit penetration of market segments with only slight variation in the basic product line.

Sociological trends stemming from economic conditions may change markets and present new opportunities. Inflation, for example, is causing people to put their money into products rather than paper. There is great interest today in buying quality products. One example of this interest is the popularity of products that are ego-satisfying because of their image of quality and exclusivity. As

Table 6-1. Measuring market success.

Critical Success Factors	Prime Measures
Volume of sales by product line*	Shipments by product
Profitability	Profit and loss statements
	Standard costs by product
Success of new products	Shipments
	Profitability
Distribution of product lines	Shipments by channel of distribution and geographic area
Market success	Change in market share

* In periods of inflation it is important to monitor sales data in units as well as dollars, since price increases often camouflage true product performance.

we examine consumption patterns, we find that the consumer is willing to pay more for quality and ego satisfaction even if it means buying fewer goods.

There have been changes in demography that should have a great effect on our marketing strategy. By 1990, nonfamily households will increase to 45 percent of the total population. These households offer a marketing target for the many products required in furnishing a home—appliances, furniture, tabletop accessories, and so forth. Another interesting market emerging is the over-50 or middle-age-and-beyond market. This population is growing at a rapid rate and accounts for a high share of consumer demand. Most of these families have completed their nest-building chores and are ready to spend their money on things that, in their minds, improve their quality of life. Even in times of heavy inflation, the middle-aged are big spenders.

In order to maintain our life styles in times of inflation, we have to work harder. This has contributed to the change in the role of the woman in households headed by a married couple. The proportion of households in which both husband and wife work is expected to grow to 70 percent by the end of the 1980s. Continued inflation will be a large factor in this increase.

We also see the emergence of the "instant gratification" family unit. These are made up of newly married working couples with combined earnings between $40,000 and $60,000 per year. This combined income permits instant gratification through the immediate acquisition of almost any material object desired. This is quite different from the situation of previous generations, which had to wait many years to achieve this position.

The shift in single nonfamily households, the growth in the over-55 population, and the increase in two-income households are all factors that will provide new market targets and opportunities for profit in the 1980s. How good a job we do in identifying and satisfying these opportunities is key to our survival and prosperity.

■ Develop a product mix that is as distinctive as possible for the market—avoid becoming a commodity in a crisis market. Innovation and creativity are usually required to make a product mix distinctive and unique for a market. Many products start out with unique characteristics and benefits that are achieved through exclusive technology, but become commodities when that technology is duplicated by competitors. Commodities usually have common benefits and are undifferentiated. Since commodities are usually bought on the basis of price and availability, they are the first to be adversely affected by the laws of supply and demand. In a crisis environment, demand decreases, supply increases, and profits evaporate under the competition for sales. A product developed around benefits that are unique and demonstrable is usually easier to merchandise and normally has sufficient elasticity in its price/value relationship to permit aggressive pricing.

Successfully positioning a product is a sophisticated process that requires awareness of and sensitivity to the needs of the marketplace. While one of the important ingredients in establishing a positioning strategy is input from market research, intuition, timing, and a marketing sense also play important parts in developing this strategy.

The development of an effective positioning strategy assumes added importance in a crisis environment, since competitors may be scrambling as hard as you, but hopefully not as wisely as you, to position their products in markets that might be eroding because of decreased demand. Very often, positioning an existing product in a new market and using new packaging and display techniques to merchandise the product benefits can achieve product differentiation at a relatively low investment, important in periods when the cost of capital is high.

A good example of the positioning of existing products to new market segments is Johnson & Johnson's positioning of its baby oil, a long-standing child-care product, as a skin moisturizer and softener for use by women. This strategy generated the additional sales volume needed to offset the declining baby-care-market sales volume at a minimum marketing-mix investment.

■ Do more new-product testing to establish the most effective and concentrated product mix. New products provide additional sales volume when positioned in new market segments and can offset the effects of diminishing demand in existing market segments. Indeed, many companies derive 15 percent to 25 percent of their current sales volume from major new products introduced over the last five years.

The failure rate for major new products is high, although not as high as the often cited nine out of ten. According to a recent study by The Conference Board, the failure rate for new products in the last ten years is about one in three.

Inflation has affected the cost of failure. New-product failures are costly under normal circumstances but disastrous in our present environment. Because of the high cost of product development, new-product introductions will probably be reduced in the near future. So we must maximize our efforts, and make sure that our new product is not the one in three that fails.

The major cause for the failure of new products is insufficient and poor market research. The next most common reasons are technical problems in design and mistakes in timing the product's introduction.

Consumer research can aid in the screening of new-product candidates, define the product concept, and test the salability of the product.

- Maintain or increase market share in crisis markets in spite of changes in segmentation and size. Maintaining and increasing market share is always important in the marketing of products in a competitive environment. Market share affects the efficiency of your marketing-mix expenditure, unit costs, and selling and administrative expenses, as well as the economic health of your competition. In a crisis environment, markets and segments sometimes shrink in size; it's important to make sure your sales volume and operating margin do not follow this trend.

Cost efficiencies in all areas of your operation and marketing effectiveness can help you maintain and improve market-share position and cannibalize the competition. Expansion into new markets and market segments can be the source of growth. Look for ways to effectively expand geographic marketing areas. Great financial rewards can be gained by the extension of geographic marketing areas without the cost of new manufacturing facilities. A key factor in accomplishing this feat is a product mix that positions well in the market and has unique benefits giving pricing flexibility that supports additional freight costs. Some products, because of size and benefits, are ideally suited to this marketing approach.

Additional volume from existing products often can be generated by distributing the product into retail outlet categories not covered by your existing distribution system. This can be accomplished by adding specialty jobbers where possible or using specialized sales representation organizations. Keeping the product in stock and promoting it are also good ways to maintain sales volume. To counter the effects of sluggish consumer demand symptomatic of a depressed economy, promote your products so they appear to offer an extraordinary value available for a limited time only. Price-off promotions are one way to achieve this. This tactic can be part of an overall strategy that encourages your entire distribution network to stock products adequately.

Financing jobber and retail inventories through some kind of dating program (postdating of invoices) can, by easing cash-flow requirements, ensure adequate inventories throughout the distribution system. This can be an expensive tactic and should be used with prudence. If you are using a two-step distribution system, financial and other incentives for the jobber salesperson can also help ensure adequate inventory at the retail level.

- Expand your product mix by adding value so as to improve profitability in an inflationary economy. The basic concept to follow is to analyze your product mix as it relates to the market, and find out how to add value benefits to that mix so you can justify higher selling prices that give higher profit margins. In the packaging industry, for example, the move away from the brown shipping carton that just protected a product to a package that both protects and acts as a merchandising tool was the way that value was added to the product mix sold. Often superficial styling changes can transform a standard product into the deluxe category justifying a higher selling price.

In a crisis environment, it is important to execute product-mix options that can be achieved quickly at minimum capital investment and that generate higher profit-margin yields.

The price sensitivity of our products is an area that unfortunately most of us know little about. In times of inflation, we tend to get aggressive about pricing, but this aggression is more a reaction to rising costs than to what the market will bear for our particular product mix. Market testing and other research techniques can help you establish a pricing strategy based on perceived value rather than on manufacturing costs. Many times, lower unit volume resulting from an increased selling price can result in improved profits.

■ Institute value-analysis procedures. In its most simple terms, value analysis may be defined as an analytical tool that determines the most efficient way to get a desired effect at the highest value in relationship to costs incurred. We normally think of applying this technique to the manufacturing process, but it also has benefit to the entire marketing process. Value analysis is a good tool to use in establishing the merchandising effects you are trying to achieve, their value, and the least costly way to achieve these effects.

In times of economic crisis it is almost axiomatic to exercise tighter controls on expenditures. Very often this means cost cutting in order to preserve operating margins. It might be prudent to consider also increasing costs in areas that could increase the demand for your products. In this way, volume and market share can be protected.

Your marketing mix is a major area for cost cutting or increasing your expenditures to stimulate demand. Here are some questions to consider: (1) What happens to your sales if you cut your advertising budget? What happens to your sales if you increase your advertising budget? (2) What happens to your sales if you cut your sales promotion budget by 25 or 50 percent? What happens to your sales if you increase your sales promotion budget by the same amount? (3) What happens to your sales if you cut your public relations budget? What happens to your sales if you increase your public relations budget? (4) Can you cut out some packaging costs without affecting sales? What happens to sales if you increase your packaging efforts?

Application of some or all of the action steps recommended is good business practice in any economic environment. The immediate implementation of these action steps as part of a crisis strategy can provide you with short-term protection of your position in the marketplace and your assets; it can enable you to make money in a difficult economic environment. ☐ *David J. Freiman*

THE ESSENCE OF MARKETING

A company's success or failure in the marketplace depends on total commitment to marketing—on whether the organization is entirely imbued with the marketing concept or whether it views its marketing as a separate entity independent of the other divisions. Commitment to marketing must permeate the organizational whole, from the very top through every major division. This is not to imply that a major division should ignore its primary responsibilities; it simply means that each division and department should be infused with the idea that the company is oriented and committed to a marketing concept. Each department gives support to the others to ensure the company's survival and growth in today's competitive field of battle.

Too often, the concept of marketing has been limited to the sole endeavor of selling. Though selling is an integral part of marketing, it does not encompass the whole of the marketing concept. The essence of marketing today is evidenced in six major areas of endeavor. To fulfill and use the marketing concept to serve the needs of the company and in turn increase the sales and profitability of the company, a marketing organization must be willing to do the following: (1) define its market area; (2) establish a product positioning strategy; (3) research consumer needs and wants; (4) develop and redevelop product and/or service to meet the demand at a selling price that generates profits for the producer and the distribution system; (5) recruit, select, and train manpower to deliver the product or service; and (6) develop its sales approach and advertising support.

Defining the Market

A person seldom begins a journey unless he knows his destination; and if he is a careful traveler, he has planned his route, his stops, and his time of arrival and has determined how much it will cost to get there. The same principles apply to marketing. Basically, there are three major markets that a company attempts to woo—the general consumer market, the industrial market, and the vast, growing government market. After a company has decided where it wants to go, it needs to find out what that market segment needs, wants, and is buying.

Positioning the Product

The product positioning strategy should be established before the product is developed, because it influences the ultimate characteristics of the product. The position a product fills might be based on unique functional benefits that satisfy a need of a market segment. The benefit can also be a price point for a product that does not have any unique functional benefit but represents a favorable price/value relationship over the other products available in the market. Sometimes the niche is a styling difference. The Freiman three-dimensional product positioning matrix (Figure 6-1) allows the visualization of a market or market segment, with competitive products defined as to price point, product differentiation characteristics, if any (styling, functional, or service differentiation benefits), and market share. This visualization with its definition of the critical factors found in the competitive market environment is helpful in positioning a product offering.

In forming the positioning strategy, product benefits as they relate to the needs or the demand the company intends to satisfy are analyzed, and then planned product benefits are compared to those of competitive products if they exist.

Researching Consumer Needs and Wants

Researching consumer needs and wants is a vital step in marketing. Here the distinction—or lack of distinction—between needs and wants is encountered. Frequently, these two elements are at variance with each other, but the possibility

Figure 6-1. The three-dimensional product positioning matrix, showing average retail price point, product differentiation characteristic, and market share.

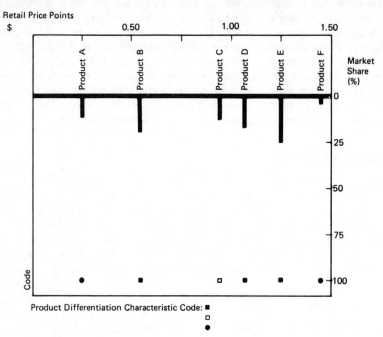

Product Differentiation Characteristic Code: ■
□
●

that a need and a want may be the same is not completely excluded. A child "needs" milk; a child "wants" candy—a simple illustration of obvious duplication. The company must realize, through research, the distinction or absence of distinction between the consumer's needs and wants. The product can then be so designed to fill each desire and sold to fit each element of need or want, or both.

Following closely on this basic research into the needs and wants of the consumer come the facts of how much the consumers are buying; when they buy; how they buy; how much they now spend; and how much they can and will spend for the need and/or want. This research is planned and carried out internally through the company's own market research department or externally through the use of outside research resources, or through a combination of both. Market research is worth the money, time, and effort needed, because it yields essential information to aid in the continuing endeavor of giving customers what they want and need.

Market research is largely an art. Its scientific aspects are largely from the social sciences—from sociology, to see how individual attitudes can affect the purchasing of goods and services; from anthropology, to see how past and present life styles can affect the presentation and advertising of goods and services; and from economics, to see how past, present, and future economic conditions can affect a product's current and future profitability.

Defining the consumer on demography alone is not effective in sophisticated markets. We must establish the psychographic profile of the consumer, which is an all-inclusive definition based on such factors as life style, attitudes, self-image, aspirations, goals, and emotional characteristics, in addition to demographic information. Thus it is to psychographics, the study of consumer attitudes, not only numbers, that marketers should give special attention.

Developing and Redeveloping Product or Service

Keeping a product up to date in the latest design, with materials that are functional, attractive, and appealing, and at a production cost that is competitive with that of similar products and/or services, is a continuing process. This is an essential, cooperative part of a company's development and production division, just as market research is essential. In the group life and health insurance field, for example, health coverages must be kept constantly in line with medical practices and costs to ensure customers' financial well-being when service is needed. This is true of any product or service, whether it is in the field of food products, clothing, heavy machinery, television repair, banking, or other areas of marketing.

New-product development is the life blood of any business. Even with the high risk of failure to position a new product in the marketplace, audacious efforts such as the successful introduction by Cuisinart of the food processor, an entirely new product concept that created a new market and subsegment of demand, demonstrate the rewards that can be reaped by good new-product development.

Marketing targets of opportunity present themselves that do not require major development but rather modification of an existing product. An example of this is the Sony Corporation's creation of the mini stereo cassette recorder. Sales after the first year of introduction exceeded 1 million units at a list price of about $200 per unit. The Sony Corporation recognized that a substantial demand could exist for a product that provided portable, personalized stereo entertainment, and it produced a product that provided it at a cost that its targeted consumer would pay and positioned it in the marketplace so well that it is going to have to share this growing market with many competitors attracted by its success.

Selecting and Training Personnel

It is often said that an organization's greatest strength and greatest wealth are in its people. This is certainly true in a marketing-oriented company. The function of recruiting, selecting, and training company personnel—from the president down through his executive staff—is vital to the successful fulfillment of a planned program of marketing. It must be evident throughout the various other divisions, both line and staff, down to the man who sweeps up after a production run or the girl who opens and sorts the mail. Each employee's knowledge, attitudes, and skills are important to the overall success of the organization.

There must be a planned program to enable employees to meet the company's personal and commitment standards. A good training program gives new employees the knowledge and security they need in order to become functional, val-

uable forces in the organization. More than this, training should be on a continuing basis to ensure that each employee can continue to function to his full
capacity. All training should be directed toward the total marketing concept and
aim to aid in the development of each individual's desire, enthusiasm, sincerity,
and ambition to enable him to become and remain a successful member of the
successful marketing team.

Developing Sales Approach and Advertising Support

It is often said that "nothing happens until someone sells something." This is
what starts the wheels moving, the production line puffing, the shipping clerk
wrapping, and the claims clerk processing. And the instigator of all this activity is
the well-trained, highly motivated, hard-working salesman.

Before selling can begin, important decisions must be made. How will the
thoroughly researched, highly developed, priced-right "need fulfiller" and/or
"want satisfier" be sold? Will the company's own salesmen or agents do the work,
or will manufacturers' representatives, brokers, or jobbers be used? Will sales be
made directly, through distributors, or by some other method? What about consignment, minimum orders, restricted trade territories, and size of customers'
companies or numbers of employees? All this must be determined before that
first sale of product or service is made. Until then, "nothing happens."

A further necessity in the marketing effort is advertising support. Advertising
must complement the overall company image and intent. However, it must not
replace the front-line salesman. Advertising can be used to whet the appetite of
the defined market, to herald the good news of the arrival of the product or service, and to inform potential customers of the places where it can be seen and
purchased. It should reach the vast markets of the general public or the more
restricted areas of industry and government. The design, purpose, and function
of the product or service should be results of the combined efforts of the advertising agency and the R&D department and marketers of the company. The company should always listen to its sales force and customers for feedback of suggestions, praise, and criticism.

The Overall Concept

The essence of marketing is more than selling, more than researching, more than
advertising, more than planning, developing, and redeveloping. It is a synergism
that encompasses all these things; it is a concept that must permeate every organizational division in order to be successfully fulfilled. There are no shortcuts in
acquiring and using the full marketing concept. If an organization is to be
groomed properly for its competitive battle in the marketplace, it must function
through a sound, well-planned, and flexible market-oriented program.
           □ *David J. Freiman* (*and Victor R. Kennedy, Jr., the original author*
                                      of this now substantially revised section)

THE MARKETS AND THEIR EFFECTS ON MARKETING

The success of every seller depends on the action of buyers. Marketing deals with influencing the action of buyers. Product characteristics, promotion efforts, and the locations where marketing action takes place—be it presenting the winning persuasion, making the purchase decision, or actually transferring possession—are all oriented to achieve the sale. Aside from the execution of the functions of design and production, the major effort exerted by the seller and his agents, from planning through implementation, is the scope of marketing.

The *job* of marketing is a different activity in almost every organization. Three key variables cause these differences:

- *The kind of purchaser:* How does he behave? Does he act for himself or for others? How does he make his decisions?
- *The product or service involved:* Is it a discretionary item or a necessity; a high-ticket item or a minor purchase; an item needed as an investment, a consumable, or an item used in the creation of other products?
- *The nature of the marketing effort:* Does it involve a precise argument based on values, or an impulse-motivating inducement, or is it based on providing the most convenient system in which consumers can act?

In the following paragraphs the factors that define markets and the different approaches to marketing are examined to determine how they pair and why.

Definitions

Despite broad understanding and adoption of the marketing concept by business, much is yet to be learned about how markets are formed, how they segment or divide, and how the marketer should formulate effective marketing strategies. A major factor contributing to the problem of this knowledge gap is imprecision in the definitions of popularly used terms and hence in the understanding of the subject. The American Marketing Association has two definitions for "market": (1) "the aggregate of forces or conditions within which buyers and sellers make decisions that result in the transfer of goods and services"; and (2) "the aggregate demand of the potential buyers of a commodity or service."

The first definition is in the context of the marketplace, which is often referred to as the market. This definition denotes various environments in which buying decisions take place, such as the New England market or the agricultural market.

The second definition has significance for marketing strategy; it is concerned with potential buyers. The key point here is the identification of the potential buyers in terms that go beyond positioning them in an environment; rather, they are pointed out in terms that differentiate between a consumer who, for example, desires cold cereal for breakfast and another consumer who has a preference for bacon and eggs. This is important because it says that the bacon-and-eggs eater is not a good target for the marketing effort of a new cereal promotion.

Note also that both definitions contain the word "aggregate." This is important, for the American Marketing Association (*Marketing Definitions*) carries this
underlying notion into its definition of "market potential" as "a calculation of
maximum possible sales opportunities for all sellers of a good or service during a
stated period."

Market potential is thus an aggregate figure, the *maximum* opportunity for *all*
sellers. Therefore, a given company's sales potential is but a part of total market
potential, depending on the subgroup of potential buyers to which it directs its
marketing strategy, or the segment of the market it selects as its target market.
This selection in turn will depend on the differentiating characteristics the company includes in its products and on its marketing resources and capabilities.

The foregoing definitions point out that a market is defined around demands
for a commodity or service, or the opportunities to sell a good or a service. That
is, markets result from needs to achieve satisfactions, and it is therefore convenient to describe them in terms of the products used. There is hazard in this conceptual expediency, since, at later times, these needs can find new ways of achieving satisfaction and vacate present product-defined markets. This is the point
made by marketing conceptualists. Nevertheless—and pragmatically speaking—
there is, for example, a very substantial market for hydraulic fluid power components today even though a new invention in subminiature electric motors could
conceivably displace it at some future date.

Market Segments

Reference has been made here to two bases for market segmentation: the environment in which buyers and sellers operate (the New England market and the
agricultural market), and classifications of potential buyers according to factors
that describe the varied nature of their demands or the opportunity for a seller to
make the sale (the reasons that classify a person as suited to be the object of a
bacon advertisement but not of a cold-cereal promotion). These two examples
illustrate that markets may be segmented in several ways. The ways by which subdivisions are made are called the modes of segmentation, and they are manifold.

In earlier days of marketing, markets were segmented by market analysts
chiefly according to demographic and classification modes. The factors for segmentation were geographic area, age group, company size, ethnic identity, home
owner or renter, income group, political party affiliation, and the like. Although
analyses on these bases permitted the improvement of marketing efforts, the reasons were more operationally than conceptually or strategically oriented. Today
studies on attitudes, motivational considerations, and other decision factors reveal that a man's breakfast-food preference might well correlate with how much
of a hurry he is in at breakfast time, which in turn is influenced by how late he
habitually goes to bed and the starting time of his job in the morning. Thus one
could propose a promotion strategy for the early-to-work market segment for
cold cereal as advertising on late-evening television programs. Purchaser value
criteria constitute another mode for segmentation. This factor aids in the separation of the markets for high- and low-cost items within a product classification.

Marketers

The other party to the marketing situation is the seller. It is important to identify him in precise terms so as to differentiate among those that compete in the supply side of the economy. They comprise the organizations that conceive of the marketing strategies and also contribute largely to the dynamic character of marketing. Sellers are classified according to industry. The U.S. government *Standard Industrial Classification Manual* states that sellers are establishments (producing economic units) that are identified by industry classification codes based on the products they produce or handle, or the services they render. Thus sellers, and in fact all industry establishments, are not classified according to what they do or the operations they perform but, rather, by the goods they produce. Therefore, precisely speaking, the metalworking industry is more like a metalworking market than an industry by the criterion of output rather than operations performed. This is an example of how markets and industries are incorrectly referred to interchangeably. Correctly, it is a matter of whether reference is to the buyer or to the seller: buyers form markets, and sellers form industries.

The problem of distinguishing between markets and industries is more complex when middlemen are included. These organizations, too, are given Standard Industrial Classification (SIC) establishment definitions according to the services they render. The question that must be considered is this: Are middlemen markets for producers, or are they industries from which consumers buy? Middlemen—agents, wholesalers, jobbers, retailers, and dealers—constitute the extracompany elements in the channels of distribution through which a company accomplishes its marketing job. Hence, they are agents of the seller, and the answer is that they are a part of the industry structure rather than the market structure. Notwithstanding, they take title to the products they sell, and therefore they constitute a group of buyers and would appear to form a market even though they are agents. It is less confusing, however, not to refer to groups of middlemen as markets, for the reason that they do not constitute final demand, nor do they convert or integrate products into other products as do OEM (original equipment manufacturer) markets. If they were considered as markets, their purchases and the purchases of consumers would erroneously combine and thus would describe a market size twice that of ultimate consumption.

Economic Groupings

Economists are not so often concerned with the marketer's problem of defining market segments as they are with production and consumption by economic sector. These sectors subclassify according to industries and markets by major characteristic.

Gross National Product (GNP)

The combined value of the product (and service) output of all economic sectors is gross national product (GNP). This breaks down into categories of final demand, capital investment, and the purchases of government, plus certain balance adjustments. The major subclassifications of GNP and their 1980 values are:

	1980 *($ billion)*
Consumer durables	211.9
Consumer nondurables	675.7
Consumer services	785.2
Nonresidential construction	296.6
Residential construction	105.3
National defense needs	131.7
Other federal and state and local government needs	534.0

GNP shows a total of $2,626 billion. In that these classifications are based on product groups by kind of need, they describe some markets.

Input-Output

Input-output theory holds that there are three major areas of economic (marketing) activity: interindustry transactions, industry/final-demand transactions, and value-added contributions by industries.

Interindustry transactions are the buying and selling actions between industries, including industrial purchases of raw materials, components or intermediate products, energy, and services. It should be noted that, as in the SIC system of definitions, wholesale and retail trade middlemen are considered industries along with producers and suppliers of services. For the purposes of input-output analysis and also business and market planning, industries break down into five sectors by type of product or service.

Final products are products of industries that sell a large portion of their output to final demand. They are in two categories: nonmetal (furniture, apparel, drugs); and metal (machinery, appliances, and motor vehicles). It should be noted that purchases of production machinery and related durable equipment investments constitute, for the purpose of these transactions, an action of final demand. Because they are transactions entirely between industrial organizations, they are often mistakenly considered as within the interindustry activity area. Purchases included within the interindustry activity area involve raw materials, intermediate products, energy, and services.

Basic products are products of industries that sell a large portion of their outputs to other industries. They also are found in two categories: metal (machine parts and primary metal mining and manufacturing); and nonmetal (glass products, paper products, and chemicals).

Energy is the product of electric and gas utilities and of the petroleum, coal, and similar industries.

Services include government, transportation, trade, and business and consumer services.

Other industries include research and development (R&D), scrap, and secondhand goods.

These sectors constitute the broad classifications of industries that supply markets, which in turn are composed of the industries themselves for intermediate products and services, plus a group of classifications known as final demand. The economic sectors that constitute the markets of final demand break down into the following classifications: personal consumption (consumers); producers' durable equipment investments (manufacturers, transportation companies, commercial farms, contractors, and broadcasters); construction (purchasers of residential, highway, and commercial and industrial construction); government (federal, state, and local organizations); and exports minus competitive imports.

Action in the marketplace is thus composed of the economic transactions that take place between sellers and buyers. The foregoing definitions of marketing terms and review of the major factors of national economics identify most of the participants.

The Marketing Viewpoint

From a marketing viewpoint, the viewpoint from which marketing strategies and approaches are formulated, markets may be broken down as follows: industry markets (basic materials and products industries, intermediate products industries, producers' durable equipment industries, utilities and transportation companies, construction firms, other service industries, wholesalers, and retailers); government markets (defense and aerospace agencies, public works agencies, and other federal, state, and local agencies); consumer market; and export markets, which may be industry-, government-, or consumer-oriented.

These classifications—except the consumer market—describe markets in terms of groups that have generally common needs and require generally uniform marketing approaches.

The final demands of consumers are for a wide variety of needs, including emotional, that call for different marketing strategies and approaches. The GNP breakdown of consumer markets by product-type demand (durables, nondurables, and services) is a good first cut of this classification. The products of these market categories may be further broken down according to whether their demands classify them as necessities or discretionary purchase items.

In actuality, each supplier-and-market combination interacts in its own way, and this determines each marketing job. It is not really correct to describe this job as just a few ways of interacting, although such must be the limitation in the scope of this discussion.

The Marketing System

The marketing system has been described thus far as consisting of producers, middlemen, and buyers. Buyers can purchase as members of final demand or as purchasers of intermediate products used to make end products for final demand (requiring further continuation of the marketing process). Moreover, one more complexity must be considered in order to understand all the many variations in the marketing system.

Just as sellers have agents that are middlemen, many buyers have agents that specify and even procure for them. For example, the consulting engineer in design specifies the needs of his client, the doctor specifies the prescription of his patient, the architect specifies the materials used in the builder's building, government organizations qualify subcontract sources, and corporate headquarters often name the suppliers whose products are acceptable at the division or retail-unit level. These behind-the-scene influences must also be persuaded, and therefore they too are the targets of many marketing strategies and plans. In general they enter the picture when the buyer is not qualified to properly specify or evaluate the seller's products and there is a technological knowledge gap separating the principals.

The Marketing Job

The marketing job consists in applying the elements of the marketing mix in appropriate balance, to the right extent, and at the right places. The elements that make up the marketing mix are activities that may be classified under the following headings: sales coverage and distribution, product information and application assistance, advertising and product promotion, distributor development and training, merchandising assistance and sales services, price administration and trade promotion, customer order service, and product and package design.

What is done under each of these headings differs in nearly every product/market situation. In total each set of activities describes the many different ways in which the marketing job is done. For the remainder of this discussion, the principal characteristics of the marketing job will be described for the following representative market situations: industrial products sold to industrial markets; defense and aerospace products sold to the federal government and its prime contractors; and consumer nondurables sold to the consumer market.

Industrial Marketing

Industrial markets are composed of purchasers of capital equipment (producers' durable equipment), intermediate products, and industrial construction. Without resorting to an input-output analysis of the economy for a value, the size of the overall industrial market is best appraised by examining the national income of durable-goods manufacturers. Excluding the multiplying effect of intermediate-products sales on the size of the industrial sector, income for durable-goods manufacturing is the largest of the national income accounts, accounting for almost 20 percent of total national income.

The elements of this market are corporations that have a rational and methodical approach in their dealings. The purchasing function is performed by a purchasing agent aided by buyers. Although it would appear that this function is the decision-making center, it acts in behalf of and under the guidance of others. The principal influences in the decision-making process are product engineers and designers where intermediate products are involved (components for production), production and industrial engineers for plant equipment, and facilities planners for construction. These persons establish the specifications of the purchase items, and, basing selection on technical evaluation, they determine or approve the vendors who are considered as acceptable sources of supply. Moreover, even this influence is not individual action; most often it is a departmental or committee action.

The purchasing agent next negotiates and executes the fulfillment of the company's need. This activity embraces obtaining the best price and terms, an acceptable delivery promise, vendors' technical assistance where useful, a reliable and dependable source of supply, specified product quality and specifications, and flexibility to meet the company's changing requirements. For his own purposes he also seeks attentive sales coverage and responsive customer order service from his vendors.

It is difficult to pinpoint a single decision-making unit in the industrial customer organization. Initially, a number of selection criteria must be met, and different persons are assigned the responsibilities of ensuring adherence to the criteria. Once a supplier and his products have been determined to be acceptable, conditions of purchase tend to be the dominant influence in supplier selection. For reasons of economy and stability in vendor–customer relations, once a source has been selected, buyers and sellers often negotiate annual supply contracts against which purchase releases are made during the year. On the other hand, distributors become involved when products are standard low-cost items and when sales are very infrequent.

In every situation, the industrial marketing job must meet the demands of the purchaser. The most critical issue is probably that of product specifications and design. It's important, however, that this be in the context of the value considerations of the buyer. Only in very rigid situations is there no latitude for obtaining a higher price for improved dependability, performance, usefulness, or rating.

Hence an industrial vendor's marketing strategy must emphasize the following primary considerations: leadership in product planning—product specifications, design, utility, and quality; a value-derived price—a price/utility balance concurring with customer value standards; and recognized dependability and service as a supplier.

Defense and Aerospace Marketing

The market for defense and aerospace products is the federal government, except for foreign governments, commercial aircraft, communications satellites, and the like. According to the latest available input-output estimates, the federal government's final demand was approximately $533.5 billion in 1980. Of this amount approximately $131.4 billion was for defense and aerospace requirements.

The government formulates general requirements for the products needed, on the basis of strategic posture decisions. The products themselves are not explicitly defined except for what they must do. Actual product development is left up to the supplier. Accordingly, there are several stages in defense procurement, the procurement of concept R&D, prototype development, and production. Definition of the product progresses with and parallels these stages of procurement.

The end products that are delivered to the government are fabricated by prime contractors. Suppliers of intermediate products, components, and subsystems to prime contractors are known as subcontractors. To prevent excessive economic concentration within the defense industry, the government directs prime contractors to subcontract many major components and subsystems. But to ensure that all intended requirements will be met, government representatives participate in qualifying subcontractors and their product designs.

Purchase decisions, both award determinations and approval of major subcontract sources, rest in the end with the government. Such approval may be as simply achieved as getting on a qualified list of suppliers or as arduous as a full design evaluation. In nearly all instances, however, subcontractors must also be the preferred sources of the prime contractors, who must bear ultimate responsibility for final product acceptance by the government.

The marketing task in this industry is unique and complex. First, as a supplier, one must stand in good stead with both the government and the major prime contractors. Moreover, prime-contract contenders often become subcontractors to their competitors after they have been unsuccessful in obtaining a prime contract. Second, one must have a well-developed market information system to be constantly informed of bid opportunities as well as the plans and unsolved needs of the government. This enables one to be prepared for opportunities and to develop, on one's own initiative, product research and unsolicited proposals directed toward perceived potential opportunity.

Because of the many levels, locations, and committees that are involved in purchasing decisions regarding defense products, and because of the many criteria that apply to successful contracting, rigorous marketing effort must be exerted to achieve success in this section. In sequence, there is the initial work of becoming known and accepted as a qualified supplier, the job of being currently informed on where developing business opportunities are, the strategy of organizing or getting on the right team of prime and subcontract suppliers, the development of an extremely comprehensive bid proposal, the intense follow-up and presentation programs to achieve appropriate recognition of an offer, and a detailed program of executive selling to demonstrate top-management interest and the company's overall capability. The defense contractor's marketing strategy must emphasize the following considerations: advanced product research and development capability with a record of proven success; adequate technological support facilities in terms of laboratory and testing equipment; adequate production capabilities in terms of methods and tool-engineering competence, production facilities and equipment, and quality control; adequate business systems for cost control, scheduling, and contract administration; adequate manpower in all skill levels—managerial, professional, technical, and shop; a deep concern, on the part of top management, for the contract; and an approach to organization that appears effective and efficient.

Consumer Marketing

The consumer market is the aggregate of all individuals acting in their own behalf or that of their immediate families. Personal consumption is the biggest figure of all in total final demand. For example, 1980 figures show GNP for consumer durables as $212 billion, for consumer nondurables as $676 billion, and for services as $785 billion.

In that each consumer is an individual buying unit, the market is not an organized structure. And because individuals possess all the different qualities and characteristics of mankind, and because they are free to act in whatever way they wish, they form an extremely complex market.

The large population that makes up the consumer market dictates that, for reasons of economy, these buyers be dealt with in large groups—hence the designation "mass markets." It is when they are perceived and appealed to as groups that the consumer market takes on a structured appearance; that is to say, the ways in which groups differ from one another and also interrelate depend on the basis that has been taken for differentiation. This basis is referred to as the mode of segmentation.

There are two main reasons for segmenting consumer markets. The first reason is to determine what sets of motivational and behavioral criteria can be applied to delineate different groups within the market. This analysis permits the formation of appropriate marketing strategy. The questions for which answers are sought are these: How do consumers perceive their needs? How do they perceive achieving satisfactions? Upon what bases do they make decisions? What inducements and appeals motivate them to purchasing actions?

The second reason for segmenting consumer markets is to determine other classification criteria that enable marketers to identify, reach, and serve the different members of the market. When strategic target segments have been identified and a marketing posture has been formulated, the job of marketing implementation remains to be done. The problem is, then, what descriptive and classification criteria best describe those members that make up the target segment so that they may be found? The questions for which answers are sought are as follows: How much purchasing power do the individuals in this segment have? What promotional communications channels best reach them? Where are they located? How can they be identified? What patterns and characteristics do they have that suggest the best ways to serve them?

A link that is unique to the consumer economic marketing sector is the retailer. Without his support the best marketing plans will come to a halt. He must be compensated and motivated to cooperate; thus trade promotion is as important as consumer promotion in consumer marketing plans. Because the population of the consumer market and its retail outlets is large, a wide variety of distributors plays an indispensable role in achieving distribution.

The marketing strategy for consumer products marketers must emphasize the following primary considerations: selecting target market segments from a motivational and behavioral analysis of the market; determining the characteristics of the population making up the target market that enable promoting to it and serving it effectively; and formulating a product design and interrelated promotion and advertising program that motivate both customers and retailers.

Marketing Approach

In industrial marketing, product considerations dominate the marketing picture. In the case of defense and aerospace markets, product development and production capabilities outweigh the current state of product design in the marketing argument. In consumer markets—granted the importance of the product as the means of satisfying the need—a well-conceived marketing strategy and plan are the keys to success. These key differences in marketing approach are the result of the differences in the markets. Further differences in marketing approach are attributable to the kinds of products and the variations in strategy by marketers. □ *A. John Ward*

THE NATURE OF THE PRODUCT AND ITS EFFECT ON MARKETING

The marketing concept asserts the absolute and fundamental importance of the market. Its dictum is: "Determine what the market wants, and deliver that product to the customer." The demand of commerce and industry is for positive affirmation that "*It* works, we can make *it*, and we can sell *it*." But the individual marketer who is to sell the product musters his arguments and directs his plans and efforts to accomplish that sale in ways that differ radically from one type of product to the next. The nature of any product category, as well as its market, very significantly influences the seller's general approach to the product's market. The intangibility and complexity of a product particularly shape that approach, as do the product's function, price, quality, and service and other after-sale characteristics.

Similar Products in the Same Market

The market's effects on marketing are indisputable. Frozen orange juice for A&P patrons, for United Airlines, or for the U.S. Army Quartermaster Corps is handled in three distinctly different ways. In each case the market dictates particular requirements related to the marketing strategy, planning, organization, research, pricing, advertising, packaging, product management, sales management, distribution, delivery, merchandising, and practically every other aspect of marketing operations. However, each market defines explicitly the manner in which *all* frozen foods are marketed; that is, the nature of all frozen foods for consumer purchase in supermarkets (for instance) dictates that they be similarly processed, prepared, packaged, advertised, distributed, and handled, right up to the time the buyer puts the item in his or her cart and heads for the cash register. Generally, all these products affirm their value in terms of appearance, preservation, taste, purity, and several other characteristics peculiar to such products. And, of course, a number of these characteristics differ from the corresponding characteristics of fresh fruit juice, fresh vegetables, or fresh meats; and they differ again from the characteristics of canned foods. Whether the foods are frozen, fresh, or canned, in each category their characteristics distinctly (and differently) affect their marketing.

Dissimilar Products in the Same Market

Just as the nature of frozen foods directly influences their marketing, this same relationship can be seen for every other product category. Contrast the industrial marketing of elevator maintenance service with the industrial marketing of frozen foods. Or contrast the marketing of electrical fixtures and supplies to the Department of the Navy with the marketing of frozen foods to the National Aeronautics and Space Administration (NASA). Each type of product, by virtue of its unique characteristics, must be defined, demonstrated, and delivered to the buyer in a way that is in some respects unique and peculiar to that type of product.

Factors of Differentiation

The unique quality that differentiates one product category from another may invite analysis in terms of product tangibility and product complexity. (There are many other differentiations, of course.)

Tangibility

The fact that a product can be felt or tasted, or calibrated or examined in operation, or otherwise physically observed and evaluated has a direct relationship to the marketing approach for that product. The more tangible the product, the more likely it is that advertising can be used to help sell it; conversely, the less tangible the product, the greater the need for personal selling. The more tangible the product, generally, the more important the display and appearance characteristics and the features of serviceability, durability, and practicality of application.

At the other end of the spectrum, the intangible services, such as the professional ones of psychiatry or law, or the highly specialized areas of consulting, depend almost entirely on personal relationships with potential customers: the sponsor of the product (service) markets himself directly; the "package" is expertise or authority or intellectuality, which the seller shares with the buyer. Thus the manufacturer of power tools and the admissions director at a boys' school market their products differently to the man who is a home craftsman and who also has a 15-year-old son. So do the information systems consultant and the laboratory-instruments maker who face a typical corporate customer.

Complexity

A complicated, intricate product or system requires a marketing approach distinctly different from the approach dictated for a simple commodity or a basic material. Thus, the understandability of a product category, the requirement for customer education, or the need for *technical* marketing variously shape the marketing approach for that product. However, this differentiation is not a matter of tangibility in terms of the physical features of the product. For instance, both an intricate, electronically controlled machine tool and a pair of shoes have substance and dimensions; telephone-answering services and architectural-engineering services have neither. The tool, because of its complex nature, requires technical selling—perhaps of a highly personal, sophisticated type. The shoes, supported by advertising, to an appreciable degree sell themselves. The answering service also sells itself, in effect; but the architectural-engineering service must be made acceptable and understandable and be expressly presented to each customer.

The tangibility and complexity differentiations of a product or service influence not only the marketing approach to the selling market but also the approach to the service and repair and maintenance after-markets. And these differentiations, in addition to others such as price, quality, and competition, definitely relate to the product as well as to the markets for that product.

Managing Products and Markets

The most elementary requirements for any marketing manager are to know his markets and know his products. His astuteness concerning his products assures his appreciation of the subtle as well as the obvious effects of the nature of those products on their marketing, and this knowledge and understanding stimulate his study of similar and different effects for various other products. As a result he is able to market his own products according to established, demonstrated standards; he is also able and willing to deviate knowingly from those standards, to experiment deliberately in the marketplace, and to test unusual or special situations.

Two such deviations in the home fuel-oil business were the initiation of ten-month, averaged installment payments to stabilize buyer expense and dealer storage inventory, and the initiation of degree-day records to permit automatic delivery when needed. In both instances the nature of the market and the nature of the product accommodated these innovations, which reduced costs, improved profits, and increased sales. Knowledgeable, imaginative marketing managers in every industry have employed similar adaptations; they have identified the effect of one product's characteristics on its marketing, relating this product to another in its market or in another market, and have tested the parallel.

More basic is the imperative need for the marketing manager to know first the nature of his own products. Chain saws are not outboard motors; transistors are not vacuum tubes; helicopters are not taxis; magnetic tape is not typewriter ribbon; yet the annals of postwar marketing abound with instances of marketing programs conceived by people who really didn't know the product they were marketing. They *thought* it had the same basic characteristics as some other product, and sometimes these misconceptions cost their companies millions of dollars.

The Matrix of Product Characteristics

As this brief study of dissimilar products has indicated, even within the dimensions of tangibility and complexity the nature of products and services does not affect their marketing consistently or uniformly. However, certain trends or standards can be established for broad areas or categories of products and services.

Basic Materials

Generally, basic materials and commodities have almost no differentiation; they are almost all marketed in bulk quantities, in relatively open markets, at narrow margins. Variously, tariff quotas, subsidies, and government regulatory commissions may influence a particular product's prices and markets; but these external factors in no way alter the essentially stable, fundamental nature of these products—such as minerals, wood products, livestock, and grain—and an extensive variety of first-derivative products and by-products. The cost of sales (extraction, production, processing, and so forth) is the most significant problem for companies dealing in these types of products. Historically, the marketer of a basic commodity such as raw lumber operates rather perfunctorily—principally, managing sales—and has not done very much market research, planning, testing, or advertising; and his organization is fairly simple and straightforward. He contracts or "brokers" large volumes at standard quality or condition levels, and he may have significant responsibilities for shipping and distribution.

In the shipping and distribution area, perceptive marketing managers of basic materials and commodities have successfully tested a number of new techniques. Not too many years ago, experimental pipelines were developed for gas and oil. Today more than half the petroleum and nearly all the gas in the United States move underground in a network of over one million miles of pipeline. Whether the idea came into fruition as a result of the oil companies' efforts or the pipe manufacturers' efforts, it was supported and nurtured by understanding of the nature of the product, of its markets, and of the technical feasibility of the system.

Similarly, a number of other handling and distribution techniques have been developed that radically affect the marketing of basic materials. Some of these might be classified as production-oriented rather than market-oriented, such as cargo-handling equipment for bulk tankers, systems for processing bulk chemicals and other materials, and computerized data systems for grading, sorting, and warehousing. But regardless of who claims responsibility for this type of innovation, the idea related fundamentally to the nature of the product and had a powerful impact on the marketing of that product.

Standard Manufactured Products

The differentiation of products that are off-the-shelf or standard catalog items, and of certain basic standard types of services, varies from somewhat more significant to very appreciably more significant than the differentiation of basic materials and commodities.

The nature of many manufactured products, particularly those that do not change significantly from one decade to the next, affects their marketing relatively little. Just as in the case of commodities and basic materials, the simplicity and stability of this sort of product minimize the explicit effect of the product in its marketing. Rivets, sulphuric acid, and corn syrup in volume, in industrial or government markets, are all sold at generally established quality levels. Corn syrup consumer marketing is considerably different, but this results from the complexity of the market, not from the complexity of the product.

Marketing complex products—electrochemical drilling machinery, high-fidelity stereophonic equipment, or biometric centrifuges, for example—is distinctly different from marketing basic materials. The nature of these types of products, even though the products are standard, catalog, production-run, off-the-shelf items, directly influences their marketing. First, the marketing manager must have technical competence; and second, he must organize to operate across a considerable range of responsibilities. His counterpart who deals in rivets generally need not meet either criterion.

The marketing manager for complex, technology-oriented products finds himself closely involved with R&D and engineering; he variously exercises responsibilities for new-product planning, technological forecasting, and commercial development; he directs a technically trained sales force and works with or directs technical services; and he may play a key role in licensing, acquisitions, joint ventures, and general business development. Threaded through all this, the need for him to know technology is emphatically demonstrated. He must recognize and understand technical ideas long before substantial development funds are committed; follow technical progress and actively participate in the resolution of new-product plans and targets; engage the customer finally, knowledgeably, and sensitively; and follow up his customers, identifying their new needs (which are technically oriented, technology-responsive) and his competitors' awareness of and attention to those needs.

His technical competence thus equips him to do the things that the product requires him to do; and in order to discharge these responsibilities, he must staff and organize his function accordingly. Overall company size will directly determine the size of the marketing group; but regardless of the number of people who report to him, he must closely coordinate with and directly relate to a diversity of functions that either do not exist or are not marketing's concerns in the company that produces rivets.

As the rate of change of technologies continues to accelerate, more and more marketing managers find their "standard manufactured" products becoming more complex.

Because of dramatic developments in materials technologies, for instance, radical changes in product composition have occurred in engineering, design, functional purpose, cost, competitive pricing, and numerous other characteristics. Technologies related to manufacturing, processing, packaging, handling, inventory, and information systems have kept the same pace. Every change in any of these technologies that serves to further product differentiation has a direct impact on the marketing of that product.

The lumber industry clearly illustrates this change in the marketing manager's job. The marketer of raw lumber, who has become a marketer of wood products, now deals in prefinished paneling as well as a wide variety of other new product categories. But in the area of paneling alone he must know and understand a great deal of chemistry; and he must keep abreast of changes in the state of the art as they advance toward the marketplace.

Product and brand management evolved, at least in part, because of the technology explosion and resultant greatly increased emphasis on new products that has taken place in recent years. Unquestionably, market differentiations that characterized the completely new market environment that began to evolve after World War II principally stirred marketing professionals to experiment and to develop the principles and tools and techniques of product management. But there were early indications that product differentiations as well as market differentiations were important, that a particular product benefited from the direction of a highly profit-oriented, generalist manager who could view his authority and responsibility, his goals and achievements, in terms of total function. Here the consideration might have been the nature of the product in relation to the company's other products or product lines, or it might have been the general differentiation of the product type.

Service

The range of differentiation of services is much like the range for manufactured products. Automobile lubrication is more complex than garbage collection and less complex than television repair. But automobile repair work, sophisticated by computerized electronic "diagnostic clinic" installations, is becoming highly complex. The overall complexity, the technical features of the product serviced and of any equipment used to provide the service, require the marketer to have a relative depth of understanding of those features. In some services, such as real estate, stock brokerage, or fire insurance, an understanding of the technical features of the service itself is the marketer's criterion.

Principally, the differentiation in services that in turn affects the marketing of those services is a matter of tangibility of results. Thus services are largely differentiated by the market and in the marketplace. A customer can inspect shirts that come back from the laundry to determine whether they are properly starched, or he can listen to a smoothly running repaired pump. In similar fashion he can generally evaluate the deal that he made with a real estate agent, he can always measure the worth of a broker's advice after he has bought the stock, and he quickly knows the worth of his fire insurance if he experiences a fire.

Custom-Made Systems

Nearly every standard off-the-shelf product or regular service can be obtained in some modified form to serve the user's particular needs. Some products (such as Rolls Royce automobiles) and some services (such as the installation of an office telephone system) are always custom-tailored to the buyer's requirements. At some point in the scale of modification, however, the uniqueness of the end product or service distinguishes it and thereby differentiates it from all the others generally like it. It is at this point that such a special version of a product or service approaches the custom-made category.

The truly custom-made product or service may be relatively uncomplicated, engineered to moderately particular specifications that are dictated by an express need; or it may be a highly structured, intricate complex of products and/or services. These combinations or systems have become more and more widely identified with the rapid advance in communications technologies and information management applications. Obviously, each custom-made system reflects a very high degree of differentiation, and marketing such systems requires technical competence, highly specialized customer liaison, and close personal management. The subtle implications of expertise and intellectuality impose here, for the seller is usually better able than the buyer to structure a system that balances capability and need. His consultations, however, are not offered free of charge, and his pricing-negotiating must be accomplished accordingly.

It is also characteristic of many—though not all—custom-made systems that the service market may be extremely important. In such a case, whether the sale involves a municipal sewage-treatment plant or an international credit-card operation, the marketer must know the economics as well as the technology of the system intimately, and he must be qualified to furnish maintenance and service for a (sometimes considerable) period after the purchase. Simply, he must be a well-grounded student of his own company's business and technology and of any customer's business and technology. His marketing counterpart who deals in rivets, however, rarely needs to meet these criteria.

R&D Systems

The mysteries of research have never been confined exclusively to the workbench. Within a company's laboratories, scientists and engineers purposely deal with unknown, unresolved problems ranging from nondirected, so-called pure research to defined development work and application and design engineering. The other management functions' varying relationships with the research group afford them little real insight into what R&D is doing from day to day. Rather, these nontechnical types for the most part identify and evaluate what comes out of research. The more technically oriented the company's products, the more the marketing manager and his nontechnical peers must strive to comprehend R&D's work—both when it is in process and as it comes out the laboratory door. Thus, in an organization devoted to R&D systems work, the marketing manager's knowledge of science and technology is highly important; otherwise, he cannot comprehend his own organization's products, nor can he recognize and understand customers' needs in terms to which his own company can respond. However, the organization's staff includes a large number of professionals, every one of whom is potentially if not actively engaged in the marketing effort. Indeed, the technical community executes a major share of the marketing functions; thus the marketing manager's relationships with it are vital.

Much though not all systems research is done for the federal government, particularly for the Department of Defense (DOD) and for NASA. These customers of course affect marketing in a great many distinct and significant ways, particularly in the requirements for detailed plans and controls that they impose: proposal procedures, contractual arrangements and terms, monitoring and controls, performance evaluations, and the like. Yet, fundamentally, it is because of the nature of this type of product, as well as the nature of its market, that both the research and the development must be thoroughly planned in advance and carefully controlled in their execution.

The marketing manager necessarily plays a key role in determining what the customer wants and in shaping the plan for getting the job and for doing the job; only if his intelligence is good can the organization effectively pursue the job. He also has important responsibilities for developing additional information that may lead the firm to decide not to bid the job. In systems R&D work the stakes are high; the business strategy and marketing strategy must be sound, for an organization cannot afford many bad decisions. Good market intelligence enables the company to submit a winning proposal. This means simply that the customer finds the approach—both technical and management—most nearly what he wants; he finds it well planned and believes achievement assured.

Another aspect of systems R&D—the breadth of technology that may be involved—also affects marketing. In a custom-made system where a variety of subsystems may be needed, the marketing manager must know where and how these subsystems will be obtained, costed, and integrated into the final system. In a major systems R&D program the marketing manager has similar responsibilities and relationships with subcontracting organizations. Inasmuch as their product, like his own, is R&D, the business-marketing judgments and decisions can be extremely difficult and highly risky.

R&D Studies

R&D studies are somewhat more abstract and less tangible but not necessarily more complex than systems R&D. The marketer here is almost certainly an advanced professional who is probably more a technical man than a marketing man. He may not need to relate to as broad a range of technologies as the systems R&D marketing manager, but he certainly needs to know the particular related area of technology that is his organization's or group's specialty. (Of course, he also needs to know the tools and techniques and philosophies of marketing.)

A review of the spectrum leading to R&D studies, from basic materials through standard manufactured items, services, custom-made systems, and R&D systems, demonstrates that the greater the differentiation in product type, the more personal selling replaces advertising. Systems, whether custom-made or R&D—and R&D studies even more so—must be marketed personally and directly by highly knowledgeable individuals. The understanding of business management required of marketers of R&D studies is not peculiar to their function; a high degree of management and business acumen is demanded of contracting people, R&D, engineering, finance, purchasing, and others. But the marketer frequently is—or becomes—the program general manager. He identifies and develops the market, responds in depth to the opportunity, wins the contract award, and directs the fulfillment. Most assuredly, this is not the marketer of rivets.

Professional Services

The range and variety of professional services span a vast differentiation. The licensed certified public accounting (CPA) firm that provides a year-end audit can almost be considered in the off-the-shelf business. Its fellow specialist firm that constructs and helps to install a computerized cost-accounting profit-center control system for a multiplant company doing business around the world operates in a far different environment. However, both firms market intangible expertise. That which they deliver will not physically pump more, dig deeper, run faster, or operate at improved efficiencies or lower costs that are positively and indisputably attributable to the supplier of the service. Always, some measure of the performance achieved after the service is rendered can be blamed on or credited to the client.

The marketer of professional services must fully appreciate the ephemeral character of his product. He must explore his client's problem in the greatest possible depth in order to serve real needs and dissolve those that may be imaginary; he must demonstrate continuing sensitivity and counsel to the client while the work is under way; and he must be alert and responsive to postfulfillment problems or needs. Thus the marketer of professional services shares many of the characteristics of the R&D marketer: he is almost always a doer or practitioner; he sells a highly personalized product; he must know as much as possible about his client in order to tailor his service to that client individually; and he finds that most of his business is built on reputation rather than advertising, for most of his business comes from direct referrals or in the form of repeat business.

Professional services differ from R&D in one significant respect: R&D attacks unknown elements of a problem, whereas services generally treat clearly demonstrated needs. R&D points the way to new hardware or new systems that may cause the future development of new philosophies or principles. Professional services focus on immediate, existing situations and concern interpersonal relationships, operating concepts and methods, and the health, education, and welfare of the client. Thus the marketer of professional services deals in human affairs. He must project his organization's capabilities to counsel, console, instruct, and advise, as well as to provide expertise and technical or professional understanding —all of which work toward a sound solution to the client's problem.

Profiling Product Effects

At best, the nature of a product or service and its effect on marketing are difficult to measure in precise terms. The variations apparent in this review, ranging from basic materials and standard products to R&D and professional services, demonstrate that intangibility and complexity are often obscure, sometimes almost contradictory. The astute marketing manager, however, knows full well that the nature of the product or service does affect marketing significantly and that his study here is essential.

A decade or more before John Kenneth Galbraith (*The New Industrial State,* Houghton Mifflin Company, 1968) wrote about the "technostructure," marketing practitioners were becoming aware of the growing necessity for anticipating and dealing with change. Vast changes in technologies and in the whole order of man's social, political, and economic affairs were introducing an increasing number of new differentiations of markets and of products and services. The marketing manager, responsible for directing "the flow of goods and services from production to consumption," became a true professional whose breadth and perception enabled him to meet the demands of the new marketing environment that was evolving.

It was increasingly clear that marketing considerations would orient management strategy and marketing decisions would platform business decisions. Among the many challenges faced by the marketing manager was the requirement to understand, more than ever before, the relationship of his products to the marketing function, and the effects of changes in those products that further differentiated the products. Today that challenge is far more significant than it was in the 1950s; today he and all other managers are most certain of tomorrow's uncertainty, most certain that tomorrow will be different.   □ *John L. Wood*

COMPETITIVE FORCES

Competition and competitive activity are commercial and economic realities. Because competition is something that all businessmen are aware of and in one situation or another constantly encounter, not only in business but in personal situations, it is an entity that has close personal identification and is readily understood.

Although the existence of competition and its measurable and unmeasurable influences are readily acknowledged, there is often a tendency toward overconcern or underconcern, and either a fatalistic attitude or complacency is the result. A deeper understanding of the dynamics of competition leads to a more positive and meaningful comprehension of the significance of competition; competitive forces; the influence and effects of competition, both direct and indirect; and the negative and positive aspects of competition.

Philosophy of Competition

It is sometimes valuable to pause and reflect upon the underlying principles from which psychological, sociological, and economic realities evolve. From the urge that impels individuals to excel to the collective efforts of groups to predominate, it is but a simple extension to the impulsion of corporate expansion and dominance. Although this may explain—at least in part—the origin of competition between individuals and provide a foundation for analyzing group competitiveness, there is an additional and fundamentally significant consideration in the dynamics of business competition. The means of economic survival under the free enterprise system are such that optimum opportunity exists for the exercise and application of judgments and techniques that will allow for the successful, profitable coexistence of a multitude of companies competing in the same or essentially the same markets.

Implicit in this analysis are the dynamics of the market itself. Since the market is in a state of constant change through alteration, contraction, or expansion—whether resulting from competitive or noncompetitive activities—technology and social evolutionary change itself must relate to marketability at any given time. Therefore, competitive factors prevail in varying orders of magnitude, and their influences vary significantly according to the contemporary status of the market. This is well summarized in the classic supply-and-demand concept; however, that concept fails to appreciate the implications of creative marketing and the effect of applying behavioral studies on the creation of demand, by satisfying unfulfilled consumer needs.

The Market

The size, nature, and posture of the market vary depending on the circumstances, but they are in a state of constant change. The manner and degree of competition in any given situation therefore vary. However, in considering competition and market as coexistent forces in a state of equilibrium, it is apparent that both affect each other and that a change in either one results in a change in the other; therefore, in order to fully appreciate competition and its effects, the nature and structure of the market must be considered.

Classically, the primary markets are three: the consumer, industrial, and government markets. This classification is obviously an oversimplification, but it is nevertheless cogent because the effects and influences of competition vary dramatically in relation to this market segmentation.

Consumer Market

The consumer market is probably the most competitive, volatile, and active of the three. The number of firms competing and the size, strength, and distribution potentialities of any given supplier are of vital importance to its ability to compete in the consumer market. Technical evolution is a determinant, and the effects of sociological change—particularly as they relate to the psychology of consumer marketing—are additional influences. Creativity in competition as a reflection of imaginative marketing is a very important consideration in analyzing competitive activity within the consumer market. Consumer appeal, new products, product modification, packaging, price, advertising, promotion, and convenience items are all employed as active competitive strategies. In the consumer market there is deep concern with less obvious competitive strategies—for example, monetary advantages, particularly consumer credit. As the trend to deficit financing becomes firmly entrenched in consumer purchasing, the use of competitive credit techniques becomes increasingly significant.

Industrial Market

There are many considerations in the industrial marketplace that parallel those of the consumer market. The differences involve the number of competitors, who are often far fewer but tend to be larger. The peripheral benefits of size prevail. The ability for sales/purchase reciprocity is not and cannot be explicit but can be and is implicit. Again, price, service, distribution, and availability are all relevant factors. New products, product development, product modification, and customer service are also important. Advertising and promotion are certainly important in the industrial market, but their value is probably not of the magnitude found in consumer marketing.

Government Market

Competition in government marketing is important, despite the very distinct differences from consumer and industrial marketing characteristics. The government, in its contractual relationship with suppliers, is quite clear in its stipulation regarding competitiveness, but competition in government marketing is most directly concerned with economics and with quality in relation to price of products delivered.

Another distinction is that although in consumer and industrial markets both the nature and means of competitors are known, competitive bidding in government marketing is often done without such knowledge but merely by assumption, on initial bidding at least. This, of course, complicates entry into the government market, since the techniques for dealing with government and specific competitors can be determined only after in-depth study.

Competitive Techniques

The object of competition is to obtain, maintain, or improve a position in a given market; traditionally, the following devices have been employed for this purpose: price, quality, service, advertising and promotion, distribution, financing, supply, product and product development, and company image.

In considering these elements one by one in the discussion that follows, it is important to appreciate that the market changes have resulted in an alteration in the general approach of competitors to effective competitive maneuvers. The face of competition has changed, with the result that the elements formerly encountered as major competitive strategies have altered, by and large, to keep pace with the dynamics of marketing requirements.

Again, to put the principal techniques of competititve activity in perspective, it is essential that opportunities for creativeness, either in the use of existing techniques in combination or in approaching the development of competitive tactics, be thoroughly considered. The opportunities for imaginative competitive response are abundant, since the principal competitive activity now centers in sectors other than those of previous years.

Price. Price is subject to manipulation. Obviously, price concessions in a given market can result in increased sales, either temporary or long-range. There is no doubt that this is the most manifest competitive technique. However, irresponsible competitive pricing results in some form of retaliation.

The use of price as a competitive technique has other serious ramifications. Management must always be concerned with profitability, and it is apparent that competitive pricing, if carried too far, can eventually lead to price attrition. When new products are considered, existing market price levels will impose limitations as well as provide guidelines.

The use of price was, for many years, undeniably the predominant competitive weapon. With the increasing number of competitors and competitive products, the product–value relationship has largely stabilized, thus necessitating emphasis on competitive strategies other than price manipulation. In recent years this change has been reflected in tremendous emphasis on service and service-related techniques. When the increased technical requirements are taken into consideration, this is a logical approach to improving competitive position, and either technical or commercial service assistance generates an entirely new competitive climate. This is not to say that price is no longer actively employed as a competitive tactic, but rather that it is usually now used as only one element in a combination of individual strategies.

Quality. Quality can be considered from two standpoints in relationship to competition: on the one hand, competitors may offer improved quality in a given product at the same price, thereby obtaining business; on the other hand, they may offer lower quality at a lower price with the same objective. Either technique can result in restrictive, temporary gains. The response to such a technique depends essentially upon the consideration of longer-range corporate objectives. Such maneuvers have at times resulted in the establishment and promotion of dual product lines whereby competition can be effected at equivalent quality and price levels.

Product quality has taken on added importance in recent years, particularly in scientific and government markets, where extremely high specifications and commercial tolerances are commonly encountered and the ability to compete is predicated upon technological or scientific improvement and related engineering installation and process assistance.

Service. Service is multifaceted, and the levels of service required in various markets differ significantly. Customer service in consumer markets most often involves resale and maintenance; in the industrial market it is technical support; and in the government market service involves predetermined, specific arrangements. Competitors can and do offer additional services to their customers regardless of the marketplace—a definite contribution, in many instances, but one that can be quite expensive to the supplier. Customer service levels either for a given market or product or for a particular product to a specific customer must be carefully analyzed from the standpoint of return on investment (ROI).

In one guise or another, service is repeatedly encountered as at least the secondary element in overall competitive maneuvers. The keys to the effective application of service as a competitive device are imagination and creativity.

Advertising and promotion. Competitive marketing activities are of most apparent and immediate concern in two specific areas—advertising and promotion.

The effects that competition can create through advertising and promotional efforts differ in the industrial and consumer markets. Regardless of the market segmentation, the influence of these efforts is dramatic, although of questionable duration in many instances.

It is not feasible or necessary to consider here all the ramifications of advertising and promotional marketing activities; most of them are well known and established. Due consideration should, however, be given to the influence and importance of effective countermarketing measures.

Distribution. Although distribution is not usually thought of either as an external competitive force or as a technique that can be used in competition, it can be and is effectively employed. If distribution is conceived of as being, essentially, the means of getting the product into the consumer's hands, it is evident that the competitor who can assure the consumer of his superior ability to do so has gained a competitive advantage. Conversely, inability to fill a demand with the immediacy so often required in active markets is a distinct disadvantage that can be capitalized on by competitors.

Financing. No longer can it be said that the customer is *becoming* credit-conscious; he is already credit-conscious. The importance of this consideration has been given added significance through the introduction of new federal legislation, the Consumer Credit Protection Act. Recognition of this factor, with proper imaginative use of it, provides a definite competitive tool.

Supply. Though supply could be considered as a subfactor in distribution, the situation in a marketing sense is of far broader implication. Supply in the more expansive concept involves totality from inception to finalization; from earliest raw material to the last point of sales support. In this broader sense, competitors who have difficulty satisfying all these requirements are not likely to be able to employ this distinct competitive factor, whereas competitors who are able to do so, do not often fully exploit the inherent possibilities.

Product and product development. The competitive force implicit in the product and in product development requires little elaboration here. It is usually the first-considered and perhaps the most obvious manifestation—second only to price—of competitive activity. Product stasis is the progenitor of market stagnation. Competition recognizes this and exploits it. Product viability creates market vitality and assures the competitor of a position of prominence in the marketplace.

Image-consciousness. The overall image of the supplier in the market is of vital concern to initial and continuing success and growth. A definite force is associated with the image of success, and image-consciousness, not alone of product or brand but of the total corporation, is a valued asset. Modern management's recognition of psychological principles as applied to effective marketing and development of image-consciousness is of concern in this area. The constant interplay of competitive techniques creates the competitive atmosphere in which marketing functions and to which it must effectively respond.

To effectively exploit the full value of image-consciousness, it is necessary to recognize the importance of promoting the total corporation and utilizing this additional strategy as a component of the total marketing effort—more specifically, of implementing it in advertising and promotional activities.

Significance of Competition

The "whys and wherefores" of competitive significance are evident from the points already established regarding the prevailing atmosphere of competitiveness in the marketplace. The importance of competition must not be underestimated, particularly since it is clearly apparent that there is a vast increase in competitive activity in contemporary marketing and that there will be a continued acceleration of such activity, particularly as international markets expand.

The force exerted by competition through implementation of its techniques is apparent. What is essential is that the effect of the force be understood. Effective marketing and product planning require not only a recognition of competition but the establishment of appropriate countermeasures and the ability to respond rapidly as well.

It is clear that competition is a dynamic force. The balancing of situations at any time, and the shifts that occur as a consequence of competitive activity, provide the conditions in which marketing operates. Effective operation within these dynamic parameters is a basic for successful marketing.

Effects of Competition

Competition, as visualized from the seller's standpoint, has very definite controlling influences that have to be considered in the marketing activity. From the consumer's standpoint, competition carries with it benefits that are sometimes not completely understood or exploited—for example, capitalization on created consumer demand. Since the consumer is the final reduction of the market to its smallest unit, he creates the demand, the satisfaction of which is obviously used as a competitive tactic. One factor to observe and guard against, however, is overreaction to competitive activity, with the needless expenditure of compromise that can ensue, based on ill-advised or premature competitive response.

Negative aspects. Management often conceives competition in its more negative aspects. There are indeed negative considerations, particularly since competition limits market share, market potential, price, and all the many factors that define total response to the given marketing effort. Viewed from this vantage point, competition undeniably has its negative side; but there is a balance in its positive aspects.

Positive aspects. No one will argue as to the value of competition from the consumer's standpoint. In this theory of sociological evolution, the importance of competition as a contributory force has been validated and revalidated. Visualized as a driving force in economic evolution, competition is again a primary motivating influence and as such expands the market internally and externally, thereby of itself effectively generating additional marketability through the creation of further opportunity for competitors. The most obvious positive contribution to business therefore is that, by its very nature, competition creates business.

Legal considerations. Management, especially marketing management, when considering actions of its competitors and of its own corporation, would be very wise to evaluate such activities in the light of federal and state legislation. Antitrust and trade regulations (the Sherman Act of 1890, the Clayton Act of 1914 and its later Robinson-Patman Act amendments, the Federal Trade Commission Act of 1914, and the Celler-Kefauver Antimerger Act of 1950), as well as local legislation, should be thoroughly considered and any contemplated competitive activities reviewed to assure that they are within the framework of existing legislation. (See the following subsection.) □ *George S. Dominguez*

THE LEGAL FRAMEWORK OF MARKETING

This discussion concentrates on situations and relationships that give rise to the legal problems most frequently encountered in marketing. Reference to the statutes and to case law is kept to a minimum. Legal problems that, although important, arise infrequently are not treated. For the sake of simplicity it is assumed that the marketing executive is engaged in marketing a product that does not require special licensing and that his company is not a member of a regulated industry.

Necessarily, the objective of these few pages must be solely to alert the marketing executive to the existence of these legal problems rather than to adivse him of their solutions. The resulting legal checklist, accordingly, will inform the reader when he has need—but not how to dispense with the need—for a legal adviser.

Consumer Problems

In a company's relationship with the consumer, the company's advertising is usually the initial area giving rise to legal problems. Other problem areas are labeling, warranties, and procurement.

Advertising. Deceptive advertising in interstate commerce is unlawful under the Federal Trade Commission Act. There are also many state and local laws that may apply. In addition there are statutes that impose special obligations with respect to special products or services. An example is the federal truth-in-lending law, which governs advertising of certain interest rates and financing terms.

No marketing executive need be reminded that there are legal problems in false advertising. But it is valuable to remember that there may also be legal problems when the advertising is believed to be true but no evidence exists as to its veracity, and even when the advertising can be proved to be literally true but is readily misunderstood by the careless or casual reader. In the former case a marketing executive may find that his company's legal department insists on advance documentation of controversial product claims in order to be prepared to deal with the controversy that may arise. The legal department may consider that even old-fashioned "puffing" cannot be tolerated if it provokes a competitor, a trade association, or a government agency to initiate an expensive legal proceeding. In the latter case—advertising which may be readily misunderstood although true—the trend of modern interpretation and regulation is to place on the advertiser the burden of making his message clear. This is because those most in need of the consumer protection laws may be unable to draw fine distinctions or extract the true meaning from carefully hedged advertising copy.

A host of more technical legal problems are encountered in advertising. One, for example, concerns the obtaining of releases when using others' names or likenesses (photographs or drawings). Advertising men should be encouraged to become familiar with these problems through the various texts and management courses available. The general rule of thumb in dealing with such situations is that a $50,000 advertising program should not be exposed to an injunction merely because a $50 release was not obtained or a slight change in wording was not made.

Labeling. Supplementary problems are involved in labeling products, because legislatures have generally considered that the most effective way of bringing desired information to the consumer's attention is to require the information to be placed before him when he reads the product label. Labeling is subject to extremely technical requirements. The federal statutes on this subject include the Fair Packaging and Labeling Act and the Hazardous Substances Labeling Act. State and local labeling requirements are numerous. Since there are frequently regulations for details such as type size and location of required information, it is obviously necessary to obtain specific information on these requirements early in the course of designing packaging for a product to be placed on the market.

Warranties. A further situation for the marketing executive to anticipate is the possibility of consumer claims after sale. The consumer may claim that the product has caused injury or is otherwise unsatisfactory. The extent of manufacturers' responsibility for injuries caused by the products they sell has been broadened greatly over the past 30 years. The outcome of a product liability claim may depend in part on factors under the control of the marketing executive, such as the advertising and labeling of the product and the accompanying instructional material. The result of ordinary warranty claims may also turn on advertising, and the marketing executive should take part in the decision as to the scope of the warranty and how it is to be advertised.

Warranties referred to in advertising must be fully stated. The warranty given may not vary from the warranty advertised. The warranty must also be reasonable. For example, a long-term warranty may be considered improper if the product is not really expected to last for the period of the warranty. At the other extreme, an unduly short or limited warranty may be considered unlawful because it tends to mislead consumers into believing that they have protection in excess of what is offered. Obviously, a key question for the marketing executive to ask about the warranty is whether it is fair to the consumer. Another key question is whether the selling price includes an adequate allowance for the estimated cost of warranty servicing. This may reduce the possibility that the company is later placed under pressure to skimp on warranty service.

Procurement. All these legal problems affecting consumers take on a different complexion, of course, if the consumer is not the man in the street but an industrial concern or a government agency. In such cases some of the laws that impose specific requirements for the protection of the public may not apply to their full extent. The Fair Packaging and Labeling Act is an example. The company's relationship with sophisticated industrial and government consumers is normally governed by the latter's sales contracts. It is obviously desirable to review carefully such a contract—whether it is embodied in a formal document, an exchange of order and confirmation forms, or an oral understanding—in order to determine if it protects the seller adequately as to essential terms such as price, quantity, delivery, quality, and the seller's responsibilities after sale.

Occasionally, in negotiations with industrial organizations, counsel may be needed because the proposed terms are too general. Vague or incomplete contracts, especially in situations where there is no established trade custom, spawn legal problems that can often be avoided by having a proper contract prepared by counsel. In dealing with government agencies, on the other hand, the marketing executive may also need counsel but for the opposite reason. Government contracts may contain, or incorporate by reference, so many standard clauses or prescribed forms that it may be practically impossible for the marketing executive to understand his obligations under the resulting document. This makes it wise to obtain legal advice as to how much of a commitment is actually being made before determining the price to be charged.

Customer Problems

Potential legal problems in the customer area are numerous. They arise chiefly from restrictions in the appointment of dealers or distributors and from pricing policy, attempts to restrain customers from buying from competitors, and attempts to control resales.

Dealer or distributor appointment.   In selecting his channels of distribution to the ultimate consumer, the marketing executive presumably will desire to sell through wholesale or retail outlets. In initially selecting the dealers or distributors to whom he will sell his products, the marketing executive of a nonmonopoly company has much latitude under the current law. Generally speaking, he is altogether unrestricted in his unilateral choice of his direct customers. He usually encounters legal problems only if he undertakes to make his dealer or distributor appointments by agreement with others, or if he terminates such appointments without adequate justification, or if he seeks to deal with his customers on discriminatory or unduly restrictive terms. One aspect of his freedom to select his customers is his freedom to determine the number of customers he will select in a particular area. To this end he may lawfully agree with a customer that the customer will be the sole distributor appointed within a certain area for some reasonably limited period of time, in order to induce him to devote adequate resources to marketing a low-volume product with high distribution costs.

Pricing.   In dealing with his customers once they have been selected, however, the marketing executive must be aware of the laws concerning discrimination in price or promotional allowances and services among competing customers. Such discrimination is not always forbidden; but where commodites sold in interstate commerce are concerned, it is closely regulated by the Robinson-Patman Act and the Federal Trade Commission Act. These acts raise extremely technical issues. Unless a seller has a uniform one-price policy, F.O.B. or delivered, and makes no promotional services or allowances available to customers, the marketing executive will almost certainly need legal assistance in the design and implementation of his pricing and promotion policy to assure avoidance of unlawful discrimination. Among the issues involved will be those of which products are sufficiently "like" to require similar treatment, when price differences may require justification, what cost savings will justify such differences, and when competition may be met.

Purchases from competitors.   On occasion a seller may desire, as a condition of sale, to require his customers to refrain from obtaining goods or services from competitors. Any such attempt, whether sought to be achieved by tying arrangements, exclusive dealing covenants, total requirement contracts, or franchise licenses, will raise serious antitrust problems.

Resales. Most other legal problems in a manufacturer's relationships with customers arise from attempts of the manufacturer to control what his customers may do with his products once the products have been purchased. For example, agreements stipulating resale prices, except pursuant to federal and state "fair trade" legislation, violate the Sherman Act and may subject the parties to severe penalties, both criminal and civil. This has been established law for many years. It has also been ruled illegal for a manufacturer to limit customers as to where and to whom they will resell products purchased by them. A manufacturer may still suggest a resale price and assign areas and markets of primary responsibility, leaving it to the customer to decide whether he will conform to such suggestions. But for a manufacturer wishing to reserve such decisions to himself, the opportunities are few. A marketing executive would be well advised to consult with counsel before discussing any restriction on resales with customers.

Competitor Problems

Relationships with competitors provide numerous matters in which the exercise of caution is essential, for this is the area most under the influence of the antitrust laws.

Agreements. The marketing executive should realize that, although the antitrust laws do not altogether forbid agreements between competitors, they tend to limit the scope and nature of such agreements so substantially that many corporations lean over backward to avoid equivocal competitive contacts. Thus corporations may, as a matter of policy, ban all business contacts with competitors except where authorized by counsel.

Whether or not his corporation has such a legal policy, a marketing executive should bear in mind that the "contracts, combinations, and conspiracies" forbidden by the Sherman Act are not confined to price-fixing agreements. For example, agreements dividing markets, territories, or customers are among the many types of nonprice agreements that may violate the antitrust laws. Moreover, conduct falling far short of formal agreement has been interpreted by courts and juries to constitute a combination or conspiracy. The general rule of thumb in this area, as in the case of price discrimination, should be to check with counsel before making a move involving cooperation with a competitor.

Coercion. Like the Marquis of Queensberry rules, the antitrust laws ban not only collusion with opponents but also unfairly aggressive conduct toward such opponents. Specifically, these laws reach monopolization and attempts to monopolize as well as contracts, combinations, and conspiracies in unreasonable restraint of trade. Moreover, monopolization of a market is not solely what the term implies in ordinary usage. A company may have active competitors and yet be a monopolist in the antitrust sense if it intentionally acquires or exercises dominant power in a particular line, and if that line is sufficiently distinct to be considered a separate part of commerce. For example, the promotion of championship boxing matches was considered to be a separate part of commerce.

The achievement of such a dominant position is not unlawful, of course, if it results simply from superior performance in the marketplace. However, the use of contracts excluding competitors from supply sources or outlets, discriminatory practices, and acquisitions of competing businesses are among the factors that have been taken into consideration by courts in ruling that a dominant position has not been acquired merely as a result of such superiority. Indeed, the marketing executive must bear in mind that even lawful practices such as long-term leases, if adopted for predatory or exclusionary purposes, may at some future time form part of the evidence in a proceeding directed against his company for an unlawful plan of monopolization.

Organizational activities. From time to time it may be advisable for a company to participate in industry committees, buying groups, and trade associations. The purpose, procedures, and scope of activities of each such organization should be reviewed carefully to ensure that unlawful conduct of others does not expose the executive and his corporation to attack.

Patents. Whether his company or a competitor owns patents and trademarks, the marketing executive must be equally on the alert. On the one hand, if he possesses such rights, he may exclude others from their enjoyment or may license their use on nonrestrictive terms. On the other hand, if a patent is held by others, it is altogether possible that the manufacture and sale of a new product could be enjoined at great cost to the executive's company or that his company might be compelled to pay royalties not contemplated at the time of the formation of the pricing strategy for the product. It is essential that all patent policies be reviewed by antitrust counsel and that all proposed new products be reviewed by patent counsel. The same principle applies to proposed trademarks. A suit by a competitor to enjoin use of a trademark after an advertising program is under way can be both costly and embarrassing.

Corporate Problems

In addition to the legal problems that a marketing executive encounters in his relationships with consumers, customers, and competitors, other legal problems are thrust on him because of the management practices of his own corporation.

Formalities. Normally, the legal department or the secretary will wish to keep signed copies of all outstanding agreements of the company. They will establish procedures for reviewing agreements before signature and assuring that agreements are signed only with proper authorization. They will wish to be kept advised of any changes, proposed changes, or interpretations concerning such agreements that are made by exchanges of correspondence or oral understandings, because these may create conflicts with other agreements, go beyond the authority given, or even raise questions of legality.

Integration. The corporation may also have policies requiring operating units to "stand on their own feet" without unfair assistance from other operating units. If he should fail to heed such policies, the marketing executive could inadvertently expose the company to liability. For example, if a marketing executive were to request the assistance of the purchasing department in making sales presentations to customers, or arrange for the purchasing department to maintain records on sales to potential suppliers, he could expose the company to charges of unlawful reciprocity. Or if he holds out for favored treatment of one branch by another branch of the company and this results in unfair treatment of the competitors of the favored branch, he may in some circumstances expose the company to liability. If the company has a dominant position in its field, there may even be attempts at divestiture by the federal government of parts of the company.

Mergers. A corporation is entitled to expand at will by internal growth, but it may not as freely do so through acquisitions and mergers. Section 7 of the Clayton Act must be considered before entering into negotiations with respect to the stock or assets of other corporations.

Records. Management needs records to operate, and the corporate marketing executive must give attention to maintaining records that are accurate as well as adequate. Reports of sales personnel tend to contain exaggerated and colorful statements, such as a determination to "clobber" the competition or to make full use of the company's "muscle." Often, such statements are not made or taken seriously. But if the company's records are later subpoenaed, such statements may be paraded before a court or jury as evidence of an intent to stifle competition. It is advisable to have written evidence indicating that the company's actual motives were not what such salesmen's reports might inaccurately suggest.

The records of a marketing department may also play an important part in assessing whether proposed mergers have been undertaken for anticompetitive purposes or may have an anticompetitive effect. For many reasons it is useful for the marketing department to work out, in conjunction with the legal department, an adequate system of records that will make it possible for the company to substantiate its legal rights and defend itself against charges of impropriety, and at the same time will be useful in giving the company's other executives adequate information on which to base proposed corporate action.

The Price of Negligence

A marketing executive sometimes asks, "What risks do I incur if I should decide to ignore these legal problems?" The answer is that—if he is challenged in an administrative or judicial proceeding—he will at best incur substantial legal expenses and at worst be subject to varying legal penalties. Thus fines, jail, injunctions, and treble damages may result from antitrust violations. "There are times when fear is good." □ *William T. Lifland and Jerrold G. Van Cise*

CONSUMERISM

Consumerism has been described as a social movement seeking to increase the rights and powers of consumers and buyers in their relationship to sellers and the government. Consumerism is not a phenomenon of the 1960s or 1970s; it has been around since 1914, when the FTC passed a law to provide administrative machinery to enforce antitrust laws and to spell out unfair and unlawful methods of competition and trade practices. Consumerism is a social movement that will change the way we market products and deal with the consumer, and it will grow dramatically in the 1980s. We are all consumers, and the successful seller satisfies the needs of the consumer in an honest, ethical manner because that is good business practice.

Consumerism can be used to the advantage of the marketer. It is so important that it is a major part of education and business. Consumerism is not limited to just consumer goods; it also includes industrial products, because, eventually, the consumer will come in contact with some form of the product. It is vital that marketing people become aware of consumerism and how it affects advertising, marketing mix, packaging, labeling, consumer letters, product recall, and warranties.

Advertising

Consumerism has a major effect on advertising. The marketing person should thoroughly understand advertising laws and what constitutes deceptive trade practice. Congress has established many protective agencies, such as the Federal Drug Administration, the Interstate Commerce Commission, and the Federal Trade Commission, to name just a few.

The FTC has the power to control unfair or deceptive business practices. Since the FTC is getting tough with unfair and deceptive trade practices, the safest way to avoid criticism is not to use deceptive production techniques to differentiate "me too" product offerings. Advertising must also support advertising claims by clarifying the research that was done to substantiate these claims. This would help reduce many claims of unfair and deceptive advertising.

There are also many technical problems. Consider, for example, the classic case where glass marbles were used in an ad photo of soup to make the beef chunks it contained more prominent. Is this deceptive advertising or creative marketing-oriented photography?

The FTC is taking a tougher stand on "bait and switch" tactics. This approach involves advertising an item at a low price to draw customers into the store and then steering them to a more expensive version. For example, a retail store might advertise a TV set at a special low price. When a customer comes in to see the set, she is told that it has been sold out and asked if she would like to see some other models. One of America's largest retailers was recently suspected of this practice and ordered to cease and desist.

Besides the FTC regulations on advertising, there are many state and local laws to be aware of.

Labeling

Legislators believe the most effective way to bring information to the public is through information on the labels of the product. Labeling is subject to legal requirements. There are federal laws, including the Fair Packaging and Labeling Act, the Product Labeling Act, and the Fair Product Labeling Act, that specify such details as content; type size; location of information; identification of product; distributor; manufacturer or packer; and quantity in package. The information required on food labels includes net weight, size of serving, quantity, nutritional information, ingredients (listed in order of amount), and date for freshness. The FDA labeling laws also require grades for canned processed foods and meats. These grades are meant to guide the consumer as to the level of quality.

In 1971, the Federal Trade Commission ruled that care instructions must be given in clothing. This ruling specifies that all fabrics be labeled as to the laundering care that will be required to maintain the garment's original character.

Deceptive graphics on labels are to be avoided, since they can mislead the consumer as to the true contents of the package when a purchase decision is made. To comply with the law, it is important to know all the latest government regulations.

Complaints and Service

In handling consumer complaints and service problems, one should always remember that consumer satisfaction is the goal of the marketer. One way to achieve this satisfaction is by answering the consumer letters promptly and adequately. This will give the consumer a feeling that the company cares, and the consumer is apt to choose that product again.

There are five steps that will help in handling consumer letters and complaints and keeping customers happy: (1) Establish a complaint policy if there is not an existing one. (2) Put the policy in writing, and let your employees know what the rules are. (3) Centralize your system so that one department or one person is handling the complaints. (4) Act promptly. This is the key. The quicker the better. This can be an easy way to have satisifed customers. (5) Keep a log of complaints that have been handled. You can learn a great deal from this, such as which products have broken parts and have been returned because of malfunctioning.

Remember that the most important goal when dealing with a complaint is not to assign blame but to solve the problem at the least cost and to the benefit of everybody. To identify and remedy the defect as soon as possible is the marketer's obligation to the consumer.

Product Recall and Safety

In product recall, promptness is also the key. The government set up the Consumer Product Safety Commission (CPSC), which has the power to regulate the production and sale of consumer products that are potentially hazardous. The CPSC not only sets up safety standards for consumer products, but also can ban manufacture and sale of any product deemed hazardous. It can seize products from the market that are hazardous. If the company does not implement a recall voluntarily, the government will. (See Table 6-2 for the federal laws governing specific recall authority.)

With consumer awareness reaching an all-time high, major retailers are swept up in an increasing number of product recalls. In a poll taken of J. C. Penney, Federated, and May Company department stores, Woodward and Lothrop, Bullock's, and Zayres, all shared the opinion that the mere fact of participating in a recall does not harm a store's image. On the contrary, the consumer likes it, since consumers like to feel protected, and the company also benefits in the process. The consumer feels that the company cares and is trying, and since everyone makes mistakes, it is a good company that can admit to a mistake and correct it. It is also an important point that the problem will be corrected.

A major study to identify various factors that influence public attitudes toward product recalls of faulty products was conducted by John C. Mowen, assistant professor of marketing at Oklahoma State University's College of Business Administration. He says there are direct correlations between how a company handles such a situation and the public perception of the firm. Among the key points he makes are: (1) The public believes a well-known company is less culpable for a defect than a lesser-known company. (2) The public perceives the company as more responsible when it acts before a government agency steps in. (3) A company is believed less concerned for the consumer welfare when it takes a long time to recall the product. (4) The company that has recalled several products is perceived as being more at fault for a particular defect than a company with few recalls. (5) Companies revealing the worst aspects of the recall first, rather than putting the brightest interpretation up front, score the highest with the public.

The study suggested that the most favorable perceptions are gained when the first report gives the worst possible outcome. Companies tend to understate their cases, and as a case escalates, with numbers becoming higher and conditions more severe, the trust level of the public goes down. However, when companies report the worst possible outcome, any results that improve upon that outcome are viewed as a plus for the company and its credibility goes up with the consumer.

Once the product recall is ordered, the four main methods of reaching the consumer about the recall are direct mail; advertisements in print, television, and radio; news releases in the media; and in-store displays. Product recall can be very expensive; not only does the manufacturer have to repair or replace the product, but it also must incur the high cost of communicating the recall to the consumer.

Product recall insurance is available. Most product recall insurance is underwritten by Lloyds of London. The two major domestic companies that underwrite such insurance are Fireman's Fund Insurance Co. and Admiral Insurance Co. Product recall insurance generally covers the administrative expenses of complying with a recall. Not too many companies use this type of insurance, because most feel that the insurance costs more than the actual recall would.

It is good business practice to make certain that before a product goes out in the marketplace, it is thoroughly tested so there is little chance for product recall. Very often product failure occurs because of efforts to cut costs coupled with inadequate product testing. Consumerism in its truest sense must ensure that the buyer is protected against catastrophic product failure.

Table 6-2. Recall authority.

Authority (Congress)	Agency	Powers	Products	Examples
Consumer Products Safety Act Flammable Fabrics Act Federal Hazardous Substances Act Poison Prevention Packaging Act	Consumer Product Safety Commission	Can order recalls; can effect recalls by threat of seizure, injunction, etc.; can make rules that can bring about recalls.	Most consumer products; hazardous substances; medical devices.	Amusement park rides; toy missiles; electric percolators.
Motor Vehicle Safety Act	National Highway Traffic Safety Administration	Can order recalls; can effect recalls by threat of seizure, injunction, etc.; can make rules that can bring about recalls.	Motor vehicles and tires.	Ford Pintos and Bobcats; Firestone "500" radials.
Federal Trade Commission Act	Federal Trade Commission	Can force recall of misleading advertising.	Advertising.	Corrective ads for Listerine.
National Mobile Home Construction and Safety Standards Act	Department of Housing and Urban Development	Can order recalls; can make rules that bring about recalls.	Mobile homes.	Tappan gas stoves.

Act	Agency	Powers	Products Covered	Examples
Federal Food, Drug and Cosmetic Act; Public Health Service Act; Radiation Control for Health and Safety Act	Food and Drug Administration	Can order recalls; can effect recalls by threat of seizure, injunction, etc.; can make rules that bring about recalls.	Food, drugs, and cosmetics; medical devices; radiation-emitting devices; biologic products.	Animal feed; pretzels.
Federal Boat Safety Act; Miscellaneous marine inspection laws	United States Coast Guard	Can order recalls; can make rules that bring about recalls; can suspend certification.	Ships; pleasure boats.	Outboard engines.
Federal Aviation Act; Clean Air Act	Federal Aviation Administration	Can make rules that bring about recalls; can suspend certification.	Aircraft and components.	Wide-bodied aircraft.
Clean Air Act; Toxic Substances Control Act; Federal Insecticide, Fungicide, and Pesticide Act	Environmental Protection Agency	Can order recalls; can effect recalls by threat of seizure, injunction, etc.; can make rules that can bring about recalls; can suspend certification.	Motor vehicles and engines; hazardous chemical substances; pesticides.	Cars and trucks.

Source: FRASER/Associates, Washington, DC.

Warranties

The FTC has set up guidelines to try to assure that warranties are not deceptive
or unfair. The FTC is concerned with warranties being unambiguous and clear.
There are basically two types of warranty: full and limited. A full warranty states
that the product must be repaired or replaced by the seller without charge and
within a certain period of time with no limitations. A limited warranty states what
is covered and not covered in the warranty and has limitations. Warranties are
known for their highly technical legal language. It is the job of the marketer to
make certain the warranty can be easily read and understood by the consumer.
In 1975, Congress enacted a federal law on warranties—the Magnussen-Moss
Warranty Act—and the FTC Improvements Act, which covers consumer products costing $5 or more. The Magnussen-Moss Act closes many loopholes that
manufacturers had included in their warranties. The act also encourages the sellers to set up informal dispute settlement procedures to handle complaints made
under the warranties.

Warranties are not mandatory, but they are in the best interest of the marketer
and the consumer. In case complaints do come up about your product, you have
a warranty to refer to for coverage. This, in turn, can make the consumer more
satisifed and apt to buy your product again. Warranties can be very expensive;
therefore, you should look closely at the product and its effect on the consumer
to see if the warranty is justified.

Consumer Relations

Consumer relations departments are important in being responsive to consumerism. In some cases, this may be the only contact the consumer will have with
your company. The employees that work in consumer relations should have a
good understanding of human relations, since they have to deal one to one with
the customer. The consumer relations department communicates with the consumer in a variety of ways. For example, it may develop consumer buying guides
to assist in the making of buying decisions; informative labeling; instructions for
use and care of products; and wording of warranties so they are understandable
to the customer. Some large companies have a toll-free telephone service to enable them to deal with complaints about products or services promptly.

Another service a consumer relations department can offer is a monthly newsletter. This can be an informative letter about established and new products and
even new legislation, or a question-and-answer page. This helps give the consumer the feeling that the company cares about him.

Many consumers think that big business doesn't care about them. Companies
need to prove to the American public that they do care. Here is a simple consumerism audit that your company can follow: (1) Find out if your company is consumer-oriented and how you handle consumer complaints and questions. (2)
Find out how employees of the consumer relations department are trained and
how good your product quality control is. (3) Study your product or service and
see if it fulfills consumer expectations. (4) Evaluate your consumer satisfaction

level and target areas of improvement. (5) Meet with department heads, discuss product improvements, and implement changes where practical.

An audit of this type should be done on a regular basis, and improvements in dealing with the consumer should be made wherever possible. A company needs to give the consumer the feeling that it does care.

In conclusion, we must recognize that consumerism is not just an important social issue but also an important marketing issue. We must accept the responsibility for consumer claims after sales and be ready to satisfy those claims. We have a social responsibility to educate the consumer, since lack of consumer education affects the poor and the elderly. These people have little extra money, are vulnerable, and can be taken advantage of in the marketplace because they have little disposable income.

Virginia Knauer, director of the U.S. Office of Consumer Affairs, said, "Business could not expect consumers to accept a decrease in government regulation unless business was more responsive to consumers." She also stated that consumers are looking for more meaningful information provided by companies that stand behind their claims.

Many of us believe that it is not in the best interests of business to incur additional government regulations and control. Therefore, we must be responsive to consumerism.   □ *Jane M. Freiman*

CUSTOMER BUYING BEHAVIOR

An understanding of the buying behavior of customers and prospects is essential to introducing a new product or service successfully and developing the full potential thereafter. This understanding must be thorough and current, since behavior is constantly changing, usually gradually but at times abruptly, because of forces outside the control of any one marketer. Nevertheless, every marketer is attempting either to change behavior or, in the case of established markets, to prevent behavior from changing.

The act of buying results when internal attitudes and intentions and external catalysts combine in the absence of constraints in the environment in such a way that it seems easy and safe to a customer for him to buy. A central task in marketing is to keep the purchase as free as possible from effort and risk in the view of the buyer.

Basic Factors

Customer buying behavior is a function of six factors: (1) the nature of the marketer; (2) the nature of the customer; (3) the nature of the product or service; (4) timing; (5) availability (where and how the product or service is offered); and (6) motivation (benefits expected and received). It is helpful to think of each of these factors in terms of two dimensions. Marketers are describable in terms of size and reputation. Customers are describable objectively (by age, sex, income, education, domicile, occupation, and other demographic characteristics) and subjectively (by less apparent psychological and other intangible characteristics). Products and services are describable as to their concept and content. Timing is most usefully approached in terms of *introduction* or initial purchasing, and *continuation* or repurchase maintenance. Availability breaks down into place of purchase and means of purchase. Motivation is a matter of benefits expected and received, and the benefits can be of two kinds: primary, direct, or positive; or secondary, indirect, or negative. Adding up these items results in 12 angles from which to view customer behavior—more than most marketers actively deal with at any one time.

Nature of Marketer

The marketer is a factor in customer buying behavior either directly or through the agents he selects to purvey his offering. In consumer products the name of the marketer may either facilitate or diminish purchasing activity, because of his size and general reputation, or because of specific experience of customers with other of his offerings. With this in mind, manufacturers decide whether to use corporate, division, or subsidiary names, especially in the case of new and revised products. In industrial purchasing the identity of the vendor, his approach to the buyer, and his capabilities are significant factors in buying decisions. In government purchasing the size of the bidder, his location, and the history of past relations all enter into the considerations of purchasing goods and services from him rather than from other possible contractors. The first task of the marketer is to prepare for his own acceptance—to ensure that customer prospects will elect to deal with him at all, or, in established markets, that they will continue to deal with him.

Consumers and the marketer. There are many examples of the varied usage of company names in retailing. One large soap company, knowing the impact of its name on housewives, allows product managers of new brands to feature the company name in introductory advertising only for a specified period of time; thereafter, the product must survive on the strength of its own image and market acceptance. A large food company knows that a subsidiary name gains more acceptance from customers for frozen foods than its own name and continues to promote that name rather than its corporate style. In contrast, a major chemicals company found that consumers would accept color film bearing its name only if associated with a better-known name in photography.

Other customers and the marketer. Business and industrial buying are no less affected by the nature of the marketer. A tobacco company buying its first computer system was less impressed by the equipment described in solicited proposals than by the number of representatives sent and the distance they had to travel, both of which were measures of installation capabilities and service intentions. A utility may divide its buying between two or three major equipment suppliers in order to ensure their survival, thereby reducing opportunity for a new, smaller marketer. Many industrial and government purchasers maintain an approved list of suppliers for which the prospective marketer must qualify. There may be several lists for different products and services, each one with different standards that the marketer must meet.

In most government purchasing, suppliers on an approved list may receive some or all of the requests for quotation that the buyer sends out. However, pre-proposal services, including considerable personal attention in one form or another, are necessary if the marketer is to receive serious consideration from the buyer. In addition the marketer is evaluated against other bidders and prospective bidders, and the secondary effect of awarding a contract to one or the other is given weight equal to or greater than the product or service itself.

Both business and government purchasers, like the consumer, favor a marketer who has done exactly or nearly exactly the same thing before in the provision of goods and services, because the risk appears to be less. In areas where the buyer has little experience contractors located near the work site or buyer's headquarters are favored, chiefly because of nominal cost saving; but other able marketers, including those providing R&D services, are usually given fair consideration if they persist. When the marketer is able to present his offering as unique, he may be given work as a "sole source" without competitive bidding. This is precisely the position that consumer-goods manufacturers hope will be accorded to them by individuals and families. Consumers and other customers alike expect higher prices to be charged by the "sole source" and are willing to pay them according to their knowledge of the marketer. Some marketers are sufficiently powerful in their respective industries to administer prices and to be price leaders. In such cases customers will not pay higher prices to smaller marketers, even for specialties, until the price leader sets the level.

In short, regardless of the marketing area, the marketer's identity affects the buyer's behavior. Many have found new sources of business from learning what people are willing to buy from them, while others have sustained losses from pushing an offering that gained little acceptance because of the nature of the marketer.

Nature of Customer

A customer is an individual acting for himself or as a member of a group, family, or organization. The customer for any product or service may be a reseller, a gift buyer, or a user of the product or service. The individual rarely purchases anything without having imagined, if not actually ascertained, the effect of his buying behavior on others, mainly people in his immediate environment. The others who are considered, even briefly, may exist in the past or in the future as well as in the present life of the individual. A consumer may be thinking of what his parents or an early mentor would say were they to learn of his purchase; he may also envision how his children would react to it in later years. An executive evaluating a buying opportunity on behalf of a corporation may look at the alternatives as he imagines the founder would, or a professor whose teachings he has always relied upon; at the same time he may be looking ahead at the effect of the purchase on those who learn of it much later—his successor, for example.

Isolated purchasing decision. The mental rehearsal of the effect of a purchase on other people may take place at the time of purchase, in the case of impulse purchasing, or, in the case of deliberative or planned purchasing, during a period of time prior to the purchase. For purchases made routinely, a customer may have gone through this process years before and closed his mind to further reflection upon it, despite the fact that in the meantime his way of life has changed in other respects. To be a prospect for some other product or service, such a customer must direct his attention to the inappropriateness of his routine habit. Customers are not necessarily loyal to their own nature but do hold to preferences for certain products and brands. Over 20 years some 25 percent of initial brand preferences may be retained. Brand loyalty is partly a function of length of use; the more something is purchased, the more likely it will continue to be purchased.

Reference groups.   The other people whom the customer considers in thinking about and making a purchase may be described in terms of nonwork activities in which the customer is a participant, such as skiing or churchgoing, or in terms of class. Classes are defined by relative amounts of wealth and personal power. Education, occupation, and income are the major overt indicators of class, and many people see differences in attitudes as well. To the extent that an individual identifies with others similar to him in these respects, buying behavior can be characterized along class lines. According to one research study, in the upper class, men buy their own clothing; in the middle class, they buy it jointly with their wives; in the lower class, women buy their husband's clothes, along with virtually all the household purchases. Other habits and tastes also vary between the classes. An automatic dishwasher is distinctly an upper- and middle-class product, despite the fact that the lower class purchases other appliances and household goods in the same or higher price ranges. In contrast, laxatives are a lower-class product in terms of the income of purchasers. The upper class was conservative in accepting television, but its housebound entertainment, requiring no social exposure or acceptance for enjoyment, was taken up quickly by the lower class. The lower class was conservative in adopting canasta, while it swept through the upper class. The middle class accepted supermarkets more readily than either the lower or the upper class. Reference groups strongly influence the purchase of cars, cigarettes, beer, and other products conspicuously purchased or used.

Pace setting and trend making are often functions of class. The bulk of customers in the lower and middle classes will reject the product or service that has not first been accepted by those whose taste they trust and whose behavior they emulate. Fiber-glass curtains failed to be profitable in their first years, not because of faulty manufacturing but because they were introduced in low-price lines without prior acceptance by the upper-middle class. Aluminum siding at first gained no more than an insignificant sales volume because it was placed on small development homes; as a result, it came to signify cheapness, wealthier home owners would not use it, and the middle class had nothing to emulate. On the other hand, customers in the highest classes may deliberately adopt styles identified with lower classes as evidence of their own recognition of practical values. Consumers without much status strongly favor popular brand-named products, whereas those whose positions and fortunes are secure can afford to buy and serve cheaper private-label and off-brand products; in fact, they account for a disproportionate share of such purchases. Disadvantaged elements of society want the "best" or the "biggest" they can buy. This behavior is unrelated to personal income or to price, to actual product performance or personal service delivered, for the customers are seeking an abstract value that confers benefits beyond the mere possession of the purchased item. Each marketer of consumer products or services must determine if status or class is affecting buying behavior with respect to his offering.

Fabric converters, who buy rolls of cloth from mills and finish and print them for garment makers, also make decisions in isolation; they are buying for their own positions and go through the mental rehearsal process when selecting material. In anticipating the reactions of their customers' customers, they try to imagine the ultimate consumer's reaction when approaching a rack of finished clothing. Quasi-technical terms, such as "look," "hand," and "feel," are derived directly from this mental rehearsal. The marketer must determine in each case which other groups are being considered in the buyer's decision.

Group purchasing decision. The apparent difference between the buying behavior of customers acting in isolation and the behavior of buyers acting within a group is attributable to the transfer of these considerations from the thought level to the speech level, resulting in direct information from "significant others" as to how they will react to various possible purchases. At the same time, nevertheless, all the individuals in a group are envisioning the effect of any purchase on still others who are either not present or outside the group membership entirely. How long this process goes on before the decision is made and the act of buying is performed is mainly a function of the customer's tolerance for anxiety rather than the size or implications of the purchase. People "should" spend more time in selecting and shopping for a refrigerator than a toaster, but often they do not. The decision to buy a piece of machinery must be made by a certain date, whether or not all the facts about competitive equipment are in. Pressure of time and other importunities aside, many customers end up buying a specific offer because they can't stand any further reflection or inaction.

Decision-making unit (DMU). As the proper body to which a marketer must address his efforts, the DMU itself affects buying behavior. The same individual will make different decisions and purchases, depending on the DMU he is a member of at the time, even on the same day. An individual desiring to purchase a new house or new furniture is heavily influenced by whether his children are in school or are grown and gone from home. The individual desiring to purchase office typewriters adaptable to optical character recognition is heavily influenced by whether he is on the administrative or the long-range planning committee or both. The same is true of individuals playing different roles in institutional or government hierarchies. The DMU takes on the character of an individual, and its members affect each other much as thoughts affect the individual in isolated buying behavior. As a result, the DMU becomes personified and enters into buying considerations. This is true even of conglomerates engaged in shopping for and buying whole businesses.

Within the same DMU, criteria applied to selecting products and services may differ. Conflicting points of view also exist in commercial and industrial DMUs. In judging a new product line, the head of a department store may be concerned chiefly with net profit contribution and the store image; the division merchandiser, with gross profit and reliability of the supplier; and the department buyer, with net revenue and turnover. The marketer, however, must satisfy each viewpoint.

Price and customer. Customers react differently to price. Some are inveterate price shoppers, regardless of the product or service, and require some semblance of a bargain before they buy. Others feel sufficiently affluent, or desire to appear so, to give very little attention to price. The greatest number of customers judge price in relation to the significance of the product or service to them. Customer awareness of, and ability to report, price is the single best indicator of its importance.

Buying power. Just as customers buy benefits (offered by products and services) on the basis of expectations, they spend in advance of income on the basis of anticipated buying power. Surveys of general customer confidence are important indicators of future buying behavior, as are surveys of intention to buy specific goods because of expectations of increased income and money to spend. The rate and amount of capital expenditures by manufacturers, representing the investment of time and effort in the anticipation of profit, indicate the confidence of the productive sector of our economy. In either case, customers buy more readily when they are confident than in a period of retrenchment, when the decision not to purchase one thing leads to not purchasing others. This is true of customers in households, service firms, factories, and government agencies.

Customers in transition. About one-third of the population at any one time is in transition with respect to buying behavior because of changes induced by ordinary life experiences: moving residence, changing schools or leaving school, entering or leaving the armed services, taking a new job or quitting a job, getting married or divorced, retiring, reacting to the death of relatives, and other events that disrupt the continuity of habits and preferences. These people soon settle into a new mode of life and reestablish a consistent buying behavior. While they are in the transitional state, however, their purchases may be erratic and unrelated to their prior life situation, and may reflect a trial mixture of newly possible patterns of purchasing. People in the transitional state may experiment with novel offerings, but they are not true innovators and are not in a position to influence many others. As many industrial salesmen have learned, sometimes to their confusion and dismay, the same transitional state is encountered in the buying behavior of organizations as they relocate, expand, merge, or diversify.

Nature of Product or Service

A benefit promised by a marketer to a customer prospect in return for money or other consideration may be in the form of a product or a service. A product may be accompanied by service or may have service built into it, as in the case of labor-saving appliances or prepared foods. A service may be accompanied by tangible goods that facilitate the performance of the service to become convertible under certain conditions, as in the case of insurance.

Buying behavior is greatly affected by the definition of the offer made by a marketer; in fact, the definition may determine whether the purchase will be made. The two aspects of an offering (product or service) that greatly affect buying behavior are its concept and its content. The concept of an offer embodies the promise of benefit and is critical in initial acceptance, while the content (what is delivered after the purchase is made) mainly determines repeat purchasing.

Concept of the offer. A compendium of information on foreign countries may fail if offered as a basic product followed by monthly updating sheets but succeed as a newsletter followed by an annual summary, even though the content is pretty much the same: whereas the first concept requires the acceptance of a sizable reading job plus regular work in updating, the second offers a light reading task and an opportunity of obtaining a one-volume reference book. Buying behavior is triggered by the proper conceptualization of the offering. For example, a gin offered as superior because of aging may utterly fail, despite several years and several million dollars of advertising, because the concept is conveyed by a yellow color that proves incompatible with user need for a clear ingredient in cocktails that must not appear to have too much vermouth. Or an automobile advertised as "designed for the young executive on his way up" fails on a conceptual basis, when introduced during an economic recession in which the customer prospect is not sure he is on the way up.

Advertising may convey a concept that differs from the content delivered. People buy promises, however; they will change their "blind" taste ratings of beer when the labels are revealed, thus conforming to the advertised image rather than to their own senses. This phenomenon exists for products and services that provide chiefly psychological benefits; customers responding to the advertising of air-conditioned comfort are soon lost if there is no such comfort.

Content of the offer. Customers must also accept the content of an offer, either before or after a purchase, if a successful market is to be sustained. Content consists of substance and structure; structure includes all aspects of composition and presentation, from size and shape to packaging and labeling. Customers' perception of a product or service is greatly affected by the way it is presented to them. Products can be made too well. Small gasoline engines must be reasonably durable, but few customers demand a 50-year life engineered into the construction. Content itself may, on inspection, influence purchase in unpredictable ways because of the absence of indicators of benefits that customers expect and insist upon prior to purchasing. Customers may select a loaf of bread because the color connotes richness, regardless of the ingredients listed on the label; a bottle of syrup because it is thin rather than pure; a small appliance because the sound of the motor connotes power, regardless of observed performance in demonstrations; or a large appliance because it has more push buttons, even though they are never used.

Packaging and labeling are part of the content of the offering and may affect customer behavior in purchasing and repurchasing by the manner in which they convey the concept and facilitate the functional delivery of the benefits promised or expected. Packaging includes the size and number of separable units in the offering. Formerly, customers were buying three or six cans of beer at a time, three or six boxes of film before vacation trips, three or six golf balls—all before packaging caught up with their preferences. When packaging is relevant to buying behavior, sales go well.

Price and the product or service. Customers have expectations based upon comparing an offering to others like it or to the cost of activities they recognize as alternatives to the offering. The key to understanding customer behavior as related to price, product, or service lies in determining what other offerings are being compared and what alternatives, if any, are recognized and considered. A jar of toasted coconut, for example, may be expected by customers to cost 19 cents on the baking-ingredients shelf of a supermarket, where it is compared with the 17-cent plain, shredded coconut beside it; when the same jar is placed next to expensive dessert toppings on a shelf over the ice cream freezer, customers may expect to pay 39 cents.

Customers who shop and compare prices, or who accept bids, feel safest with a price close to what most marketers quote; they are suspicious of the lowest figures because credibility is undermined. A proportion of customers generally in any field, and specifically for any one product or service, buy on a price basis alone without considering other aspects of the concept or content of the offering. Bargain hunters and price switchers as a group form a significant number of customers when the marketer emphasizes low price. However, product quality and delivery capability are two considerations that often override the lowest price offerings to individual customers.

Timing

There may be no more critical aspect affecting customer buying behavior than timing; the same offering in all particulars can utterly fail at one time yet reach the heights of success at another. The first step in understanding the effect of timing on buying behavior is to discard the belief that there is any possibility that timing is not important. Too often, casually deceptive comments such as "they buy all year 'round" or "a sale can be made at any time" have led marketers to a false conception of customer buying behavior. Virtually nothing in customer behavior happens evenly "all year 'round."

Seasonal buying. Men buy the bulk of their purchases of photographic film in May, women in September. More men buy watches in the first six months of the year, and more women buy them in the last six months of the year. Low-priced watches sell well in December; high-priced, in June. Toothbrushes peak in June (before summer camp) and September (before school). Educational products not ordered or budgeted for in the spring have little chance of acceptance until the following year. Most consumer products and services have cycles built around the change of seasons and the holidays.

Commercial and industrial activity cycles are also functions of these cycles but, because of variations in production and distribution volumes, develop sometimes unique patterns of their own. The heaviest sale of canned tomato products is in September, when distributors take large positions at favorable prices, even though consumption peaks later in the winter. Sporting-goods lines and toys are designed more than a year before ultimate retail sale to enable the trade to screen, order, and stock before peak consumer demand in season. Products or services offered in disharmony with such cycles have little chance of success.

Superimposed on these cycles of purchasing and use are the annual budgets of corporations. Items to be purchased in the summer for use in the fall are often inserted in preliminary budget requests the previous October, approved in December, and funded in January.

Primacy. Being first in a market affects buying behavior for a long time to come. The first filter cigarette or light scotch introduced in a given metropolitan area dominates there for many years even though latecomers may gain supremacy nationwide. But the introduction of an offering may be "before its time." For example, safety belts introduced by one auto maker in advance of public readiness to accept them cost the company many unit sales one year, but several years later the same belts became a standard item on all cars.

Passage of time. The behavior of individual customers changes over the years. Customers age and either grow out or die out of the market. A sizable proportion of teen-age cola drinkers graduates to beer, and a sizable proportion of young beer drinkers goes on to mixed drinks. The customers for home remedies brought out more than a generation ago slowly reduce these purchases, yet their continued usage impedes the acceptance of the product by younger prospects.

Generally, the earliest purchasers will form the nucleus of heavy users, and the bulk of those who follow will be occasional or light users of a product or service. With the passage of time, the product or service itself ages, as first more and then fewer customers have the opportunity to become aware of the offering and to purchase and repurchase it. For this reason, products have cycles of their own.

Recency. Another time-related factor that affects buying behavior is recency. Whereas primacy may have great overall impact on customers, the recency of exposure to an offering may have a greater effect on triggering the actual purchase. The reason for this is simply that people generally forget—mainly, because other matters intervene—about 70 percent of what they could report the previous day. Their attention is continually directed elsewhere. As a result customers need to be reminded of what they initially learned. Some purchases are determined on the basis of the last advertisement seen, the last store shopped, or the last salesman to call. The strongest reminder is the purchase of the offer and satisfaction with the purchase. For prospective customers the multitude of unsolicited influences impinging on them every day is the source of reminders. Marketers must determine if recency is significant in the behavior of their customers and prospects.

Price and timing. Price is closely related to timing. Customers may be willing to buy something once at a given price, but not repeatedly. Seasonal prices are recognized by customers as natural, although some price cycles are artificially induced by marketers to even out seasonal peaks and valleys in inventory or sales volume. For example, because customers came to expect tire sales at discount prices on the Fourth of July, competitors are locked into this seasonal variety of price although most tire sales are normally made at this time (prior to vacation trips), whereas in other industries sales at lower prices are usually made in the off season when purchaser volume is normally low.

Availability

Where and how the product or service is purchasable is a major factor in customer buying behavior. To the customer, shortage or surplus of supply is significant only in his personal experience. Major effects on decisions and actions are related to place and means of purchase, which are determined by the marketer's policies in distribution and selling methods.

Distribution. For many years motor scooters had limited sales because prospects preferred not to purchase from the motorcycle dealers who dominated distribution. Then a foreign producer, heeding the repeated findings of American market research studies, set up a network of outlets with an upper-class appeal. This basic break stimulated buying behavior and opened the way for the expression of latent demand. Similarly, lottery tickets in New York State failed to meet sales forecasts until they were made available in stores where customers could feel comfortable in buying them.

Selling methods. Selling methods interact with customer behavior. Because of past habits or current situation, customers favor one form of purchasing over another. The interaction of selling method and customer behavior is demonstrated in the contrast between mail-order and door-to-door sales. People who buy by one method resist anything sold by the other method; thus a large door-to-door seller of vacuum cleaners learned that his customer lists were useless for direct-mail offers. For the same reason the best mailing list for a product sold by mail is a list of those who already have purchased something by mail, preferably similar in type and price level.

Customers who prefer to buy on credit, either in a store or from a route man, will be more easily sold other products on the same basis even though they may be able to pay cash. At the same time, customers who habitually pay cash tend strongly to stay with their preferred form of purchasing. Offering 28-foot inboard cruisers on the installment plan has no effect on customer behavior because such customers have the cash, expect open-account credit, or are trading in a smaller cruiser making up more than half the price of the new boat. The selling method chosen by a marketer will open some parts of the market to him and close others, even though the product or service is the same. For nonconsumer products and services, the same holds true.

Some buyers prefer to be called on; others delight in making outside investigations, either directly or through trade shows or in leisure activities. In the same way, some customers demand contact with headquarters or national representatives, while others find local agents reassuring. These preferences exist independently of size of order or account, need for service, or other factors that also influence buying behavior. In the farm product market, for example, company men often find that though they provide more personal service and information than local dealers, the customer still prefers transactions in nearby establishments to ordering direct. At times, customers may change their preferred modes of purchasing. Generally, however, the familiar has a much stronger influence on buying behavior than the unfamiliar.

Price and availability. Price acceptance by customers is related to the availability of the offer. Supply, whether surplus or short, is recognized by customers as a factor that affects price and alters their expectations and willingness to buy. The place where the offer is purchasable also influences price acceptance; the most dramatic examples are found in retail stores that have high-class or low-class images. The same phenomenon influences nonconsumer customers; often elabo-

rate showrooms or high-caliber salesmen are necessary to sustain high-priced offerings, and without them customer price expectations are substantially lower.

Selling methods not only interact with customer behavior but induce different
price expectations as well. Cost per month, rather than total cost, is the "price" in
installment sales, and higher amounts are accepted by customers because of budget or cash-flow convenience. Products sold without service features have accustomed consumers to "discount" prices. For services sold at higher-than-average
prices, customers expect and usually receive tangible evidences of value in the
form of gifts, premiums, or helpful aids of one sort or another.

Motivation

The question of why customers are buying a product or a service is best an-
swered in terms of the net benefits anticipated by prospects and experienced by
users. These benefits can be direct or indirect, primary or secondary, positive or
negative. At times the indirect, secondary, or negative benefits are the most important in motivation. Once discovered, they explain seemingly irrational buying
behavior.

Primary and positive benefits. Presumably, some need is being met by a purchase, but this need may or may not be reportable by the customer or observable
by others. The customer may be expecting one major benefit or a combination of
benefits after accepting the marketer's offer. His motive may be to achieve economy, identity, prestige, or the indulgence of vanity. Economy is possible not only
in money but also through limiting time and effort. In seeking to be provided
with personal identity by virtue of the purchase, the customer may be expressing
either venturesomeness or conservatism. Prestige may be conferred by indicating
membership (conformity) or by signaling exclusivity for the user. Finally, in ca-
tering to the customer's vanity, a product or service may serve to demonstrate his
achievement or personal qualities. It is the constant seeking by customers to fulfill
these motives, in various combinations, that causes flux in the market, creates dissatisfactions that open opportunities for other marketers, and is responsible for
cycles in what is fashionable.

In the initial marketing of a product or service, the most important motivation
of customers is that of venturesomeness. Innovators or leaders may contribute
only 10 to 15 percent of the ultimate users, but they are critically important at the
outset. To obtain a foothold in the market, the marketers of any product or service are well advised to seek out those among customer prospects who are unusually willing to try new things.

Secondary and negative benefits. Usually, when the customer considers
others in order to obtain their approval or acceptance of a purchase, he is attempting to satisfy their expectations. In an unknown proportion of instances,
however, the customer is more intent upon displeasing certain people whose
reactions to his purchase he anticipates. This is a secondary benefit. A negative
benefit is desired at times by individuals and organizations in order to purge
themselves of unwanted feelings or possessions through the purchase of specific
products or services. In the case of consumers, some buy a marketer's offering in

order to punish themselves for real or imagined guilt or as a means to come to terms with their superegos or consciences.

Negative motives include those mildly felt, such as simply not wanting to buy some other offer or to please someone else, and those intensely felt, such as outright defiance, hostility, or rage toward another product or service, person or group, or idea connected symbolically with the marketer's offering. Negative motives in organizations are quite varied: the desire to reduce surplus to sustain losses, to use up profit so as to avoid lower prices or rate base, to resolve tax problems, to obtain subsidies, and other means of coming to terms with the private sector's superego (usually in the form of a regulatory government body). When faced with buying behavior that does not seem to make sense on the surface, marketers may look for indirect, secondary, and negative benefits for a possible explanation. This is true of all buying behavior, from minor consumer items to major industrial expenditures and government orders.

What customers get out of a product or service is often different from what was intended by the marketer. For many years a large proportion of the packaged onion soup sold was used to make cocktail dips. When this use was discovered, direct advertising and competition to serve this customer motive opened a much broader market that included the less imaginative elements of the society. In another instance, resistance to the purchase of equipment for manufacturing intravenous solutions in hospitals was experienced by one company, despite the motivation of large cost savings and prestige for the pharmacist, because health insurance companies reimbursed hospitals for 70 percent of the high-priced bottled solutions, with an added allowance for overhead. The underlying motivation of customers must therefore be detected and provided for in relevant form before a product or service can succeed.

Combinations of benefits.   Some motives are interlinked. Customers who state they selected a car because of initial price also mention style in nearly equal frequency (and trade the car in earlier); customers who state durability as a major expected benefit also mention operating-cost economy more often than expected (and trade the cars in less frequently). For any given offering, a marketer is well advised to determine which set of expected benefits his best prospects seek so as to avoid conflicts in conveying the concept. However, customers perceive selectively and believe what they want to believe; it is perfectly possible for customers with different motives to see promises of satisfaction in the same offering. In fact, satisfying many different types of customers at the same time is what creates a mass market. The real danger is that the concept or content is insufficient to confirm the hopes of specific types of customers so that they do not care if somebody else's motives are fulfilled by the same product or service.

Belief in the future potential of a product or service can justify purchasing when it is bolstered by prestige benefits, even though economic benefits cannot be demonstrated. Most first-generation computers were purchased on this basis, and often without detailed evaluation.

Price and motivation.   Price in itself, either high or low, may serve as a benefit that satisfies any or a combination of customer motives. What price signifies must be determined empirically for each situation. A relatively high or low price for a given offer may have different meaning for different customers. Expensive shoes may be justified in the working class as "more economical in the long run." Lower-priced mowers may be justified by commercial gardeners because heavy use burns out the expensive ones almost as fast, and the cheap mowers can be discarded when worn out without investing time and maintenance expense. Depending on the stage of development of the product field or service classification, a customer can be expressing venturesomeness or conservatism, membership or exclusivity, by favoring a higher- or lower-priced offering. Finally, customers unable to express personal achievement or qualities by paying a higher price may revert to the lowest-priced offering to do so. The role of price in customer motivation must be determined by each marketer for his proprietary array of offerings.

Generally, customers want to upgrade themselves in ways that are meaningful to themselves. Determining how to put together a product or service that taps this underlying motivation in a specific area is often the key to opening up a whole market.

Other Factors in Buying Behavior

Other factors in a wide array affect customer buying behavior, either directly or indirectly. The most direct and immediate is a personal salesman calling on the customer or prospect without notice or by invitation. The most indirect and remote is the environment, nationwide and worldwide, which affects the customer's outlook and orientation and the mix of products, services, and alternative activities from which he can choose. Between these extremes a multitude of influences presses on the customer, both solicited and unsolicited by him.

Direct Sales Effort

A customer buys from direct salesmen, either company representatives or agents, chiefly on the basis of familiarity: that is, the perception of the marketer's agent as similar to himself or to his self-image in important respects. Usually, the customer must consider the individual making the offering to be acceptable as a friend before he buys from him. The most significant indicator of this potentiality is that the customer thinks of the salesman as having the same education as himself, or better, and the same or higher income; or as belonging to the same political party or religion.

Unsolicited Influences

At times the customer is basically passive, receiving suggestions or observing the practices of others to which he simply conforms. Convention and custom are strong factors in the marketplace. The purchase of missals or prayer books is a good example of this kind of influence on individual purchases. People generally buy the missal they see others using and do not shop or make comparisons or evaluations. For this reason one publisher may have 90 percent or more of a given geographic market, and it is extremely difficult for another publisher to penetrate without waiting for gradual population changes over a long period.

Similar concentrations of brand preferences are found in the outboard motor field, where one lake may be "Evinrude" and the next all "Johnson," even though the brands are manufactured by the same corporation and competitive dealers are located reasonably nearby. Attempts to break customary procedure by providing equal or better availability, price, terms, and other offers still meet resistance from those who prefer the "tried and true." In general, unsolicited influences are especially operative for products and services that are used frequently by customers or are used by many other people in an area.

Advertising. Advertising acts, in most cases, as an unsolicited influence on buying decisions and has a cumulative effect in creating familiarity. Exposures to such influences range from several hundred to several thousand daily in the life of the customer. At most, he is aware of and can report only a few dozen of them. Research has shown that he is indifferent to at least 80 percent of television advertising, for example. The effect of advertising on the passive customer is to create awareness after getting his attention. Later, in a buying situation—either impulsive or planned—the customer may recognize the product or service as familiar. In this way the sense of effort or risk in purchasing is reduced. Generalized or institutional advertising is directed chiefly toward creating attitudes prerequisite to buying decisions favorable to a marketer. It is usually inadequate for active prospects who use advertisements as they use expert opinion.

Sales promotion. Sales promotion efforts affect customer behavior by adding value to the content rather than the concept of the product or service. A customer prospect who otherwise might fail to understand or develop interest in the concept of the offering may purchase on the basis of content alone because of the added value he receives from the sales promotion, which fits into or fulfills his own felt needs. Sales promotion devices, directly or indirectly tied to the purchase, are highly varied: free samples, contests, coupons, premiums, trading stamps, and so on. Most premiums offered as sales promotion are barely suitable for their purpose. Some prove more popular than the product or service itself. A drug chain in Washington, DC, found that discounts on purchases of prescription drugs had no value in holding or gaining customers because people do not expect or shop for discounts on medicine and few remember receiving them. Customer behavior is influenced most when the sales promotion is relevant to other aspects of the marketing task.

Customers themselves become unsolicited influences on customer prospects by spontaneously telling of their satisfactions or even of their favored expectations. Such influences are usually termed "word of mouth" and are extremely effective in creating awareness and familiarity prior to actual purchase decision situations.

Solicited Influences

At times, chiefly for products and services used infrequently, the customer seeks advice and relies on the recommendations of an expert or leader or the consensus of a group of persons whose approval is important. At least one and possibly as many as three out of five buyers of such an offering are likely to have done this. In these cases the role of certain individuals or organizations has a disproportionate influence in the marketplace. When this behavior is probable, the key to obtaining a good market position may lie in identifying those whose opinion is sought. An example of such a consultation is found in the individual who seeks advice on the best bank for mortgages or special loans although willing to use any convenient bank for an ordinary account. The persons asked are those whose general knowledgeability is highly regarded by the customer or by others he is acquainted with and respects.

The same seeking out of influences takes place for services and products that do not directly involve the consumer. Mechanical engineers have infrequent need to specify adhesives, for example. When they do, they seek the suggestions of the most experienced user they can find. Often this turns out to be a specialist in insulation installation. In this way, a few individuals can virtually control the preference for type and brand of a product in a large city, and the marketer who wants to understand customer buying behavior is well advised to identify those who influence the purchasers.

Advertising can perform as a solicited influence when the customer is "in the market" and actively seeks out advertisements as part of collecting information and advice. If an advertisement in a magazine is read by 25 percent of the readers, about 10 percent of them will be buyers or prospects; an outstanding advertisement may be read by 75 percent of the readers, of whom 20 percent are buyers or prospects. When a product is advertised in a magazine, about 15 percent more readers buy it than when it is not advertised.

In the field of construction, customers rely almost wholly on solicited influences—firms or individuals who perform design and planning services in return for a percentage of the owner investment. Architects and engineers, either in the principal organization or on the staff of professional firms, specify products and services that will be used and take responsibility for satisfactory completion of the work on behalf of the owner. Customers are so heavily dependent on these intermediaries that marketers spend the bulk of their effort on influencing them.

Life Style and Environmental Changes

Buying behavior is greatly influenced by way of life, defined by stage in the life cycle and place in the social and economic sphere. This position in turn allows varying degrees of personal expression in purchasing by individuals. In consumer goods and services, innovations are introduced by those in the highest and lowest echelons of the society who have least risk (little more to gain or to lose) and, in the United States and similar countries, are validated by the most venturesome in the economically secure portion of the broad middle class. Innovators, who are the initial purchasers of new products or services, are only 2 to 3 percent of the customers; another 13 to 14 percent at most are sufficiently venturesome to be called early adopters. Later, when new modes or forms of purchasing behavior are adopted by the conservative working class and finally by the economically insecure, the process is completed and market growth is stabilized. The same pattern holds true in industrial goods and services. Growing organizations have much in common in their purchasing behavior, regardless of industry, as do firms with high earnings. Experimental or radical new designs or concepts are most quickly accepted by the largest and richest companies or by the smallest entrepreneurs, who have little established position or commitment to custom.

Young people are disproportionately represented among innovators, either because they are supported by their parents (thus resembling the upper class) or because they have nominally abandoned aspiration to membership or status in the established society (thus resembling the lower class). In both cases they have little or nothing to lose by innovating and little or nothing to gain by conforming. The extension of this period of youth portends greater amounts of change in the types of products and services purchased and a weakening of the loyalties and steady habits that have sustained many marketers in the past.

Environmental changes, such as major events affecting the economy of the nation, alter customer buying behavior markedly. The effect may be direct, as with war or depression, or indirect, as with new laws, shorter work hours, longer time for education, higher interest rates, less mobility because of housing shortages, and so forth, which ultimately change life styles and living habits. Marketers are well advised to reevaluate their offerings when overall changes are taking place in the environment.   □ *William J. McBurney, Jr.*

STRATEGIC PLANNING

For a company to grow profitably past certain limits, it usually has to have a strategic plan that integrates and focuses all the corporate efforts, assets, and capabilities toward achieving a growth goal. In its simplest explanation, the strategic planning process takes corporate objectives, goals, and aims, and establishes policies and program strategies to achieve them.

Each organization is unique. Therefore, a single planning model that fits all organizations does not exist. But successful planning does have common fundamental characteristics, despite differing operational details. While planning is basically a simple process, implementation is often difficult and requires discipline and commitment by all parties responsible for executing the plan.

There are two types of planning. The first is informal, intuitive-anticipatory planning that is the work of one person. It often does not result in a written set of plans. It usually has a short time horizon and a short reaction time. This type of planning usually is heavily based on past experience, gut feel, and the judgment and reflective thinking of the chief executive. If an organization is managed by intuitive geniuses, it has no need for formal planning.

The second type is formal planning—an organized system that is developed on the basis of a set of procedures, is explicit, and is based on research. Formal planning involves the work of many people and results in a set of written plans.

Determining the Planning System to Be Used

The first step in developing a corporate strategic plan is to design and specify the planning system to be used. As previously stated, each company has different needs and objectives, so the specific planning system used should be customized for that company. The goal is to adopt a planning process that gives the most immediate planning benefits and results in a sound corporate strategic plan.

The planning system most generally used is a top-down approach, which starts with a general situation analysis that includes internal and external factors and the company's strengths and weaknesses in both. Objectives are then established and followed up by strategies and action plans as they relate to corporate operations and ongoing businesses. The final portion of the plan is concerned with implementation, controls, and follow-up.

The strategic plan should be broken down into phases, with completion dates, individual tasks, and responsibilities defined. Effective strategic planning requires the planners to be committed, logical, disciplined, and objective. Planning for the future usually involves dealing with change. To deal effectively with change, there can be no "sacred cows."

The strategic planning process should start with the development of the preplanning guide, which is the document that specifies the information inputs needed for the plan.

Preplanning Guide

Strong statement of the CEO's commitment to institute a formal planning system as an essential management tool.

Glossary of terms that will be used in the planning system so everybody is speaking the same business language.

Specification of data required for the planning system, who is responsible for providing the data, and a schedule of data flow. These data will include information on past performance, the current situation, and the future.

Any specific planning rules. As an example, do we plan in current dollars or constant dollars?

Situation analysis. Which elements of our business, past, present, and future, are the most significant to our success?

Strengths, weaknesses, opportunities, and threats. We must identify these factors from an overall corporate standpoint, since these factors affect future growth potential.

Goals. The goals of the strategic plan should be identified and defined. They may include such things as (1) the personal aims of the CEO; (2) the philosophy, creed, and purpose of the organization; (3) the mission of the organization; and (4) core objectives, which are usually concerned with sales volume, profit level, and ROI.

It's important to remember that there is no such thing as a single aim or objective of a company. Each company has a series of different aims, each of which is developed differently in the planning process and must be clearly stated.

Outline of a Strategic Plan

Phase I. Internal and External Analysis

A. Internal Analysis
   Corporate philosophy.
   Resources
   1. People.
   2. Finances.
   3. Manufacturing facilities.

Personality.
Corporate structure.
Description of the businesses we are in.
Sales and profit history by business.
Present sales forecasts.
Problems and opportunities.
Internal strengths and weaknesses.

B. External Analysis
Profile and growth patterns of the markets that are served by our businesses.
Competitive market forces.
Threats (foreign and domestic).
Environmental factors
1. Political.
2. Social.
3. Economic.
4. Cultural.
5. Technological.
6. Changing distribution systems.
7. The changing consumer.

PHASE II. SETTING OBJECTIVES

A. Personal aims (CEO).
B. Governing philosophy, creed, and purpose for the organization.
C. Mission
1. Grand design.
2. Specific thrust.
D. Specific objectives for key result areas
1. Core objectives, corporate
(a) Sales.
(b) Profits.
(c) ROI.
(d) Margins.
2. Other
(a) Research and development.
(b) Productivity.
(c) Diversification.
(d) Facility replacement.
(e) Employment of assets (financial, manufacturing, and human).
(f) Labor content of the products.
(g) Manpower development.
(h) Social responsibilities.
E. Objectives by businesses
1. Core
(a) Sales.
(b) Profits.
(c) Margins.
(d) Market share.

2. Other
   (a) New-product development.
   (b) Specific program objectives.
   (c) Materials purchases.
   (d) Machinery purchases.
   (e) Production goals.
   (f) Salesmen's goals.
   (g) Distribution goals.
   (h) Research goals.

PHASE III. DEVELOPMENT OF STRATEGIES AND POLICIES

The strategies and policies developed are targeted to attain the objectives of the company.
A. Master Strategies
   These include organization missions, purposes, philosophies, policies, and long-range objectives.
   1. Define.
   2. Develop.
   3. Evaluate and set priorities.
B. Program Strategies
   These would be directed toward specific objectives for the business concerned. They would be medium- and long-range.
   1. Define.
   2. Develop.
   3. Evaluate and set priorities.

PHASE IV. ACTION PLANS

These are developed from the finalized strategies on a short-, medium-, and long-range basis.
A. Corporate
B. Business
   The business plan would be in the standard format and include such things as:
   1. Sales goals.
   2. Margin goals.
   3. Product mix.
   4. Key-account strategy.
   5. Product-quality standards.
   6. Pricing policy.
   7. Channels of distribution.
   8. Sales-force deployment.
   9. Sales promotion.
   10. Advertising and publicity—strategy and budgets.
   11. Market surveillance and marketing research.
   12. Research and product-development direction.
   13. Manufacturing aspects of the marketing plan.
   14. Overall budget.

15. Timetable.
16. Measurements of performance versus plan.

PHASE V. IMPLEMENTATION OF THE PLAN

A. Translate plan into budgets.
B. Monitor performance.
C. Recycle the plan annually.
D. Develop marketing plans for specific products.   □ *David J. Freiman*

ESTABLISHING OBJECTIVES

The establishing of objectives is a fundamental activity for all echelons of business management. However, it is of major significance to top management, in that objectives represent the ultimate distillation of those significant aims of the corporation that, once established, represent the elements required for obtaining and maintaining its position and ensuring its growth. Visualized in this manner, objectives represent statements of corporate intention that can be developed only by top management itself and that inherently require top-level organizational commitment. The responsibility for establishing corporate objectives cannot be delegated to subordinate management levels; these objectives must be the creation of executive management.

It is also imperative that the purpose of objectives be clearly comprehended after they have been established. While established objectives do act as statements of corporate intention and thereby become operational guidelines, they simultaneously—and perhaps even more importantly—become instruments for the measurement of achievement. In effect, therefore, established objectives provide a basis for determining corporate performance, not alone in the sense of the company's ultimate relative position in the marketplace, but as a device for the assessment of its internal performance and its ability to achieve its own stated objectives.

Clearly, then, it is essential that top management fully appreciate the implications and concerns that these objectives convey within the corporate structure. Once the objectives are established, endorsement and commitment by executive management are prerequisite to their successful execution. It is essential that corporate management both implicitly and explicitly endorse the objectives and recognize its responsibility with respect to their development, implementation, and promulgation. Without this top-management commitment, the entire validity of the structure is undermined and the accomplishment of objectives seriously jeopardized.

Marketing Objectives

After corporate objectives have been thoroughly examined, marketing objectives can be considered more critically. It should be noted here that the marketing plan, whether it be short-range (one year) or long-range (five years), can be essentially one of two basic documents.

In many companies the marketing plan stands on its own and constitutes the total planning effort. In such cases the marketing plan becomes somewhat more expansive, and the scope of the stated objectives is enlarged to contain a greater number than would normally be found if the plan were limited to the more specific areas of marketing concern alone. It then, in effect, becomes the vehicle for the statement of most if not all the corporate management objectives.

The strategic-plan approach is the often encountered technique of total planning, wherein separate operational or functional-area plans are used as individual elements to create a total strategic plan for the company. In such cases the marketing plan is only one integral part of the whole, and the statement of objectives contained in it would logically be limited to those specifically of marketing concern.

Regardless of the approach used, there are certain basic criteria that any objective should meet and that should be employed in testing the objective before it is established. If it fails to meet the following requirements, the objective is questionable—if not invalid—and should be reconsidered: feasibility, suitability, realism, quantifiability, and alterability. An examination of many stated marketing objectives has revealed that they do not always meet these criteria. Enthusiasm is commendable, but in planning let it be tempered with the judicious application of the necessary criteria.

The most difficult of all tasks in creating marketing objectives is the consideration of how to identify and state the objectives themselves. The main reason that marketing objectives are difficult for most people to state is that they—and the market itself—are conceived of as somewhat illusive, ephemeral entities rather than as the realities—though intangible—that they are.

Identifying Product and Market

Marketing is concerned with the distribution of goods—getting the material into the hands of the consumer—and with profit. This means dealing with two separate yet intimately related concerns: the product (no matter what it is) and the consumer (no matter who he may be). Simple though this sounds, it is central to the problem, for many times the seller does not really know what his product is or who his customer is. This may seem incredible, yet how often it is the case: a situation frequently comes to light—for which the planner can be grateful—in the marketing planning preparation, thus leading to the consideration of these two factors (product and market) as they relate to the development of the plan and the statement of objectives.

To identify the product and the market would seem a simple matter; but when it involves making a dispassionate analysis of both, the degree of confusion that can exist is, more often than not, quite surprising. Additionally difficult is the identification of intention, once agreement as to present status has been obtained. There is a universal tendency to think that the areas to which the company ultimately wants to direct its efforts and objectives are known, and it is a painful revelation to find that this is not the case. While this may be an unpleasant reality, it is one with which the marketing planners must cope.

By now it should be abundantly clear that careful and complete scrutiny of all available data regarding the situation of company, product, consumer, and market—both current and projected—is necessary in order to formulate the marketing objectives. These are data on number and nature of products; manufacturing capabilities and limitations; available capital; market share; market potential; market direction; areas of attrition; competition; financial outlook (government, marketing, and corporate, and the possibilities of mergers or acquisitions); R&D (actual and potential); status of product life cycles; and opportunities and problems.

Most, if not all, of these factors are those normally considered in the development of any operational or marketing plan. But the emphasis and the perspective taken in the formulation of the marketing plan itself differ somewhat, in that the ultimate concern is the relationship with the marketing function; and it is from this viewpoint that these factors must be visualized. Upon determination of the statistical data to be used in the composition of the plan, the planner must also come to grips with the marketing "art work" of subjective analysis as it relates to the development of the marketing objectives. As has often been said, there is no substitute for personal judgment, and in the marketing area this is especially true. The resulting objectives reflect the analysis made, on the basis of the data submitted and the individual assessment of the market, which comprises the totality of marketing knowledge integrating the internal corporate goals and capabilities, present and future, with the market status and requirements—again, present and future.

Flexibility in Planning

Among the most trying problems are those caused by changes constantly occurring in the marketplace. Nowhere else is the rate of change as rapid as in the marketing area, and it is not incorrect to say that every marketing plan is in effect obsolete before it is completed. This is not the result of inaccuracy in planning or of invalidity in the marketing planning concept; rather, it is caused by the evolution of the market and the prevailing dynamics, which make obsolescence inherent in the conditions of the plan. Additional elements for concern, therefore, are the flexibility and alterability of the plan. Any plan that is formulated must have the capability of change or alteration as dictated by the market. This can be accomplished either through formal, periodic review (an essential element in any meaningful plan) or through alteration based on the requirements of specifics as they develop. Either way, it is important that this need be clearly recognized in the planning operation. As this consideration relates to objectives, reflection must be more careful, since the necessity to alter objectives does not necessarily parallel the need to alter marketing strategies and tactics. This consideration is fundamental to validating the formulation of the plan. Objectives, if valid, represent relatively stable elements; it is the mechanism to achieve them that changes.

Identifying and Developing Marketing Objectives

As previously discussed, marketing objectives are built up from a comprehensive data base that encompasses all spheres of the corporate operation and the most thoroughgoing market knowledge, coupled with and subject to the evolution and interpretation of appropriate marketing management. This brings the planner to the state of knowing his position and being able to determine where to go and how to get there. However, he faces the problem of identifying the objectives that should be specifically indicated and, where possible, quantified.

In identifying the specific elements, consideration must be given to sales, distribution, profit planning, and the market itself.

Sales. The sales factor is usually the most readily appreciated in identification and quantification during the planning operation. Sales on the basis of geographic area or market segment are obvious factors. Regional or specific market sales identification is important, but equally important is the estimate of potential sales. The identification and establishment of sales potential provide a mechanism for performance assessment, and in this sense the plan serves a dual function.

Distribution. To consider sales without paying respect to the ever-increasing concerns of the distribution of goods is to ignore one of the most critical marketing areas. Yet this unfortunately often happens, and marketing managers tend to leave the matter entirely—or, at best, too much—in the hands of others. It is not the function of marketing to control all the channels of distribution, but distribution is so relevant to the effective marketing effort, from the viewpoint of either economics or customer service, that marketing has an obligation to itself to be deeply concerned in the formulation of distribution policies. The objectives to be sought in the establishment of clear and profitable distribution channels require identification and commitment.

Profit planning. "Planning for profit" is an oft-heard but nonetheless expressive phrase. It is clearly the responsibility of marketing to plan the profits to be generated from the sales it creates. In instances where separate product management exists, it is customary to locate the profit-planning function with product managers. Whether profit planning is the responsibility of product management within the marketing operation or of the marketing group itself, it must again be quantified. Profit planning can be based on individual product, product line or brand, or total, by salesman, territory, region, or on a national basis. Profit planning is both short- and long-range, and the identification of profitability (both gross and net) is necessary, not only for the structure of the marketing plan, but also as an element in the overall operational plan as it relates to the assessment of the corporate position and capacity.

Market. Objectives related to the market as a consideration separate from sales and profit imply consideration of market share and potential, creation or exploitation of market objectives, and careful analysis of market shifts. These are necessary inputs required in the total development of the plan.

Relation to Total Business Effort

Naturally, the formulation of the marketing objectives requires a comprehensive review of the total business effort. Harmonious interpretations between marketing and other operational and functional areas are prerequisites for successful performance. The marketing concept clearly implies and is predicated on this integration of effort. In the generation of the marketing plan, the establishment of clearly defined marketing objectives affords the opportunity for clarification, provides operational guidelines, and sets forth the expectations of the marketing group.

Because the significance of objectives cannot be overstated, it is extremely important to comprehend clearly the nature of their establishment and of management's responsibilities regarding them. These considerations can be reduced to the following major elements: (1) objectives must be established directly by top management; (2) management must indicate, explicitly and implicitly, its endorsement of established objectives; (3) in establishing objectives, consideration must be given to the primary requisites of feasibility, suitability, realism, measurability, quantifiability, and alterability; (4) objectives are used as instruments of measurement of performance; (5) objectives must be communicated within the organization. □ *George S. Dominguez*

THE ANNUAL MARKETING PLAN

The annual marketing plan is a commitment to marketing action. In *form* it is a written blueprint, a manager's manual of affordable methods of allocating a portion of total corporate resources and predicting their contribution to corporate profit. In *substance* the marketing plan is an information system that correlates three types of data:

- ▫ Areas of agreement about the existing situation on which marketing action will be based; this is the plan's *situation survey,* and it represents the point of departure for marketing.
- ▫ Statistical projects from the situation survey and the plan's *objectives,* which, if achieved, will become the base of the next year's plan.
- ▫ The ways and means by which the objectives can be achieved, outlined in the form of *strategies* and their *controls.*

Basic Marketing Planning Concepts

Four basic concepts underlie the marketing planning process: pinpointing a market as the planning base and assigning it a customer-oriented definition; isolating the market's key accounts and heaviest-using customers as the planning target; isolating a year as the planning unit; and embedding each individual marketing plan into a harmonious relationship with the total corporate family of plans.

Planning Base

A market must be the base for every marketing plan. In this context a "market" is best defined as "a group of customers who heavily share a common need." The definition of this shared need becomes the definition of the market. This means that markets cannot be categorized in terms of corporate product and service systems but according to the type of customer need that exists for them. Thus a marketing plan for an office-typewriter manufacturer would be entitled, "A Plan to Market Typewriters to the Office Information Systems Market"; a marketing plan for a hydraulic-motors manufacturer would be entitled, "A Plan to Market Hydraulic Energy Systems to the Construction Equipment Market"; a marketing plan for an airline would be entitled, "A Plan to Market Commercial Air Transportation to the Business Traveler Market." In this way the planning company acknowledges the nature of the markets it serves in the same terminology that the markets themselves use to describe their needs. The planning base thereby becomes market-oriented.

Planning Target

An annual marketing plan may be said to have one overriding purpose: to ensure for one more year the premium-pricing acceptance of a company's product and service systems. In the last analysis, there is no other reason to plan. If premium pricing is to be achieved, two conditions must be met: the product/service system must deliver preemptive benefits, and these benefits must be custom-tailored for the heaviest users in the marketplace. Heavy users are customers who use the greatest volume of a product/service system, who use it with the greatest frequency and continuity, and who are willing to pay a premium price to obtain its specific benefits. These key-account customers are generally described by the "20-80 theory," which suggests that only about 20 percent of all customers in any market may be heavy users, yet they can account for up to 80 percent of all profitable sales volume. Heavy users, both actual and potential, must therefore be every plan's target. This does not mean that lighter users, switch-brand users, infrequent users, or specialty users will not be served by the plan's strategies. They will be. But they will not be planned for, since they may account for ony about 20 percent of profitable sales.

Planning Unit

A year is a convenient period of market-planning time. For the most part, it is administratively convenient. It fits budgeting and accounting frequencies, sales forecast projections, and traditional corporate reporting procedures, among other annually recurrent operations. It also matches competitive practice. But the choice of a year as the basic planning unit is an artificial convention, practical from a managerial standpoint but a contrivance from the standpoint of how markets buy. No market's needs, or preferences for product and service systems to supply them, change automatically at the conclusion of a calendar or fiscal year. A market's purchasing preferences have their own cycles, which are—except coincidentally—irrespective of "planning years." The annual marketing plan must therefore take this cyclical disharmony into consideration by engineering two controls into its management: first, the annual plan must always be regarded as a single snapshot in an ongoing motion picture, and the snapshot must continually be related to what has preceded it and what can be expected to follow; and second, the annual plan must allow for at least a quarterly review to keep it aligned with the inevitable changes in market behavior that will not necessarily coincide with the planning year.

Planning Interrelationships

Just as an annual plan is one part of a long-term, ongoing planning process that is multiyear in duration, it must also be interrelated with every other corporate marketing plan that impinges on the same market. A company that serves one market with a variety of product and service systems needs to harmonize the plans for these various systems so that the market is addressed with a single image and the additive benefits of synergistic marketing can be obtained. Each individual plan may therefore be regarded as one member of its company's family of plans for a particular market, all of which will be coordinated at the highest levels of management by a master plan for each major market.

Paralleling the family-of-plans concept is the family-of-planners idea. Most plans are the product of a family approach, involving the contributions of marketing staff officers; marketing line managers—who may be known as market, brand, or product managers; nonmarketing managers, especially in R&D, engineering, and finance; and, of course, top-management reviewers and approvers. Some companies prefer to combine the planning and operating functions and place them almost entirely in their line officers. Others assign heavier initial responsibilities to corporate planning staffs, then require each of the line officers to customize the basic situational information to his own needs and derive his own objectives and strategies from it. A plan must never be imposed on the man who will be responsible for its achievement. But it is a rare line operator who will conceive and execute his plan without multidisciplinary corporate assistance.

The Marketing Planning Process

The annual marketing plan is a basic information exchange system. Its inputs are composed of what has already happened in the planning situation inside and outside the company and what is happening now. Its outputs are the strategic ways and means of altering the planning situation in the company's favor. Inputs are therefore historical. Outputs, in the form of a planned strategy mix, are creative. Once put into effect, each plan's creative strategies become a part of the next annual plan's historical situation. In this way strategies exert their long-term effect on corporate marketing.

Because strategies are a plan's outputs, a marketing plan can rightfully be regarded as an instrument of change. Its objectives therefore become the plan's single most important component. Objectives quantify change. They predict what will most likely happen to the present situation if the plan's strategies are put into effect. As a result, a plan is really the servant of its objectives, for they will in the short run determine its strategies, and over the longer run determine its success.

As a sequential system, a marketing plan has three basic components. The planning process treats these components in rank order, since each is predicated on the component that comes before it: this year's situation survey is predicated, at least in part, on last year's strategies; the plan's objectives are outgrowths of the situation survey; and the plan's strategies are suggested by its objectives. In turn, this year's strategies will influence next year's situation survey.

This sequence is true for all planning companies regardless of age or size or industry. It is for this reason that the following basic outline for the annual marketing process can be suggested. Because it concentrates on essentials, it will serve all companies well. But it will probably serve no company exactly, because many individual markets exert their own peculiar requirements on the planning process, as do specific corporate philosophies, organization structures, and product/service systems. Any of these major variations can, however, easily be interwoven with the basic outline.

Situation Survey

The situation survey is composed of two parts: the first is an analysis of the external situation, and the second analyzes the internal situation.

External situation survey. The analysis of the external situation describes a company's or division's market and its socioeconomic and competitive context.

- The *market situation* is covered in two sections, each of which deals with the key-customer market.

Key-customer market segmentation is described by means of key-account profiles based on heaviest-using customers and their influencers, with (1) demographic description of age, sex, education, position, size and type of purchasing unit, and other relevant factors; and (2) psychographic description of needs that determine the life style of heaviest-using customers and their influencers and that underlie the specific benefits required of product and service systems and their distribution, promotion, and pricing, which are designed to serve these needs.

The section on key-customer market segment growth and development calls for a one-year and longer-term three- to five-year projection from recent growth trends among heavy customers in terms of (1) their number and (2) the numerical and dollar volume of their purchase commitments in product and service systems related to the plan. It includes up to ten-year long-range demand forecasts based on growth trends, as well as anticipated changes to be required in satisfaction of qualitative alterations in demand. It also identifies the quantitative changes in product mix and volume that may be required over the long range because of changes in key-customer market segments' size, composition, education, affluence, purchasing options, and rank order of needs.

- The *socioeconomic situation* is analyzed in four parts in the external situation survey.

First, the social environment for marketing is covered in a description of recent past and present life-style social trends that predispose, or at least correlate with, key-customer market behavior; a one-year and longer-term three- to five-year projection of these trends, with documentation for assumptions of continuity or change; and a projected life-style profile of key-customer markets one year hence.

Second, the section on the economic environment for marketing contains a description and statistical enumeration of key economic indicators of the recent past and present that predispose, or at least correlate with, key-customer market behavior; a one-year and longer-term three- to five-year projection of these indicators, with documentation for assumptions of continuity or change; and a projected economic profile of the market one year hence.

Third, the survey investigates the scientific environment for marketing through a description of recent past and present scientific and technological inventions that predispose, or at least correlate with, key-customer behavior, and a one-year and longer-term three- to five-year projection of these inventions, with documentation for assumptions and implications on market demand, potential product and service system innovation, and marketing system obsolescence.

Finally, the survey's section on the legislative environment for marketing calls for a description of recent past and present legislative trends and enacted laws that affect market behavior or marketing policy (packaging legislation; antitrust, merger, and acquisition legislation and interpretation; regulatory-agency pricing policies; and consumer protection legislation) and an estimate of their degree of influence on market penetration; cost/price policies; product/service system manufacture, distribution, or promotion; corporate image; and competitive reaction.

▪ The external situation survey's section on *competition* contains an analysis of competition, both direct and indirect, and a forecast of new competitors.

The direct-competitor analysis is a qualitative and quantitative analysis of assets and liabilities of the company or division compared with and contrasted against existing direct competitors, showing management, fiscal, and marketing capabilities and resources; marketable product and service systems; basic promotional systems and budgets; market penetration; and corporate image profiles.

The indirect-competitor analysis reveals the management, fiscal, and marketing capabilities and resources of existing indirect competitors—that is, suppliers of alternative product and service systems; their marketable product and service systems; basic promotional systems and budgets; market penetration; and corporate image profiles.

The new-competitor forecast deals with the prediction of new competitors (either direct or indirect) whose entry can be anticipated within the planning year, and the marketing or scientific basis for their competitiveness; and with an estimate of degree of threat and potential maximum loss of market penetration and erosion of corporate image, together with minimum retaliatory costs and strategies required to neutralize their inroads.

Internal situation survey. The internal situation is described according to business positioning and capabilities.

The business positioning coverage provides a market-oriented charter for the business that defines its objectives, capabilities, and strategic commitments in terms of rendering a preemptive service to the market being planned for.

The business capabilities situation is described in terms of the basic capabilities and their supporting financial resources currently being directed against the market for which planning is being done.

Productive capabilities and financial resources are in two categories: established product and service systems and new product and service systems in the current year. The two categories are broken down for each product/service system by (1) investment or capital employed; (2) ROI or return on capital employed; (3) net profit after taxes; (4) sales volume in dollars, units, and share of market; (5) brand image positioning; (6) life-cycle positioning; (7) marketable assets and liabilities compared against competition; and (8) cost/price relationship.

Promotional capabilities and financial resources, for each product/service system, are described under the headings of (1) sales management capabilities, strategies, and investment; (2) distribution management capabilities, strategies, and investment; (3) advertising and sales promotion management capabilities, strategies, and investment; and (4) packaging management capabilities, strategies, and investment.

Other capabilities and financial resources, also for each product/service system, are (1) marketing management manpower capability, organization, and investment; and (2) plant and equipment capability and investment.

Objectives

Objectives are threefold in nature. First and foremost, objectives are financial. The most essential objectives of the planning process are therefore numerical, and the numbers they refer to are profit figures. A secondary denomination of objectives are the quantitative data that form the statistical basis for profit. The third category of objectives is qualitative, concerned with the image goals that are the conceptual foundation for profit. Because objectives are expressed chiefly in numbers, the objectives section of the annual marketing plan is always the shortest element in the plan. By the same token, it is the most important.

- □ *Financial objectives* are expressed in terms of ROI, or return on capital employed, and net profit before or after taxes.
- □ *Quantitative objectives* are expressed in a profit-to-sales ratio and in sales volume in dollars, units, and share of market.
- □ *Qualitative objectives* are the company's overall corporate image and individual product/service systems images.

Strategies and Controls

Strategies are the action elements of the marketing planning process. They represent the creative mix by which the plan's objectives are to be achieved. Each individual strategy must therefore meet one essential qualification: it must contribute to the plan's objectives. Taken as a group, the total strategy mix must serve two criteria: the mix should be composed of the smallest number of individual strategies, and its overall investment should be the minimum expenditure required to complete the plan.

For the company as a whole, the overriding strategies will be business strategies. These top-level commitments will decide what is marketed and how, and what its source of supply will be. Business strategies determine corporate growth and development and influence such major issues as growth into related new businesses by venture development or growth into unrelated, conglomerate business by merger and acquisition. Within corporate business strategies, there are three basic marketing strategies that must be annually planned and executed:

product and service system strategies, by which the plan manipulates what is offered for marketing; promotional system strategies, by which the plan manipulates the way its products and services are offered for sale; and pricing system strategies, by which the plan manipulates the market value assigned to its products and services offered for sale. Promotional strategies and pricing strategies may be used as correlates of each other, each reinforcing the other's market effect. Or promotion and pricing may be used as alternatives to each other, with promotional strategies receiving emphasis in order to limit the need for pricing strategies, or with pricing strategies used as a replacement for promotional investments.

Controls are the constraints applied against strategies in order to keep their costs in line, monitor their progress, and evaluate their contribution. There are three principal means of control: financial controls, which are largely exerted through the assignment of a budget to each strategy; information controls, chiefly the findings of sales research, market research, or technological research, which can be used to predict the market performance of a strategy or to certify its operational efficiency; and judgmental controls, which are discretionary judgments applied against a strategy in areas where an information control would be too expensive or too time-consuming or is simply regarded as unnecessary or impossible. In a sense, a judgmental control is a subjective information control. Either a judgmental or an information control, along with its budgetary control, should accompany every strategy.

Using the Marketing Plan

The marketing plan should be used as a management tool for market leadership. This means that the plan must be worked as a practical guide to the three fundamental attributes of leadership: branded product and service systems, preemptive market positioning for them, and acceptance for their premium pricing. Since unbranded or commodity products and services cannot be positioned preemptively to justify a premium price, they need not be planned. Thus the marketing planning process is the basic management alternative to commodity marketing.

An annual marketing plan has, by definition, a predetermined life cycle. Its obsolescence is built in. For this reason its greatest relevance comes over the first half of its useful life. Over the last two quarters of the planned year it becomes progressively less applicable unless on-line revisions are updated into it. At any time its reliability as an action base is therefore inversely proportional to its age.

This fact helps explain why judgmental controls must always be applied to the creation and use of marketing plans. It is generally better to adopt a policy of flexible interpretation of the plan than to interpret or adhere to it rigidly in spite of its wear-out rate, the human fallibility that is implicit in its structuring, or the market dynamics that form its restless base. Even though a plan is designed to help marketers operate with greater economy and efficiency, no plan can ever encompass all marketing wisdom. The crucial 10 percent that can separate marketing success from failure can often be generated by the man who manages the plan. Because markets are people, only marketers—not plans—can ever serve them with sensitivity or elasticity, let alone the intuition that is the hallmark of the entrepreneur.

Outline of an Annual Marketing Plan

A marketing plan is a plan of action for the marketing of a product and is an important part of the planning process. It derives its direction from the strategic plan and its content from the specific tactics of the product plan. The headings in the plan outline in Figure 6-2 give an indication of the content of an annual marketing plan for the AB Company, a medium-size industrial-products manufacturer.

The sequence of the plan is important, as it follows a logic that allows for a complete assessment of the company's present position and prospects. Most marketing plans move through the following process: (1) situation survey, (2) statement of objectives, (3) statement of strategies, and (4) description of specific actions for implementing strategies. In the sample plan, the first two sections comprised the situation survey, objectives were then stated, and strategies and

Figure 6-2. Annual marketing plan for AB Company—table of contents.

   I. Position of AB Company in its markets
       A. Our major markets
           1. External analysis
           2. Competition
       B. Our position in these markets
           1. Our capabilities
           2. Our unique strengths
  II. Problems and opportunities
       A. Internal (capabilities)
       B. External (socioeconomic and competitive)
 III. Objectives
       A. Key assumptions for AB in each market
       B. Goals
           1. Financial
           2. Quantitative
           3. Qualitative
  IV. Strategies to realize objectives
       A. Overall strategies stated
       B. Strategies for each market
   V. Action plan
       A. Actions to be taken by market
       B. Target dates and responsibilities
       C. Control and review procedures
  VI. Summary of plan impact on profit and loss statement

the action plan followed in support of the objectives. Although the section headings and relative importance vary significantly from plan to plan, the basic process remains the same.

Case Histories

The following two brief case histories demonstrate how widely divergent planning goals are achieved through a common process. These cases are based upon the marketing plans of a metal-stamping plant and an actuarial and benefits consulting firm. The first plan addressed itself to major customers within a specific region, while the second addressed the needs of a nationwide client base.

Case A: The Thump and Crunch Stamping Co.

Thump and Crunch (T&C) has used a marketing plan as a critical input to its budgeting and financing process for ten years. T&C's major markets have been stable for about 20 years until the energy crisis forced the automobile industry to increase the pace of material substitution. So, the plan shown here addresses the company's turbulent major markets through a well-established planning process.

Annual marketing plan

I. T&C's Present Position

Our major markets continue to experience great changes in the amount and type of metal stampings used. It is the belief of management that these basic changes will continue due to pressure from both government and the automobile-buying public. The impact of these changes on our major markets is detailed below.

A. Automotive industry—passenger

The passenger-car manufacturers expect the following trends for metal stampings to continue:

  □ Large metal parts will be reduced in size and subject to an increasing possibility of material substitution.
  □ Smaller parts will be combined into few, more complex parts.
  □ Aluminum will become important despite cost disadvantage.
  □ Treated and laminated metals will become more common.

For the following year, we have identified the following new parts programs that best match our experience and equipment.

  □ The Q-car gas tank program at AB Motors.
  □ The aluminum bumper program for the 19XX Hound at XYZ Motors.

We do not anticipate the loss of any high-volume parts this year. Those parts lost last year were especially vulnerable to change, and the remaining parts are well positioned in terms of both application and model life.

B. Automotive industry—truck.

C. Farm-implement industry.

D. Other customer groups.

II. Objectives for 19XX

T&C will remain active in the markets it now serves. The following year will see changes similar to that experienced last year in these key markets served, although our position is more secure.

We have established the following financial targets for this year:

□ Total revenues of $257.6 million.
□ Pretax profits of $19.3 million.
□ Return on net capital employed of 17 percent.

In addition, we believe we can obtain the following specific marketing objectives:

□ An increase in share among the big three automotive companies from 3.2 percent to 4.5 percent of independent stamping firms.
□ An increasing share of revenues from nonautomotive customers, from 15 percent last year to 21 percent in 19XX.

Also, we have established the following performance objectives:

□ To be asked to bid on every new automotive metal part, appropriate for our equipment, let out for bidding by the big three automakers.
□ To develop business at the new Nikko Motors plant in Indiana for late 19XX.

III. Strategies to Meet These Objectives

The increase in automotive share plus the decreasing dependence on this market imply a major increase in volume for 19XX. In fact, our revenue goal is 27 percent higher than last year. The essence of our strategy is to step up our business development effort at the time when our competitive independent stampers are in disarray. Consequently, we propose to undertake the following strategies:

□ Add four automotive and two nonautomotive sales representatives.
□ Develop working relationships with DEF Aluminum and the ZIPCO Alloys division to gain a competitive edge in being referred by metals producers.
□ Position T&C as a former of a wide range of metals, not simply steel, through an industrywide promotion campaign.

A. Strategies for automotive industry—passenger.
B. Strategies for automotive industry—truck.
C. Strategies for farm-implement industry.
D. Strategies for other customer groups.

IV. Responsibilities for Strategy Implementation

The following charts detail the responsibilities of senior managers in implementing the strategies outlined for 19XX above.

Task Description	Responsible	Due Date
Sales Recruitment		
Job Descriptions	Marketing Mgr.	1/15/XX
Place Advertisements	Personnel	1/31/XX

Screen Candidates	Personnel	4/15/XX
Hiring Decision	Marketing Sales	3/1/XX
Sales Training		
Assemble Course Material	Sales Mgr.	1/31/XX
Design Course	Sales Mgr.	1/15/XX
First Session	Marketing/Sales	3/15/XX
Second Session	Marketing/Sales	5/1/XX

Etc.

V. Impact of Strategies on Projected Revenues and Profits

The effect of these strategies will be the increase of both revenues and the degree of profitability as plant utilization rises. Alternative B below shows the impact of these strategies.

Revenues and Pretax Profits 19XX
($ million)

	Alternative A No Strategic Change	Alternative B Full Strategic Implementation
Sales	202.3	257.6
Pretax	10.1	19.3
Capacity (%) Utilization	73	87

The result of the change in strategy proposed will be improved financial performance for T&C in 19XX. In addition to this internal improvement, we anticipate an improved position in all key markets served.

Case B: Slough and Stodgy Actuarial Accountants

Slough and Stodgy (S&S) was founded so long ago no one remembers the precise date. But marketing planning is so new that none of the partners has actually succumbed to it. Nonetheless, changing markets have forced the partners to re-examine their business on a region-by-region and practice-by-practice basis. The following plan summary is derived from an actual first-pass nationwide marketing plan.

I. Our Present Situation

In terms of our capabilities, the firm has never been in a stronger position. We have industry leaders in most areas of actuarial services, benefits, and, recently, compensation. We now have 11 offices across the country. Our client base has been steady. Yet, we have not grown at a time when the market, particularly for benefits and compensation services, has been growing quickly.

A. The Houston branch

This market has been growing rapidly in about every conceivable measure. In 1969, we opened this branch with two actuaries and one assistant. By 1975, we had five actuaries and four assistants, and this number has remained essentially constant. Our most active competitors in this market include seven of the ten leading national firms.

While we have not grown significantly since 1975, five of the other national firms and all the regional firms have expanded their practices. Most of our major clients have been approached by at least one other actuarial/benefits/compensation consulting firm in the last year. We believe that we have lost share and have become less visible in the Houston market.

Sections B to K: Situation analyses for other branches.

II. The Firm's Objectives

The analyses provided by each of the head actuaries at the branches point to declining positions in all but two markets. It is the prime objective of the firm to reverse this erosion of our position. Therefore, we have proposed the following objectives for the whole firm:

An increase in billable man-hours of 10 percent for the coming year.

An increase in fees of at least 12 percent for the coming year.

Objectives for the individual branches vary, but these objectives above are the firm's overall objectives for this first plan.

III. Our Approach to These Objectives

In this section, we outline the critical strategies that will be used to meet these objectives. These strategies will apply to all branches, but the detailed application will differ from branch to branch.

The firm will achieve these objectives by organizing its business development efforts for the first time. This organization of effort will begin at the practice level, continue at the branch level, and finally be monitored by the National Office. The following strategies will be implemented.

□ Individual actuaries will list present and potential clients.

□ Present clients' present services used will be listed with their value.

□ Potential clients will be approached by mail, then by telephone, to increase awareness of the firm.

□ The National office will undertake to support the branches through a selective advertising campaign.

These strategies will allow the firm to organize internally, while undertaking its first planned business development effort. It is expected that the return on this effort will meet our current objectives.

IV. Branch Marketing Plans

The firm's objectives are the composite of branch and individual-practice goals. These plans are detailed below for each branch.

A. The Houston branch

The plan for 19XX is shown below for the individual practices. Each actuary has been responsible for the analysis of his present and potential clients.

(*i*) *Practice A*—John Good, Actuary

Services and Value ($000)

Present Clients	Actuarial Services	Benefits	Compensation	Total
Southeastern Trust	73.5	—	2.5	76.0
Henway Aircraft	12.0	4.5	—	16.5
Alice Brown	1.5	—	—	1.5
LMG Co. Inc.	9.6	2.4	1.3	13.3
				107.3

Due Date

Potential Clients	Initial Contact	Mail	Initial Meeting
Citizen's Bank	2/15	2/28	2/28
Texas Steak	2/15	2/28	4/1
House XYZ Co.	2/15	2/28	4/14

There is an estimated additional $15,000 available at today's billing rates within the existing clients. The potential clients could add another $10,000–$15,000 in the following year. My revenue forecast for 19XX is $146,000, or 36 percent above last year.

Subsections (*ii*) to (*x*): Practices B to E.

Sections B to K: Plans for other branches.

These two case histories summarize two very different planning situations. The first case presented a plan for an established supplier of established products using an established planning approach, but facing rapidly changing markets. The second one showed the first attempt at using a planned approach to reverse a slow decline. But the commonality of these cases is found in the process used in both plans. They:

- Reviewed the key elements in their internal and/or external situations.
- Outlined principal objectives for the coming year.
- Detailed strategies in support of those objectives.
- Gave an indication of specific actions and responsibilities to support the strategies.

Again, while the individual planning situation changes, there is usually a common logic to the marketing planning process. Flexibility in presentation and in emphasis of certain parts of the plan, a logical progression in a format strictly adhered to from situation and analysis through objectives, strategies, and actions or tactics, should ensure that the planner has touched all bases as he produces the plan. □ **Mack Hanan** *and* **Rod Lawrence**

ORGANIZATION

When a chief marketing executive first assumes responsibility for managing the marketing function, one of his initial tasks is to decide how he will organize his group. This task often is approached by finding out how other companies—competitors in particular—that sell similar products are organized. Such research can be highly instructive; but the astute marketing executive realizes that his company is different from every other company he might examine, and that slavish copying of another company's organization plan—even that of the most successful company in his industry—probably is not his best answer.

The "Ideal" Organization Plan

In starting to design an organization plan that is truly his own and the best possible for his company, the marketing executive is well advised to develop first his idea of an "ideal" plan. In doing this he disregards completely any limitations related to availability of funds, number of people, or capabilities of individuals already on the payroll. He may go one step further and say to himself, "I'll accept any approach except what we've already tried."

Once freed from these restrictions, the marketing executive focuses his attention first on the markets in which he must sell. What motivates people to buy the products or services he offers? How can he present his product most compellingly to prospective buyers? What is important to buyers in making their buying decisions? In short, what are the requirements for selling successfully in these markets?

A study of this kind leads naturally to some conclusions about the functions that must be performed by the marketing organization and about their relative importance. In an organization selling standardized commodities, for example, it may be that pricing and physical distribution are the most important factors in the market; thus concentration on these areas may be highly desirable. In an organization selling high-fashion merchandise it may be necessary to put the greatest emphasis on ability to detect style trends earlier than the competition. In any event, the marketing executive develops a list of the tasks that must be performed by the marketing organization and the relative emphasis to be placed on each task.

With the aid of such a list, it should be relatively simple to decide how these tasks might be divided most effectively among a group of qualified individuals, assigning high-priority tasks to specialists and combining less important tasks in the job descriptions of other positions.

Rarely can a company afford the luxury of implementing the "ideal" organization plan at once. The exercise of developing such a plan is valuable, nevertheless, not only because it provides a solid foundation for developing the immediate organization plan but also because it sets a useful target for long-range building.

Need for Balance

When the marketing executive has his ideal organization well in mind, it is time for him to face up to the adverse realities that he disregarded at the outset. The ideal organization almost always is more costly in money and people than the company can afford. More significantly, the people available to staff the organization, and those the company can hope to recruit, seldom if ever match precisely the qualifications demanded by the ideal organization plan. The point of compromise has arrived.

By far the most important consideration in this compromise is that the organization plan is, in the end, nothing more than a description of how real people are expected to interact in achieving a common goal. One may hope that each individual will do whatever needs to be done in accordance with his own talents, resources, and motivation; but an organization plan so loosely conceived is more apt to result in chaos than in success. Thus it is necessary to decide in advance how responsibilities will be divided among the people in the marketing organization; but it is well to recognize that no assignment of responsibility will cause people to do things well that they are incapable of doing or unwilling to do. The first compromise is to modify the organization plan according to how the people in the organization, or those who reasonably can be expected to be brought into the organization, will work together most naturally and effectively.

In designing the ideal organization plan, it also is tempting to opt for structural purity and simplicity of control. In a multiproduct company, for example, the most comfortable choice might be either a specialized sales force for each product or a single sales force doing across-the-board selling on the entire product line. A close look at the market might suggest, however, the use of full-line salesmen in most areas but of specialist salesmen in concentrated markets or with major customers. Responsiveness to the market never should be sacrificed merely to attain either structural purity or a simple accounting and control system.

In any event, the marketing executive's objective at this stage is to strike the best possible balance between what the market requires and what he really can hope to achieve with the resources—financial, human, and others—that he has at his disposal. If he leans too strongly in the direction of the ideal organization plan for the requirements of the market, his sales expenses may be quite out of line with the sales volume realized; but if he leans too far in the other direction—toward building the organization plan around resources immediately available—he may find himself with an organization that is unable to reach its full potential and upon which it is difficult to build for growth.

Typical Organization Plans

It should be clear that there is no single approach to organizing a marketing department that applies equally well to all kinds of companies, nor even a single plan that would be equally good for quite similar companies in a single industry. Every plan must be carefully fitted to the market, the product, and the company itself. It is conceivable that two different companies might develop identical ideal plans, but even in this case they probably will end up with different actual plans because each company has a group of people with differing personalities, capabilities, and interactions.

In fact, the term "ideal plan" can itself be somewhat misleading. It is often the case that in a single company there are two or more alternatives—equally suitable and sound—to the organization of marketing. One of these may provide more stimulating interaction among the people in the organization than the others, but it should be recognized that any plan that really does not inhibit the achievement of marketing objectives may be adequate. The deciding factor may be simply, but validly, the personal preference of the chief marketing executive.

If these dangers of accepting generalizations too literaly are recognized, it is useful to observe some basic differences in the typical patterns found in organization plans in various types of industries.

Probably the greatest single cause for these differences is the fact that the more intangible the product or service, the more important personal selling becomes as a key factor in the marketing effort.

If the product is highly standardized and can be compared easily with competitive offerings, personal selling rarely exercises a strong influence on a customer's buying decision. In such cases much greater weight is placed on advertising, point-of-purchase promotion, and packaging. Many such products are sold through self-service retail outlets, with the result that personal selling is virtually eliminated.

If the product is completely intangible, as in the case of personal services, the customer's buying decision often is determined solely on the basis of personal salesmanship. In fact, in many such cases the professional skills of the person doing the actual selling are the "product" being sold.

The effect of this factor can be seen clearly in the following discussion of typical organization plans in four basic types of selling operations: retail companies, manufacturing companies, contract R&D companies, and personal-service companies.

Retail Companies

A frequently heard comment is that the key to success in retailing is smart buying. The basic function of a retail store is, after all, that of displaying attractively and conveniently merchandise that is well matched to customer buying preferences. If the merchandise is truly well selected and displayed, a major part of the selling task is already done. Personal selling support may be needed for many types of fashion merchandise, but the trend in retailing over the years has been increasingly toward self-selection of merchandise. Where self-selection occurs, the duties of the sales personnel are limited essentially to keeping the display areas orderly and filled with merchandise, receiving payment from customers, and handling other procedures incident to the sales transaction. Sales people may or may not be required also to prepare inventory records.

In these circumstances it is clear that the key function is that of buying, and the organization plan is constructed largely around the buyer. In a small store this may be the proprietor himself. In larger stores, separate buyers—often called department managers—may be designated for different types of merchandise. In either case the buyers typically supervise directly the sales personnel in their departments. Thus the group of employees under the administration of the chief buyer (who often has the title of vice president of merchandising) usually is the largest group of employees in the store. The other major groups found on most retail organization charts are a financial group and an operations and personnel group. The former handles all accounting matters, including customer accounts;

Figure 6-3. Organization plan of single-store retail company.

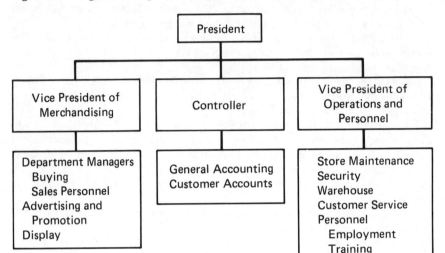

the latter handles the housekeeping functions in the store and the recruitment and training of all types of personnel. Thus a simple but rather typical retail organization plan for a single-store operation is as shown in Figure 6-3.

In multi-outlet retail organizations, buying is commonly done at the corporate headquarters level by a number of buyers, each specializing in a particular type of merchandise. Selection of items to be offered through the stores, including decisions on such matters as style, color, mechanical specifications, and retail price, is made at this level. The quantity of each item to be carried in inventory at the retail level is determined, however, by a store manager, who is also the supervisor (often, through department heads) of the store sales personnel. Thus a highly simplified form of organization plan for a multi-outlet retail organization might appear as in Figure 6-4.

Manufacturing Companies

It is among manufacturing companies that the greatest variations occur in organizing the marketing department. This is because there is such wide variation in size of company, type of product, breadth of product line, and channel of distribution.

The simplest form of organization plan for manufacturing companies involves a division of responsibility for the major activities of the company among three or four key executives, each reporting directly to the president. A common plan of this type includes a sales group, a manufacturing group, an accounting group, and perhaps an engineering or R&D group. This elementary form of organization is found in most small companies, as shown in Figure 6-5 or in some close

Figure 6-4. Organization plan of multi-outlet retail organization.

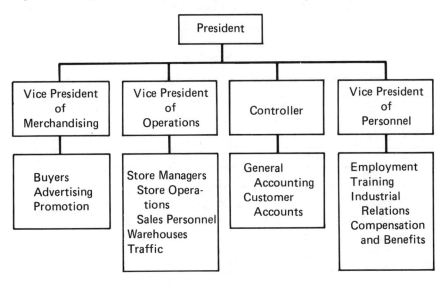

variation. The sales group is headed by a sales manager, who is responsible for all aspects of selling the product: managing the sales force or sales representatives, marketing planning, advertising, pricing, and other marketing functions.

The major difficulty with this form of organization is that, more often than not, the sales manager must spend a disproportionate amount of his time in direct supervision of the sales force and possibly in making sales calls himself. This leaves inadequate time for other marketing activities, particularly for planning. The problem can be especially severe if the company is growing rapidly.

Consequently, the most common change from the basic organization plan shown in Figure 6-5, after the company has reached somewhat larger size, is to separate the responsibility for overall marketing management from that of direct supervision of the sales force. The chief marketing executive begins to spend his

Figure 6-5. Organization plan for small manufacturing company.

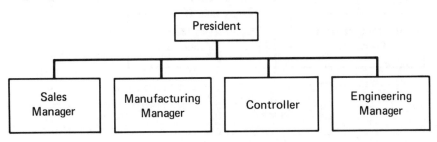

Figure 6-6. Organization plan for a manufacturing company, using functional specialists.

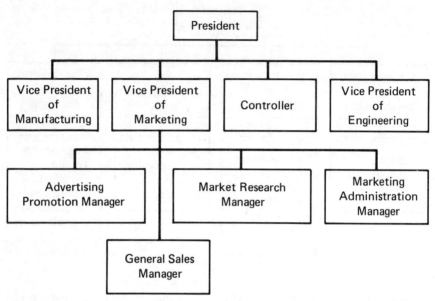

Figure 6-7. Organization plan for a manufacturing company, using product managers.

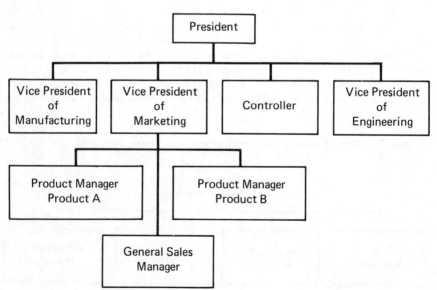

time primarily on planning and on managing the various indirect forms of marketing effort such as advertising; responsibility for direct supervision of the sales force is delegated to the sales manager at the next lower organizational level. With further growth it may become desirable to assign responsibility for some of the indirect marketing activities to specialists in those fields reporting directly to the chief marketing executive. Thus the company may have an advertising manager, a market research manager, a manager of marketing administration, or other specialists. This type of evolution is illustrated in Figure 6-6.

If the product line is relatively broad, specialization may evolve in a somewhat different direction. Instead of assigning specialists on his staff to various functional areas such as advertising and market research, the chief marketing executive may elect to assign a person to handle all the functional responsibilities except direct selling for a given product or group of products. This is the product manager concept. The product manager is responsible, principally, for planning all aspects of the marketing effort for his assigned products and communicating these plans to the sales force for implementation. This form of organization is illustrated in Figure 6-7.

If the sales force is very large, and particularly if it is divided into a number of subgroups along product or geographic lines, two completely separate departments may be established for marketing planning and sales force supervision, each department headed by an executive reporting directly to the president. A plan constructed along these lines is illustrated in Figure 6-8.

The four plans discussed are basic variations in the way marketing organization can be approached in a manufacturing company. As indicated previously, the choice among them should be determined with an eye first to the characteristics of the markets being served, and second to the marketing tasks that need to

Figure 6-8. Organization plan for a manufacturing company, with separate marketing and sales departments.

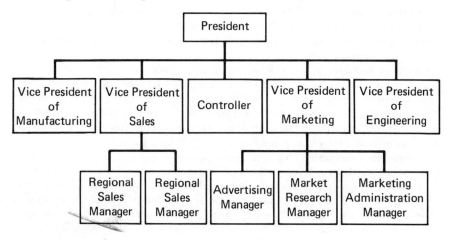

be performed and the relative emphasis to be placed on each. Except in the smallest companies, it may be that the best answer is some combination of these basic forms. Perhaps the most frequent combination is the use of both functional specialists and product managers on the staff of the chief marketing executive.

R&D Companies

Two characteristics of most contract R&D companies have a strong influence on the type of organization plans most suitable for them. First, the thing being sold by such companies—the collective experience and skills of a group of technical people—is intangible. Second, each prospective sale is a relatively unique situation and usually requires substantial technical analysis and tactical business planning before the sales presentation is made.

Because of these factors, the technical personnel themselves play a vital role in the overall marketing effort. It is they, much more than the marketing personnel, who can determine the feasibility of each prospective contract, decide on the technical approach to be used, and estimate the amount of technical effort required to complete the contract. These are all critical decisions in developing the sales presentation. Furthermore, the buyer's decision is often influenced heavily by the personal qualifications of key members of the technical group; therefore, these people frequently must participate heavily in the personal selling contacts.

In a typical R&D company, there are four primary functions of a marketing nature that must be performed by some group. Whether they are performed by the marketing group or by the technical group depends almost entirely upon the relative capabilities of the two groups. In some R&D companies, senior members of the technical group have established strong professional reputations of their own and also are thoroughly articulate in both oral and written communication. In such companies the technical group assumes almost total responsibility for the marketing effort; the marketing group—if any—is responsible only for routine, essentially clerical activity in support of that effort. In other R&D companies the technical group may be less well established professionally and less articulate; in such cases the marketing group must assume much greater responsibility for the direct implementation of the marketing effort. In either situation the four functions about to be described must be performed by one or the other group or by some combination of the two, the balance being determined by the relative competence of the two groups.

Contact with buyers. Some person or group in the R&D company must maintain close contact with primary buyers of the types of services being offered, thus functioning as the eyes and ears of the company in the marketplace. Through this activity the individual or group interprets basic trends in the market and assures that the company will have an opportunity to submit contract proposals to as many qualified buyers as possible.

Determining marketing strategy. Some person or group must use this knowledge of the market to develop an overall marketing strategy for the company. The person or group assuming this responsibility leads the way in determining what types of work should be pursued most aggressively and what the company should do to enhance its position and image in the appropriate market sectors.

Contract proposal preparation. Someone must assume responsibility for the preparation of contract proposals. The material for these proposals is drawn largely from the technical group, but it must be shaped into the format of a persuasive selling document. If the technical-group members are highly skilled and articulate in such work, they may assume total responsibility for this effort. In large R&D companies there may be a staff of technical writers and technical illustrators who can be assigned to support it. In other companies the most skilled communicators are found in the marketing group, and ultimate responsibility for preparing the contract proposal is assigned there. In this case the marketing group functions as the funnel for communications between the technical group and the prospective buyer.

Customer relations. Someone must assume responsibility for continuing customer relations after the company has been awarded the R&D contract. It is inevitable that the technical group will be involved to some extent in this effort, because it is responsible for ultimate performance on the contract. On the other hand, it is often useful to have some other group in the company functioning essentially as the customer's representative, assuring that contract work is progressing productively and on schedule and that the customer is receiving an adequate flow of information about progress and results. In such cases this responsibility often is assigned to the marketing group.

Bid committee. Each contract proposal represents a unique marketing problem; thus many R&D companies establish a group commonly known as the bid committee. In its most typical form, the bid committee consists of members from the technical group, the financial group, the manufacturing group (if production is involved), and the marketing group. The bid committee may be chaired by either the chief marketing executive or the chief of the technical group, depending on the relative professional status of the two groups. Each time the company has an opportunity to submit a contract proposal, it is the bid committee that weighs the technical feasibility of the task in view of the company's resources, and also the probability of capturing the contract against the expected competition. On this basis the committee makes the initial decision on whether a proposal will be prepared. If the decision is affirmative, the members of the committee agree among themselves on the part that each will play in preparing the proposal.

After the individual assignments have been completed, the committee plays a major role in fitting the pieces together effectively and—most important—making the contract pricing decision. In actual practice, of course, this sometimes means that the principal role of the bid committee at this point is to assure documentation of informal commitments previously made by individual committee members. After the committee's work has been completed, the formal proposal is presented to the prospective buyer. Again the roles of the marketing group and the technical group in this process are influenced heavily by the professional reputation and communication skill of the technical group.

Personal-Service Companies

In personal-service companies the outstanding example of marketing based on personal selling can be observed. This is true particularly among companies selling advisory services—attorneys, architects and engineers, auditors, management consultants, and the like—but it is nearly as true of companies producing somewhat more tangible services—advertising agencies, office designers, and employment agencies, for example.

In such companies the decision of the prospective buyer of services is influenced heavily by his confidence in the professional competence of the individual who will render the service personally or direct the professional personnel who do so. Consequently, it is essential that the sales effort consist primarily of direct and intimate contact between key personnel in the professional-services company and the prospective buyer. In such contacts the key people have an opportunity to demonstrate their insight into the buyer's requirements and relate it to their own personal expertise and experiences, and the buyer has an opportunity to assess the degree to which the necessary intellectual and temperamental rapport would exist between himself and the person with whom he would be working. The personal selling activity may be supported by secondary tools such as brochures, proposal letters, lists of prior clients, and documentation of professional qualifications; but the success of the selling effort nearly always hinges on the effectiveness of the personal selling phase.

Personal contact is so overwhelmingly important in the marketing of personal services that the introduction of a third party, in the form of a sales representative or marketing specialist, almost inevitably reduces the effectiveness of the marketing effort. Consequently, it is relatively unusual in personal-service firms to have personnel whose total responsibility is in the area of sales.

Except in very large companies that sell personal services, there is thus rarely a separate and identifiable marketing group. Responsibility for the overall marketing effort is imposed on the professional staff itself, and each key member of that staff is made responsible personally for developing some portion of the firm's total billings. The chief marketing officer is in effect the senior partner or chief executive officer of the firm. He determines the firm's overall marketing strategy and often takes personal responsibility for such matters as developing brochures and other promotional materials.

Although this approach is eminently practical for most personal-service companies, it does lead to the risk that the total marketing effort will be somewhat disjointed, uncoordinated, and poorly planned. Major market opportunities may be overlooked because nobody on the professional staff has particular interest or acquaintance with people in the area of the market where the opportunity exists. As the professional personnel become heavily engaged in client work, they may subordinate their selling activities to the point that a continual inflow of new work is not maintained. Because the development of each new client situation ordinarily requires considerable time, this weakness may result in substantial peaks and valleys in the firm's billing level. Also, supporting marketing materials (brochures, client lists, and so on) may be developed hastily to meet an immediate requirement and consequently may not be prepared as well as if a more concentrated and systematic approach were taken.

To overcome these difficulties, some of the larger personal-service companies have established a position for a chief marketing executive, usually with the title of director of client relations or director of development. The responsibilities of such a position are quite different from those of the chief marketing executive in any of the three types of companies discussed previously. In this case the individual is clearly in a supportive role and has little personal participation in the direct selling effort. On occasion he may accompany professional personnel in their contacts with prospective clients, but in a background or coaching role only. Normally, he is responsible for seeing that a comprehensive marketing plan for the firm is developed for execution by the professional staff. Subsequently, he monitors the activities of professional personnel in securing new business and works with them to ensure that the marketing plan is being implemented as it was conceived. Typically, he is also responsible for developing and directing the firm's public relations program and preparing supportive marketing materials. In some cases he may have the additional responsibility of training younger professional personnel in techniques of business development. □ *Richard J. Steele*

PRODUCT MANAGEMENT

The product manager concept has emerged as one of the more remarkable developments of modern marketing. Its adoption by a great number of consumer-oriented companies has substantially affected both the organization and the management of marketing operations. As planner and coordinator of all major activities related to his assigned brand, the product manager occupies a managerial post of considerable responsibility. He must generally carry out his mission without having line authority over any of the various company departments whose cooperation is essential for the market success of the product. In order to understand this difficult job, there is need to explore the product manager concept, the functions and qualifications of the product manager, and the organizational requirements for success.

The Product Manager Concept

In recent years the marketing of consumer and industrial goods has reached a state of enormous complexity. In this environment an administrative apparatus that would ensure survival in an era of line diversification and product fractionalization was urgently needed. The product manager system has found overwhelming acceptance in achieving the objectives for which it was developed.

Rationale

Some of the specific reasons why a company may need a product manager system include the following: (1) constantly changing customer needs that make sensitivity to them essential for prompt action; (2) the need to extend greater amounts of technical service to help customers to use products more advantageously; (3) the need to monitor competition and develop strategies and counterstrategies; (4) the threat of product obsolescence as a result of the multiplication of new products and the need for alert, aggressive marketing management to maintain market position; (5) the possibility of multiproducts spread too thin, with insufficient attention given to certain product lines; (6) the problem of launching new products efficiently and successfully; and (7) the need for more selectivity in selling, concentrating on the most worthwhile prospects and opportunities for profit.

The major advantage of the product manager position is that it provides sufficient individual attention to the planning, development, and sale of each product in each market. Properly applied, the product manager concept provides an overall approach to the product as it relates to the entire company.

Market Manager

Several approaches similar to the product manager concept exist under different names. Often these variations are found within the same industry. A close organizational and functional equivalent of the product manager is the market manager or industry manager. A market manager is oriented toward a market rather than a product. The need for a market manager may develop in companies where a particular product or group of products is sold to several markets, each of which is sufficiently differentiated from the others and important enough to the company to justify specialized staff attention. For example, a computer manufacturer may sell the same equipment to various different user industries— retail department stores, hospitals, and aerospace industries. Some companies have both product managers and market managers. In any case, many features of the product manager's job and that of the market manager are similar.

Consumer- and Industrial-Product Managers

It is generally recognized that the product manager in the consumer-goods field is often largely concerned with advertising and promotional matters and the product manager in the industrial-products field tends to be more technically oriented. The promotional orientation of the consumer-product manager is often a result of the need for extensive advertising and promotion in mass markets and the fight for shelf space in retail stores. The industrial-product manager is more concerned with such activities as technical assistance, service to customers, and analysis of the implications of changes in customer requirements.

A typical product manager in consumer-goods companies is usually less than 35 years old and has a formal education, often with a master's degree in business administration. His background is generally with several employers, usually in advertising, selling, or sales promotion. He tends to associate largely with advertising-agency people and with marketing people in his company and is highly mobile, with a strong possibility of switching to another employer. If successful, he is highly promotable.

A typical product manager in industrial-goods companies tends to be in his forties and has a BS degree in physical science or engineering. He is likely to have served his entire career with his present employer or no more than two employers. Such a product manager is experienced in laboratory or technical-service work and generally associates mainly with laboratory and engineering personnel in his company. He tends to be stabilized in permanent employment with his present company, with promotions relatively slow but sure and earnings about 10 to 15 percent less than in consumer-goods companies, though with exceptions. In either case a typical product manager is a decision maker and a risk taker. If he is right, he moves; if he is wrong, he is moved.

Functions of the Product Manager

Despite observable differences in the orientation and duties of product managers in different companies, there are a number of fundamental similarities in the work done by all product managers. Regardless of the kind of product they deal with, the size of the company, or their place or title in an organization, most product managers are likely to have job descriptions that use such words as "plan," "organize," "develop," "recommend," "motivate," "implement," "coordinate," and "control." A product manager basically has the following functions: to recommend sales objectives for his product; to create marketing strategy for products that are to be promoted; to develop promotion programs to be executed by advertising and field sales departments; and to coordinate all activities relating to his product.

Strategy and Planning

At the core of the product manager's job is the marketing plan that sets the strategy and tactics for a 12-month period. Strategy means taking into consideration all marketing movements, with projections of anticipated results; tactics are the practical carrying out of that which has been directed by strategy. The product manager has complete responsibility for the development, preparation, and implementation of the annual marketing plan for the brand. It includes basic objectives, strategy, budgets, forecasts, income, and profit and generally details all aspects of a marketing program for a brand for one year, including copy, media, promotion, trade incentives, packaging changes, and research.

In developing the marketing plan, reliable background information in regard to the brand is essential. This usually requires studying the product in detail, including costs, profit margin, packaging requirements, and distribution channels; analyzing competitive products to determine their strengths and weaknesses; and obtaining information on competitive changes and technological innovations.

The product manager must also familiarize himself with every feature of the market for his product. This usually means gathering detailed market information and statistics; analyzing market trends and changing buying habits; conducting market research to determine customer needs and wants; exploring existing and possible future market opportunities for the product; and examining all marketing problems that threaten the future growth of the brand.

The next state is the actual development of plans and programs. This usually involves developing a basic sales forecast for the product; recommending short-range and long-range objectives for the brand; producing strategies for the attainment of marketing objectives; and planning sales, sales promotion, and advertising campaigns for the product.

Functions in Other Areas

In addition to his major responsibilities for developing strategies and plans for his brand, a product manager also has important responsibilities in virtually every other major function in the company. It is up to him to use all the resources of the company in order to successfully market its products.

Sales. In the area of sales the product manager is usually responsible for developing a basic sales forecast on his product and reviewing it with the sales department; consulting with the sales department on product information specifications, distribution changes, and all matters of a sales nature; soliciting new customers and solving customer problems; preparing presentations and delivering them to all levels of sales meetings; and for certain products, setting policy relating to such concerns as warranties, pricing protection, sales allowances, and returns.

Field trips. Generally, the product manager does not engage in direct selling, although in industrial-product firms it is part of his duties to sell to selected accounts. A product manager generally undertakes some field trips periodically so as to get a firsthand feel of the market and familiarize himself with customer needs and the situation in the trade. In most companies the product manager spends some time with customers, sales representatives, and service personnel in order to evaluate the effectiveness of sales and service programs and maintain an awareness of field problems.

Advertising, promotion, and merchandising. Product managers are deeply involved in all aspects of advertising, promotion, and merchandising on both strategic and tactical levels. Substantial differences exist, however, from company to company, in the authority of the product manager in these areas. A delicate relationship generally exists between the product manager and the advertising agency. Copy and media components of the marketing plan are often prepared by the agency. Even if it does not prepare the entire annual plan, the agency is often a partner in presenting the plan to upper management for approval.

Because of the enormous size of advertising budgets, other marketing management executives often become engaged in evaluating agency work. This tends to dilute the strength of the product manager system and the concept of decentralized responsibility and authority. Nevertheless, the product manager directs advertising, promotion, and merchandising effort and develops the advertising budget for higher-management approval. More and more product managers are being drawn extensively into media decision making and are instrumental in media planning, selecting flexible media, developing media budgets, and directing creative effort.

In the area of sales promotion, product managers exercise more independent authority than elsewhere. However, this part of their function is generally quite sensitive because of the sometimes touchy relationship that exists between sales and marketing. For this reason, a sales promotion planning department may be established. The extent of product manager involvement in designing specific sales promotion programs varies widely. Most product managers do everything themselves, working with outside or inside promotion-planning groups. Also important is the coordination of sales promotion with sales personnel. In some companies the product group sets sales promotion objectives and timing and dollar commitments, and the promotion department recommends strategies and plans and is responsible for implementation. In other companies the product manager has complete responsibility for all sales promotion, including couponing, display activity, deals to the trade, and selecting contests, sweepstakes, and premiums.

Packaging. Another function of the product manager is to determine packaging changes and variations. His responsibilities range from developing specifications of marketing objectives, through coordinating all phases of development of objectives, to making recommendations to higher management. The product manager rarely is involved in the technical aspects of packaging, but he is responsible for the end product. These responsibilities are particularly critical during test marketing and new-product-development programs.

Pricing All the critical information needed to make decisions on pricing is available to product managers. If a price adjustment is necessary, they are usually the first to realize it. Because prices are relatively stable and are often simply linked to competitive activity, only a limited amount of time is spent on analysis and recommendations. However, monitoring the competitive pricing situation is an ongoing function. Most often the product group is strongly instrumental in establishing the price and determining, with upper-management approval, the actual selling price.

Market research. The product manager's role in market research is determined by several factors: the quality, strength, and experience of the company's market research department, if there is one; company policy in respect to interpretation of research findings; relationship with the advertising agency, and the agency's capabilities in market research; and the product manager's expertise in this area. Three distinct types of working relationships seem to exist between product management and market research. In some companies the market research department initiates and interprets nearly all product-oriented effort. Under such circumstances the product manager is obligated to respond positively. In other companies the market research department is a service to product management. In these situations, product managers initiate research programs and are entirely responsible for their interpretation. A final approach somewhere in the middle of the road is most commonly found. Initiating and interpreting are functions equally shared by the product manager and the market researcher assigned to the brand. Generally, market research activities to be included in the annual marketing plan are developed jointly by the product manager and the market research staff.

New Products

A typical function of a product manager is handling line extensions, modifications of existing products, and the development of new products in his line. Otherwise, the degree of involvement in new-product development depends on several factors: the strength of the new-product-development group, the positioning of an independent new-products product manager, and the timing of the assignment of a new item to a product manager who is already handling established brands. Within the framework of new-product-development extensions and modifications, a product manager is generally aware of other new products and innovations within his category and is responsible for the creation and recommendation (to the R&D group) of new and additional products. He is also responsible for approving all alterations or modifications of a major nature.

In companies with a new-product-development group, completely new products are dealt with there. The group generally has its own staff and research personnel, who do market testing and sales testing through the company's sales organization. Once a product is established, it is turned over to the regular marketing organization and is assigned to the product manager in whose category it logically falls. In some companies the product manager becomes involved at the concept stage; in others, after test marketing is complete. It is rare for product managers to come in as late as a regional or national rollout.

Qualifications of the Product Manager

Because the product manager's job carries such varied and exacting demands, it calls for a very special combination of personal characteristics and experience. One essential characteristic associated with the product manager is flexibility, and it is desirable that he have a broad background—as broad as possible.

Educational Background

Regardless of whether the product manager is working in a consumer-goods or an industrial-goods firm, a college degree is almost universally required. Consumer-goods firms generally look for men and women who have degrees in business administration—preferably, in the marketing field—but industrial-goods firms seek those whose studies have been in technical areas (the physical sciences or engineering). Increasingly prevalent are product managers who have higher degrees (mostly MBAs) or who have done or are doing postgraduate work. In business areas where advertising, promotion, and selling are of paramount importance, graduate studies in marketing are regarded as excellent background to broaden an individual's experience but are not required if broad experience exists.

Business Experience

The product manager also has to be a highly knowledgeable executive—in effect, to be able to manage his own business. For this reason many companies tend to place great emphasis on the person's previous business experience. A broad background knowledge of total company operations, as well as intimate familiarity with customer needs and opportunities for product development and market expansion, is looked for.

Sales. Most companies prefer that a prospective product manager have, as a minimum, some exposure to sales work. In fact, the sales force is one of the primary sources of supply for product managers in companies where sales work is the major route for promotion.

Advertising. A major second area of exposure for product managers is in advertising, promotion, and merchandising. This background could come through a job in an advertising agency or through the advertising department. In some cases it could be obtained through close association with advertising agencies or the company's advertising people while working on a product.

Production. In industrial-goods firms, a product manager must know a great deal about the product—how it is made and what can be done with it. As a result many product managers come from the manufacturing department and are engineers, chemists, or metallurgists. Often they have worked in the plants and have been involved in making the product, which qualifies them as experts on the product.

Personal Characteristics

Personal characteristics often make the difference between the successful product manager and the one whose achievement is mediocre. The product manager must know his market, his competition, and his product. He must have the ability to create new ideas in strategy, to innovate, to use all the resources of his company in the marketing of his product, to communicate ideas, and to sell programs to others. He should have leadership ability, persuasiveness, and understanding. He should have administrative ability, a well-organized mind, and a great deal of drive. In other words, the qualities necessary in a product manager are much the same as those for any other responsible managerial position.

Organizational Requirements

In order to reap the full benefits of a product manager system, it is necessary to provide the product managers with support and latitude consistent with the multitude of tasks they have to perform.

The product management concept, in the 15 years or so that it has been accepted by top management in American companies, has not been without its problems. In order to obtain maximum advantage of the product management system, a number of organizational requirements must be met.

Scope of responsibilities. Experience with the product manager concept reveals that product managers function most effectively when the scope of their responsibilities includes making recommendations for product investment, production scheduling, and participating in the total distribution process, pricing, and profit policy. They should be able to participate in new-product selection, timing, and development from a market viewpoint. A product manager should be considered the most capable member of the corporate team on matters pertaining to his product lines.

Adequate resources. Often it is not difficult to secure financial resources for market development. However, the assurance and allocation of selling power are quite difficult. In many cases the product manager lacks a staff and must handle many details alone. The problem is not solved by simply making available the services of inside and outside specialists. The product manager is faced with the problem of how he alone can best use these people and find the time to deal with them.

Simplified decision channels. Decisions in developing the proper marketing strategy and determining the best mix of resources to allocate to a product are exceedingly difficult for a product manager to make. The time and communications required to transmit these decisions to higher management for approval necessitate the simplest decision channels. Simple channels clarify decision making, identify accountability, and minimize loss of communication and distortion of planning.

Managerial authority. Unless a product manager is given managerial authority, the greatest advantages of the system are lost. The three chief reasons why little authority is generally given to product managers are doubt of their capabilities, opposition of entrenched senior functional managers, and lack of understanding of the basic organizational principles of the product management system. It is essential that product managers have the authority to plan, create, develop strategy, and marshal resources for their product lines. Their authority should include the power to command resources to implement their programs—subject, of course, to the concurrence of their superiors.

Assumption of responsibility. When fully implemented, a product management system should create the means for assumption of profit-and-loss responsibility. The product manager, when provided with the proper levels of company resources and the authority to insist on their delivery, should assume the responsibility for profit and loss, sales, share of market, and distribution performance of his brands.

Management development. The great mobility of product managers is well known; average duration in the job is about two years. Few product managers have sufficient tenure to work their way out of difficult situations and develop their abilities. Often there is an imbalance in education, background, and experience. Competent product managers should not be expected to develop without some of the formal training that has become standard procedure for most other responsible positions. Emphasis in training should be on the compilation and analysis of data, on the specification of research requirements, and on quantitative decision making. In this way the problems of selecting and developing qualified manpower may be significantly reduced and the ultimate promise of the product management system brought a great deal closer to fruition.

□ *David B. Uman*

MARKET ANALYSIS: DEVELOPING, USING, AND MAINTAINING THE MARKET INTELLIGENCE SYSTEM

This discussion deals with the critical, but often shortchanged, two-thirds of the marketing process—before-the-fact environment analysis and after-the-fact progress evaluation. Before-the-fact analysis is commonly referred to as the environmental situation analysis, the foundation of the marketing plan. During implementation of the plan, after-the-fact analysis measures progress against the strategies and the objectives in the plan, as well as changes in the environment that occur during the plan implementation. If marketing planning is viewed as a continuous process, as it should be, the environmental portion of after-the-fact analysis and before-the-fact environment analysis become a single process.

Rationale for the Market Intelligence System

The market intelligence system is the foundation of a sound marketing effort. Just as one would not build a house on sand, one should never undertake a marketing program that is not built on a firm foundation of market knowledge. To do so would be to run a high risk of rendering substantial marketing expenditures ineffective and, perhaps worse, of raising in the minds of top management significant doubts regarding the effectiveness of the marketing function.

Importance of a Market Intelligence System

Any business exists at the pleasure of one or more markets. If the market chooses not to buy, the game is over. So the traditional marketing concept of "find a need and fill it" is sound, virtually unassailable. Concentrating on identifying and satisfying market needs is the route to continued long-term profitability. Not doing so is the route to unprofitable operation and, ultimately, business failure.

But despite the compelling logic of the marketing concept, examples of its effective implementation are still the exception rather than the rule. Only rarely do we see an example of successful implementation of the marketing concept such as Xerox, which created an entirely new business based on solving customer communications problems, or Polaroid, which successfully addressed the desire of people to have a record of their good times . . . instantly. Far more commonly do we see products or services that must be withdrawn from the market because of the lack of market acceptance and companies which, though once prosperous, learn with apparent suddenness that the market is no longer interested in their offerings.

Why does this happen? It happens because of an innate tendency in an organization to focus inward on the desires of the organization rather than outward on the needs, values, problems, and concerns of the marketplace. Companies, like people, tend naturally to think more about themselves than about others. In the process, the market—in reality, the lifeblood of the company—gets short shrift. It is this natural and usually insidious tendency, this inward focus, which must be overcome if we are to achieve a true market focus and a long-term profit success that accompanies that market focus.

The best indication of the existence of a true market focus is the existence and common use of an effective market intelligence system. Yet, it is remarkable and alarming how little managers of businesses really know about their markets and the other elements of their outside environments. A U.S. supplier of expensive technology to a large firm in Brazil, for example, lost the contract because the Brazilian customer was losing market share in *his* market. The reason for the share loss was a competing product that used more up-to-date technology that was more appropriate for the Brazilian market. Specifically, the competitive technology was based on the dual assumptions of inexpensive labor and expensive materials, circumstances quite descriptive of Brazil, whereas the U.S. firm's technology was based on the opposite assumptions—expensive labor and inexpensive materials. This is an example of the type of market knowledge that should be routinely available to marketers, if they are to prosper through a true market focus. In short, the marketer should understand his customer's business as well as he understands his own.

A domestic marketer discovered, to his dismay, that he lacked a clear understanding of the dynamic situation that existed among the channels through which his product got to market. Everything looked fine, because he was becoming more and more dominant in one major channel. What he failed to realize, however, was that in the mix of channels, the channel in which he was dominant was losing market share. He overlooked the fact that the channel is only a means to an end. This same marketer also had inadequate understanding of his competitors' cost structures, making it very difficult for him to develop effective competitive strategy.

There is nothing whatsoever altruistic about market-focused management. It is nothing more than common sense, reflecting a realization that we exist at the pleasure of the market. Similarly, there is nothing elegant or luxurious about the existence of an effective market intelligence system. Without it, one simply cannot be market-focused. With it, one's chances for long-term profitability, through effective addressing of market needs and problems, increase dramatically.

Market Intelligence — the Basis for Effective Marketing Effort

In any competitive environment, marketing is a struggle for market share between competition and one's own organization. This is true even in a rapidly growing market, because, in most instances, it is reasonable to assume that the competitors in a rapid growth market have, among them, targeted more business volume than will actually exist, notwithstanding the fact that it is generally easier to gain market share in a growing market than in a mature one.

Marketing success involves focusing on market needs, wants, problems, and concerns and bringing to bear on those issues the firm's relative marketing strengths while at the same time maximizing competitive disadvantage. There are, of course, legal constraints involved. Nevertheless, marketers tend to operate in a closed-loop dynamic system in which share increases to one marketer are at the expense of another.

Given the nature of the marketing battle, it follows logically that an effective market intelligence system requires input from three areas: the market, competition, and one's own organization. A fourth broad category includes economic, natural, societal, technological, governmental/political/regulatory, and owner issues.

Steps in Developing a Market Intelligence System

Conceptually, development of an effective market intelligence system is simple and straightforward. It involves the following steps: (1) MIS content determination; (2) locating information sources; (3) people and money commitment; (4) data collection and analysis; (5) continuous use of market data in strategy development, plan implementation, and progress measurement; and (6) system maintenance, with upgrading as required. Each of these key steps will be discussed in depth. It is important here simply to note that the market intelligence system represents a chain of events that progresses continuously. If any link in the chain is weak, the chain will, of course, break.

Content of the Market Intelligence System

The content of the market intelligence system represents the meat of the system. What follows represents an ideal market intelligence system content. It should be realized that one seldom achieves an ideal. Nevertheless, one should continuously strive to obtain *all* the information outlined here.

There is a mistaken notion that the more data one compiles, the better one's market intelligence system is. The reality of the situation is that, if there are too many data, it is impossible to work with them. All the information content outlined here, however, is necessary to the performance of an effective marketing job.

It is important to note at the outset that one must not confuse channels of distribution with markets. All demand is derived demand, as many an industrial marketer or OEM supplier who lacked effective end-user intelligence has learned to his dismay. While it is not a foregone conclusion that a marketer will aggressively "market" to end-user markets in the merchandising sense, the marketer must nevertheless make it his responsibility to understand the dynamics of his end-user markets. In the following discussion, market information is therefore treated differently from channel information, although both are important.

Market Information

The following key elements of market information should be included in the market intelligence system: segment identification; segment size and growth rate; segment perceptions of competitors' and own firm's quality; identity of key buying influencers and purchase decision mechanics for each segment; and unfulfilled needs, wants, and problems of each market segment.

Segment identification. A market is a group of individuals or organizations that share a common generic need. Thus, for example, there are consumer markets for pain relief and personal transportation, and there are industrial markets for energy management and logistics. A *market segment* represents a subgroup within a market whose members each have a common set of secondary needs, wants, problems, values, and concerns beyond the generic need. Thus, in the consumer markets cited, one segment of the pain relief market might be suffering from severe chronic pain whereas another segment suffers milder pain only periodically. In the transportation market, there might be a segment aimed toward luxury while another segment is predominantly concerned about economy.

In the industrial markets cited, one segment of the energy management market might be concerned with minute amounts of power, whereas another segment might be concerned with extremely large amounts. In the logistics market, one segment might have a periodic need to move small volumes of material short distances, whereas another segment might have a far greater and continuing need to move larger volumes of material longer distances.

To be sure, markets can and should be segmented more finely than in the examples given. But the examples explain the basic concept.

Note that in the discussion of market and market segments, there was no mention of products. There are no markets for products. Markets represent groups of people or organizations with needs and problems. Products represent marketers' individual attempts to address those needs and problems.

There are several reasonable bases for market segmentation. Commonly, in the industrial sector, marketers look at different Standard Industrial Classifications. The SIC system represents an effort to organize companies along the lines of their manufacturing activity. Although such an approach often represents a very sound basis for segmenting an industrial market, it is not the *only* approach available. One might also segment industrial markets geographically, by size of customer operation, or by function.

In consumer markets, it is common to attempt to segment according to such demographic considerations as age, sex, race, religion, income, and education. These bases, too, are frequently sound, although they do not represent the only rational basis for market segmentation. More recently, marketers have become concerned with psychographic considerations aimed more at what people think and believe than at their demographic characteristics.

The important point to note is that whether a market segmentation basis is sound or not depends not on the marketers' conceptual capabilities but rather on the market itself. If the market is willing to buy into a marketer's approach to segmentation, the approach is sound. If the market is unwilling, the approach is unsound. Competitive advantage is often gained through a novel approach to market segmentation, but it is imperative that the market understand and accept the novel segmentation approach.

Segment size and growth rate. It is not uncommon for market segments to grow at varying rates. Thus, for example, while the luxury segment of the personal-transportation market may be shrinking, the economy may indeed be growing. In industrial markets, the need for emergency fast shipping might be stable whereas the need for improving customer service through a total logistics concept might be growing.

It is common to speak of "growth markets." But today, the marketer must focus not only on the growth of an overall market but also on the growth of the individual segments of that market.

It is important also to note that market growth rate or market-segment growth rate can vary with the segmentation bases used. This phenomenon is most commonly observed in the case of a geographic market segmentation basis. A market in North America may be static, but when viewed from a worldwide perspective, the same market may be in a state of growth. This fact becomes critical when one views one's competitive situation, because more and more North American marketers today are finding themselves in competition with international competitors who view the *world* as their market.

Segment perceptions of competitors' and own firm's quality. Recently, quality has been identified as one of a handful of factors that have a significant positive effect on profitability. The higher the quality, other things being equal (which, of course, they never are!), the higher the profitability.

There are two important factors the marketer should keep in mind regarding quality. First, the *market's* definition of quality is far more important than the marketer's. It is common to hear arguments about the definition of quality. Such arguments overlook the important fact that quality is whatever the market thinks it is. A second important consideration is that *perceived* quality is often at least as important as and frequently more important than any measurement of quality that might be devised in the quality-control laboratory. This view of quality says that the Cadillac is a superior automobile simply because the market perceives it that way.

Perceived quality of the individual marketer's offerings is not the only important consideration. Rather, in the market's eyes, quality is a relative issue. If one marketer's perceived quality is bad and his competitor's perceived quality is excellent, that is bad news indeed—far worse news than if the quality of *all* competitive offerings is perceived as bad.

Identity of key buying influencers and purchase decision mechanics for each segment. Most purchase decisions are effected by more than one individual. This is especially true in industrial marketing but often in consumer marketing as well. An effective market intelligence system must identify each of the key purchase influencers.

Just as important as the identification of each key buying influencer is an understanding of the role of each specific influencer and the interrelationships of each individual with the other purchase influencers. There are several categories of influencer. One is the individual who actually makes the final decision. A second important category, however, includes all those individuals who *influence* the final decision maker as he makes his selection. Some of these influencers, of course, exist *outside* the purchasing organization. A third set of key purchase influencers consists of those who essentially *protect* the decision maker or the other decision influencers. Frequently this category includes secretarial and clerical personnel as well as purchasing personnel in many cases. The effective marketing intelligence system identifies each of the individuals important in the decision process.

Unfulfilled needs, wants, and problems of each market segment. In a competitive environment, which includes the situation of most marketers, there commonly is no shortage of generic products. Thus buyers are free to decide between many brands of tires or many brands of axles.

In such a competitive environment, the secondary benefits sought—satisfaction of the wants, needs, values, and problems of the individual purchase influencers—typically become far more important than the generic needs. Thus, in an industrial situation, the vice president of finance might be concerned chiefly about long-term costs, whereas the purchasing agent might be more concerned about purchase price. The vice president of manufacturing may be more concerned about packaging than the quality-control chemist, whose primary concern might be product purity.

It is important that the market intelligence system realize that each buying influence, as well as each segment, has varying needs. In fact, the determining factor in market segmentation, as has already been indicated, is this bundle of secondary needs. An effective marketing effort addresses *all* the needs of a market segment, especially those which competition is ignoring or addressing ineffectively.

Channel Information

As already indicated, it is critical that the marketer not confuse the channel with the end user. To say that, however, is not to imply that it is unimportant to know what is going on in channels of distribution. The opposite is true. The following paragraphs list and discuss critical information on channels of distribution.

Markets served and share earned.   For each important channel of distribution, it is important to know which markets or market segments it serves and what share of the business of that segment it enjoys. There must be some historical perspective on this, preferably three to five years, because it is important to know, for example, not only that a particular channel enjoys 25 percent of the end-user market but also whether the percentage enjoyed by that channel is increasing or decreasing. It would be disastrous to inadvertently rely on a channel that historically has performed well but which is declining in importance. It is also important to note that channels of distribution seem to follow a life cycle of their own.

Analysis of marketing functions performed.   The economic justification for the existence of a particular channel of distribution is that it performs some marketing function. It is important to identify the marketing functions being performed by each channel and, conversely, those not being performed. For example, in some cases, a channel merely makes the product available to the end user, whereas in other cases the channel also aggressively sells. In some cases, the channel is good at providing technical service, and in others, it is not. It is important not to make a value judgment here. That a channel sells aggressively or not, that it provides technical assistance effectively or not, is inherently neither good nor bad. But having identified what the channel does and does not do, the marketer is in a position to understand better what gaps in the marketing function exist and must be performed by the marketer himself or by someone else.

Business health and growth prospects.   The supplier/channel relationship represents a "mutual back-scratching" effort. The term "profit partners" may be corny, but it is descriptive of the situation that should exist.

It is important that the marketer understand the profitability of the channels with which he is working. If profitability is inadequate, health is not good and the marketer can count on having to work through other channels of distribution in the future. This point is related to the historical perspective on share, but it goes beyond that point in that it represents a required effort to *forecast* into the future, on the basis of past performance and present status.

Quality of relationship.   This refers not only to whether or not the supplier and the channel have a cordial relationship but also to the balance of power between supplier and channel. As an example, historically the marketers of grocery products in the United States have had greater power than the grocery retailers. Today, because of consolidation of retail and the growth in importance of a handful of large retailer organizations, that balance of power is shifting in favor of the retailer. Similarly, chemical distributors have been relatively unpowerful in relation to chemical manufacturers historically. In recent years, however, that situation has changed because of the growing aggressiveness and market focus of chemical distributors. If the relative balance is shifting in favor of the channel, the marketer must know this and must either take steps to correct it or be prepared to see his profitability in the future decline.

Long-range appropriateness. A channel of distribution that is appropriate at one stage of the market life cycle may well be inappropriate at another. For example, in the embryonic stage of a product/market situation, a channel capable of providing education and technical assistance may be most appropriate. Later on, however, after the end users have learned how to apply the product in question, it may well be that the marketer should be looking for less education and more effective distribution on the part of his channel. In viewing channel relationships, the marketer should look not only at the present situation but also into the future.

Competitor Analysis

Given the closed-loop nature of most competitive market situations, as described earlier, competitor analysis is just as important as market analysis. Generally speaking, the marketer should have two types of information about competitors. The first of these covers competitor *capabilities,* and the second, competitor *personalities.* The marketer wants to know, in other words, what each major competitor is *capable* of doing and what each major competitor is *likely* to do.

In analyzing competitors, it is important to go beyond direct competitors and to include indirect competitors as well. A classic example of this is the calculating market in the 1950s. Here, a slide-rule manufacturer should have analyzed not only other slide-rule producers but producers of hand-held calculators as well, since calculators perform the same user function as slide rules.

In performing competitor analysis, the following specific categories of information are important: market definition and segmentation approach; share estimates; assessment of marketing objectives and strategies; estimate of cost structures; level of integration; and summary of competitor key strengths and weaknesses. Each of these points is discussed below.

Market definition and segmentation approach. As already indicated, one's approach to definition and segmentation of the market can often provide a substantial competitive advantage. Geographic considerations are a major example of this. If your firm has defined the market as all of North America and a competitor has defined the market as the entire world, the competitor may well be proceeding on the assumption that the market is rapidly growing, whereas you are proceding on the assumption that the market is a mature one. Similarly, if you have segmented the industrial market by SIC and the competitor has segmented it, for example, by customer size, he may be better able to focus on a certain category of customers than you are.

A good example of the foregoing is a firm that has segmented a particular industrial market into two segments: one with corrosion-resistance requirements and another without corrosion-resistance requirements. For a number of years the company enjoyed a dominant share of the corrosion-resistance segment of the market. More recently, however, a competitor resegmented the market, in a manner the market found acceptable, on the basis of a need for a systems approach. In the process, the new competitor overlapped the other supplier's historical market area and is gaining share effectively.

Share estimates. Estimate of competitor market shares is critical. In many cases, the greater the market share, the lower the cost structure. Generally, competitors with the highest market shares are able to maintain a price umbrella as well. Hence, the high-share supplier has the best of both worlds: high prices and low costs.

Historical measurement of share becomes important as a measure of progress against one's strategies in the marketplace.

Assessment of marketing objectives and strategies. This portion of the market intelligence effort requires an evaluation of what each major competitor appears to be trying to accomplish in the marketplace and his means for achieving it. Is he trying to improve his market share, for example? Or is he simply attempting to maintain share? How much does he spend on marketing communications? Does he tend to resort to price as the ultimate marketing tool, or does he make better use of the other elements of the marketing mix? What about the competence of his sales force? Is he overreliant on the sales force or does he have sales personnel properly balanced with other marketing communications tools? Information on each competitor's marketing objectives and strategies, coupled with the segmentation information already developed, can point out areas of opportunity available in the marketplace.

Estimate of cost structures. This is perhaps one of the most significant bits of competitive intelligence required. Naturally, its collection must be handled with special attention to legal and ethical constraints. Nevertheless, a great deal of competitive cost information is available for the asking through perfectly legal and ethical channels.

Estimate of competitors' cost structures allows the marketer to assess possible competitor responses to actions contemplated. For example, if an elastic condition exists in the marketplace, the marketer may wonder how well prepared a competitor is to respond to a reduction in price. If the competitor's cost structure is more desirable, such a move might be ill advised and a different basis for competition may have to be sought.

Level of integration. Is the competitor marketing a product in the open market for which other divisions of his company are also customers? If this is the case, of course, he may be using the open market as a safety valve, in which case competition could be very difficult.

A second aspect of the issue of integration pertains to his ability to produce the raw materials going into a product, as well as his handling of the product after manufacture. The steel manufacturer also in the steel service-center business would have a competitive advantage over another steel manufacturer who was not in the steel service-center business. Similarly, an electronics manufacturer who also produced the subassemblies going into the products produced might well have a competitive advantage over a competitor who did not have subassembly-production capabilities.

Summary of competitor key strengths and weaknesses. Once all the competitor information has been analyzed, it should be summarized into a brief listing of major competitor strengths and major competitor weaknesses. Inability to do this readily is an indication that inadequate competitor intelligence has been compiled.

Other Key Factors

The core of an effective market intelligence system includes information about the market, competition, and one's own operation. This group of considerations is discussed shortly. A second category of factors, however, is significant in that the factors in this category can and often do have a major influence on a business, often changing the business dramatically, or at least strongly influencing competitive practices. Each of these other key factors is discussed below.

Technological developments of importance. Technology, probably more than any other factor, can have a dramatic influence on a business. In bicycles, for example, technology improvements have changed the industry significantly. In calculating, the technology for hand-held calculators has resulted in the extinction of the slide rule and, in the process, a dramatic increase in practical market potential. It is important for the marketer to have a handle on major technological developments that can influence the business.

Key economic issues. In some situations, an economic phenomenon can have a dramatic influence, while the identical phenomenon might have a far more limited influence in another area. For example, in financial services, inflation has had serious negative ramifications for savings and loan associations, whereas its effects on grocery retailing, though real, have been far less significant.

In some cases, the effect of an economic change might well have a tremendous impact on an industry, actually resulting in a redefinition of that industry. Continued high transportation costs, for example, may ultimately have the effect of eliminating or causing a restructuring of many retail institutions.

Societal trends affecting business. Just as technological improvements have influenced the market for bicycles, so have societal trends. In this case, the tendency of a segment of the population toward a greater concern for physical well-being led to an increased desire for exercise. In the field of public education, tuition credits, long vehemently opposed by the vast majority of people, are growing in popularity because of societal changes. To the extent that such changes might have impact on the business, the marketer must be cognizant of them and track them carefully and continuously.

Natural issues of significance. Natural issues such as ecology and pollution represent very important considerations in many business environments. To the extent that this is true, obviously, they should be ignored. However, in some situations, natural issues become critical ones. This is certainly the case, for example, in the dairy industry. In fact, anyone dealing with natural resources in his business must be concerned with issues of nature.

Not uncommonly, there is limited freedom to deal with natural issues. On the other hand, once critical natural issues are identified, the marketer has a greater chance of dealing with them successfully than if they had not been identified at all. Thus, for example, the General Electric Company purchased Utah International as part of a very long-term business strategy involving natural resources.

Government, political, legislative, and regulatory issues. This category involves an understanding of what is going on in state and local governments as well as the federal government. It has become a major full-time function in many market intelligence systems. Not only must the marketer be abreast of marketing limitations originating in the government arena, he should also keep in mind that in many cases, government can become a key purchase influencer.

Internal Considerations

Ironically, having adequate internal information can often be one of the most troublesome aspects of the market-intelligence-system development. Having adequate internal information requires an understanding on the part of top management of the necessity of such information as well as the cooperation of service groups in data processing and accounting.

Market share by segment. The importance of market share has already been indicated in the discussion of competitor analysis. Naturally, the marketer must measure his own market share by market segment and track it continually.

Market share has been identified by a leading marketing strategy study as one of a handful of elements that have a major positive correlation with profitability. This is not the same as saying that a marketer ought always to be trying to increase market share, because there are clearly circumstances in mature and declining markets where this is not the case. Nevertheless, market share is a critical indicator of profitability and an essential component of the market intelligence system.

Share trends. Just as it is important to measure share at a point in time, it is also critical to keep tabs on share over time. Especially in a rapidly growing market, it is entirely possible that sales revenue may be increasing nicely while market share is actually declining. This, of course, is an indication of an inadequate marketing effort and needs to be spotted.

Profit contribution by segment, major customer, customer size, and product. For purposes of developing sound marketing strategy, profit contribution is a far more important measurement than gross margin. To be able to measure profit contribution correctly, however, requires an investment in and close cooperation from the accounting group.

Contribution accounting is a technique that permits the marketer to assess profitability of an *entity* by associating with that entity those costs, and only those costs, that exist because the entity itself exists. In such an approach, costs are broken into two major categories: variable and nonvariable. Nonvariable costs are further divided into *specific* and *general.*

The behavior of costs is the factor that determines the category into which they fit. The different behavior patterns are shown in Figure 6-9. Variable costs, as the figure illustrates, vary with amount produced. Examples are direct materials and

Figure 6-9. Variable and nonvariable costs.

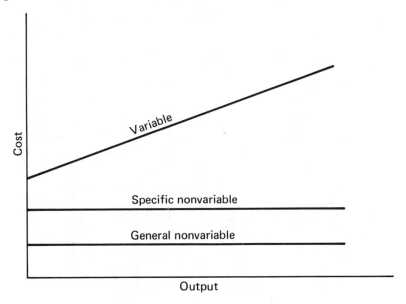

direct labor. Nonvariable costs, as the diagram also illustrates, do not vary with output. But there is a significant difference between *specific* nonvariable costs and *general* nonvariable costs. Specific nonvariable costs are specific to the entity being measured, whereas general nonvariable costs are not.

In contribution accounting, one is concerned only with the variable and specific nonvariable costs directly associated with an entity, and contribution of the entity is determined by subtracting those costs from revenue provided by the entity. Thus, if one were measuring profitability for a particular product for which there was a product manager, the salary of the product manager would be a specific nonvariable cost, whereas the salary of the president of the company would be a general nonvariable cost. An effective contribution accounting system will allow the marketer to measure contribution by segment, by major customer, by customer size, by product, and in some cases by other entities indigenous to the type of business.

Evaluation of strategy. This section of the market intelligence system must not be confused with strategy development. It is aimed only at assessing current strategies in practice, whether they have been determined formally or informally. Elements of strategy that must be evaluated include product and service offerings, marketing communications, pricing, sales effort, and customer service.

One effective technique for assessing *product and service offerings* is a market/product matrix as shown in Figure 6-10. Using such a matrix, market segments are listed on the horizontal axis and products offered are listed on the vertical axis. Varying amounts of information can be plugged into the boxes thus

Figure 6-10. Market/product matrix.

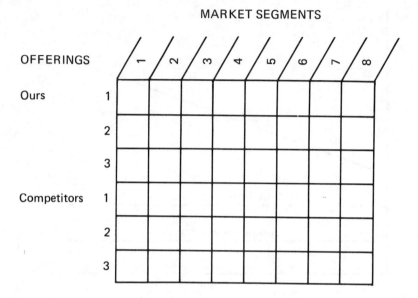

created. For example, one might subdivide each box and, using a predetermined code, indicate one's share, competitors' shares, and segment growth. There is nothing magic about the technique, obviously, but it is a good thought organizer.

In evaluating *marketing communications* strategy, it is important to assess whether a task-focused strategy has been used or a budgetary approach. Although the situation is finally changing, in many cases, particularly industrial, the budgetary approach is still the more common one. It sets aside a predetermined percentage of anticipated sales for expenditures on "advertising and sales promotion." The task approach makes far more sense. It assesses the tasks that need to be performed by marketing communications, selects the appropriate marketing communication tools, and then develops budgets based on the task at hand.

There are basically two approaches to *pricing:* cost-oriented and strategic. The cost-oriented approach simply involves assessing all the costs associated with an entity, adding a factor for profitability, and then establishing a price based on cost plus profit. The strategic approach, conversely, starts with the market and works back into the company. A contribution accounting system is essential if a strategic approach to pricing is to be taken.

In analyzing *sales effort,* it is important to note whether the sales effort has been based on opportunity or history. If the latter is the case, then the situation needs to be changed. Not uncommonly, the sales effort of an organization is *not* well coordinated with the rest of the marketing effort, and in evaluating the situation, the marketer should be alert for the existence of this possibility.

Very often, *customer-service* people have more contact with customers than anyone else in the organization: Hence, changes in customer service often represent excellent opportunities for improving the marketing function. In assessing the customer-service effort, the marketer should be alert to such opportunities and to such factors as whether customer service is being used as a training ground to the exclusion of an effective continuous customer-service effort.

Information Sources

Development of an effective market intelligence system has been compared with assembling a jigsaw puzzle. To a great extent, assembly of the necessary data sources and specific bits of information is very similar to that pastime. Another similarity is that one can obtain a reasonably good picture of the situation even if a few of the pieces are missing. Naturally, however, the more of the pieces recommended here one can obtain, the better.

Assembling the necessary information for an effective market intelligence system is easier in the United States than in virtually any other country in the world. A great deal of the information required is available through secondary sources in the United States, and the necessity to rely on primary research is therefore less than elsewhere. Information availability in Canada and Europe is somewhat less satisfactory than in the United States, and it declines rapidly when one goes beyond those countries.

Naturally, one must collect market intelligence in a forthright, ethical, and legal manner, and all the sources recommended here are based on that assumption.

Information sources are divided into two large categories: external and internal. Although there will be no attempt to present an exhaustive list of all available information sources, there is a listing of each major *category* of source, together with enough examples of specific sources to enable the marketer to dig more deeply into each major category to build an information system appropriate to his needs.

External Information Sources

Most necessary information exists outside the company. Each major outside category is discussed in detail below.

Annual reports and 10-K reports.   Every public company issues an annual report. These reports are available from the company itself or through a third-party source. Brokers often provide them, and there are other firms that can make them available as well.

Annual reports provide information that is of limited value in some cases. For example, if a firm is in more than a single line of business, it is commonly difficult to learn from the annual report how much business comes from each line. Nevertheless, the annual report is a basic element in competitive analysis.

10-K reports are required by the Securities and Exchange Commission for every public firm. These, too, are available directly from the firm in question or from third-party sources. The 10-K report provides much more detailed information than the annual report. For example, it *does* provide breakdowns of revenue by major business line. In addition, the 10-K provides business and personal information on the firm's major officers—information that can be of help in one's efforts to evaluate a competitor's personality.

Trade/industry reports. These represent an excellent source of both market and competitor intelligence. There is in the United States an industry or trade association for virtually every field of endeavor. Furthermore, they are all listed in a directory entitled *National Trade and Professional Associations of the United States and Canada and Labor Unions,* published by Columbia Books, Washington, DC 20005.

Trade associations for particular industries often compile excellent information on the industries they serve. Obtaining the information is a question of identifying the appropriate trade associations and contacting them. The best that can happen as a result of such a contact is that the marketer can get an excellent picture of the market in question; the worst is a wasted telephone call.

There are industry directories available that view markets very broadly, looking, for example, at all consumer markets or all industrial markets, rather than at such specific markets as food processing or automobiles. Examples are *Survey of Industrial Purchasing Power,* which is published annually by Sales and Marketing Management, and *Survey of Consumer Purchasing Power,* published annually by the same organization. These directories can be very helpful to the marketer in establishing sales potentials by industry for industrial supplies or geographically for a variety of consumer products.

Standard and Poor and Dun & Bradstreet publish industrial directories that provide exhaustive listings of all industrial establishments in the United States. Information provided includes primary and secondary type of business, address, names and titles of officers, sales volume, and number of employees

Government reports. The United States government makes so much marketing data available that a major problem is locating it!

The foundation for government market data is the Standard Industrial Classification System. Under this system, all economic activity in the United States is divided into 11 categories, each designated with a two-digit SIC code. Within each two-digit code, industry subgroups are defined by a third digit, and further subdivision results in a fourth digit. For example, category 34 contains all manufacturers of fabricated metal products. Category 347 refines the activity further to coating, engraving, and allied services; and category 3471 includes only plating and polishing. The full classification system is contained in the Standard Industrial Classification Manual published by the Office of Management and Budget.

Government reports built on the SIC foundation include *U.S. Census of Manufacturers,* published every five years; *U.S. Survey of Manufacturers,* published annually; *U.S. Industrial Outlook,* published annually; and *County Business Patterns,* published annually.

The foregoing list of U.S. government information is by no means intended to be comprehensive. Additional information to the marketer includes reports of export opportunities published by the Bureau of International Commerce and very specific reports dealing with a broad range of business topics of interest to the marketer. So substantial is the amount of data available through the federal government, the U.S. Department of Commerce publishes monthly the *Marketing Information Guide,* a worthwhile publication for anyone with interest in developing and maintaining a market intelligence system.

In addition to data published by the federal government, listings of companies and their activities are made available by each of the 50 states. The quality of these directories varies somewhat from state to state. In general, however, the directories include a listing of each company, types of products manufactured, company locations, and sales volume.

Finally, the marketer should seek out and evaluate data made available by various county governments. In many cases involving larger counties, this information can be quite helpful.

Investor reports.   Investment firms regularly do studies of industries and of firms within those industries. A typical report on an industry includes forecasts for sales growth within the industry. A typical report on a firm within the industry includes information regarding markets served, products offered, facilities, profitability and cash-flow highlights, scope of marketing effort, and research and development activities.

Market research firms.   Market research firms regularly supply information on markets. Predicasts and Frost and Sullivan are two organizations that frequently do industry studies and make them available to marketers for a fee. Predicasts, as an example, issues forecasts for industries by product. Included in the forecasts are short- and long-term production estimates and estimated annual growth figures, along with a listing of the sources from which the information was obtained. The forecasts are essentially statistical in nature and not strategic, but represent an excellent value for the amount invested in them.

Suppliers.   Suppliers represent an excellent source of information on competitive activity. If a firm purchases new equipment, its competitors are often among the first to know. Availability and utility of this source of information is largely dependent upon the quality of the marketer's communications with his purchasing group.

Popular and business press.   Articles periodically appear in the popular press that describe either the activities of competitors or of some company in the customer/prospect group. These can be helpful to the marketer in building his market intelligence system, provided someone in the organization has been charged with the responsibility of routinely scanning for such articles.

The trade press can provide a wealth of information about markets. Although not all publications do so, many make it a point to develop expertise in the markets they serve as a part of their strategy of marketing the publication. When this function is performed well, as it is by many publications, the material made available to the marketer can be instrumental in the market intelligence system. Not uncommonly, for example, publications perform an annual survey of the market they serve, which not only serves to update census data but also provides a forecast of industry buying intentions.

To learn of publications available in one's area of interest, the marketer need only check with his advertising agency or with *Standard Rate and Data Service* in the public library. The latter publication lists all trade and consumer publications, together with circulation figures and statistics regarding audience reached.

Competitor literature.   Finally, competitor literature is an important link in the market intelligence system. Most organizations have such literature, but it is not always systematically and rigorously collected, as is required in an effective market intelligence system.

Internal Information Sources

In a market-focused organization with an effective market intelligence system, the accounting and data processing departments should work with marketing in providing information in a market-focused manner. Also, the sales force plays a key role in market intelligence, especially in an industrial situation. The market research department, too, plays a key role, often serving as the market-intelligence-system management group. Each of these internal information sources is discussed below.

The accounting department.   The accounting department has the responsibility for providing data in a format and timetable appropriate to market conditions. The outward focus referred to throughout this discussion is also an important consideration here, because often accounting reports are neither particularly timely nor market-focused. They are often, in other words, *not* available on a timetable in keeping with circumstances in the marketplace, nor, for example, on the basis of market segments.

There is much lively argument between accountants and marketers regarding the merits of a contribution accounting system. Accountants point out, often correctly, that marketers abuse a contribution accounting system, accepting "deals" that provide the most modest of contributions to general nonvariable expenses. To be sure, viewing the organization overall, there cannot be one penny of contribution to *profits* until all general nonvariable expenses have been covered. Such a criticism on the part of accountants, however, valid though it sometimes is, is a criticism not of the concept of contribution accounting but of its misuse.

Whether or not a contribution accounting system should be implemented is not an accounting-department decision at all but a top-management decision. Suffice it to say that such a system often is the key to long-term profitability in a global competitive environment, and that without it sound strategic pricing is virtually impossible.

The data processing department.   Just as the accounting department must be market-focused, so must the data processing department. Often this is not the case. Rather, the marketer must wade through several reports and perform some calculations of his own before he can learn what he needs to know about a particular product or market segment. Careful coordination among marketing, accounting, data processing, and, as necessary, top management is required to assure that data are available in an appropriate and timely manner. This is not to say that the data processing group serves marketing, but that the entire organization, including data processing and marketing, must serve the market.

The sales force. The sales force should be an integral element in the market intelligence system, notwithstanding the bias usually unavoidably present in market information reported by the sales force.

Data generated by the sales force are usually very short-term in nature, product-focused, and very much oriented toward individual customers, whereas the approach required of a modern marketing effort is longer-term, segment-oriented, focused on augmenting the generic product, and causal. The correct conclusion is not to ignore information generated by the sales force but to view it, at the marketing level, integrally rather than piecemeal.

The sales force should be encouraged in the information-generating portion of its job, with an easy-to-use and effective means of reporting made available to it. In some cases, cassette tapes or an incoming WATS line will be very effective.

The marketing research department. Marketing research is treated separately under that title. Not uncommonly, however, because of the similarity between the effort described under marketing research and the broader market intelligence effort described here, the same group in the organization is given responsibility for both functions. If that is the case, the marketing research department should report directly to the vice president of marketing. If the two areas are treated separately, there should be close coordination between them and that coordination should be provided by the vice president of marketing.

Management Commitment

Obviously, development and implementation of a market intelligence system require management commitment to both the financial and human resources necessary to make the system work. It is easy to be in favor of "good market intelligence" but far more difficult to commit the human resources and the money necessary to develop and implement an effective program. In many cases, market intelligence is perceived as "intangible" by management, and when that is the case, management has a hard time making a "tangible" commitment. Thus, getting management commitment often requires *education* of top management as to the need for sound market intelligence.

The cost of an effective market intelligence system need not be enormous, but it nevertheless is significant. One well-known consumer-goods manufacturer makes it a point to speak directly with one quarter of a million consumers a year! Significantly, that manufacturer is very profitable, despite the cost of this aspect of the market intelligence effort. More typically, the cost is far lower than the cost incurred by this marketer, but there is still cost.

The areas of MIS content determination, information source location, and data analysis are managerial in nature. Information collection, on the other hand, typically is a clerical task. In a company with sales in the range of $50 million to $100 million a year, the managerial aspects of the market intelligence system can probably be handled by the vice president of marketing. In addition, there would probably be a need for a full-time clerical person to handle the actual collection of data. Total annual incremental cost for such a system, including salary, cost of outside materials, and modest adjustment of accounting and data processing systems, might be in the $30,000 to $60,000 range.

System Use

Use of the market intelligence system must be continuous. There are two general categories of use. The first involves the continuous reassessment of environmental changes, and the second involves measurement of the marketer's progress against strategies developed.

As indicated at the very beginning of this discussion, if marketing planning is viewed properly, the environmental analysis before planning and during plan implementation will merge together to form a single continuous process. If the marketer is to have an idea of the effectiveness of his marketing strategies, a continual measurement of such factors as relative changes in market share and changes in profitability is also essential.

System Maintenance

System maintenance and system use go hand in hand. As already indicated, collection of the data is a continuing clerical task. As the situation changes, however, it will undoubtedly be necessary to upgrade the system. The need to do this must be identified by marketing management. The market intelligence system that is perfectly satisfactory today will be obsolete tomorrow unless such upgrading is performed. ▫ *Ivan C. Smith*

MARKETING RESEARCH

The primary purpose of marketing research is to systematically assemble information and data and through the analysis of these data, to identify a marketing problem or aid in the solution of a marketing problem.

Marketing research is undertaken in a series of related steps: (1) The need to have additional information is identified. (2) Specific information objectives are formulated and put into writing. (3) Alternate research methods are examined. (4) Timing and cost considerations are taken into account, and the most appropriate method is chosen. (5) A questionnaire format is designed and a questionnaire written. (6) The data are collected. (7) The data are coded and tabulated. (8) Analysis of the data is made. (9) A report is written summarizing the results. (10) The information is reviewed, and appropriate action steps are identified.

It is important to note that marketing research is not a substitute for a management decision. Some managers expect the research to make a decision for them. Research can and does provide direction based on individual interpretation of the data, but it is only one of the many factors to be considered when making a management decision.

Management Uses of Marketing Research

As managers, we communicate information about our products and services to our target audience through our sales force, our product's packaging, point-of-sale material, and our advertising message. This is a one-way communication, because we are removed both geographically and mentally from our customers. Through marketing research, we can complete the communication circle and find out what our customer thinks about our products, packaging, or advertising messages.

Marketing research can provide information to managers in two very important ways. First, it helps identify opportunities for management. This is done by providing information that locates areas for new-product development; new channels of distribution; new geographic markets with the highest potential for growth; and so on. Second, marketing research identifies problems. It tells a manager what problems customers have with products/services in your category and more specifically with your particular product or service. Marketing research can further help by developing alternative solutions to the problems and suggest some idea of the risks and consequences associated with the alternative strategies or plans you've developed. Most marketing research is done in five key areas:

Advertising-and-promotion research, which includes motivational research, copy testing, media research, and research on advertising effectiveness.

Business, corporate, and economic research, which includes short- and long-range forecasting, trend analysis, acquisition analysis, diversification studies, pricing studies, plant and warehouse location studies, and personnel studies, including attitudinal and communication information.

Corporate responsibility, which includes ecological-impact studies, social values and policy studies, and government regulations and their implications for the consumer.

Product research, which includes acceptance of and attitudes toward existing products, modification of existing products, competitive analysis, packaging testing, and new-product development.

Sales and market research, which includes market-share analysis, sales analysis, customer profiles, distribution-channel studies, target-market identification, consumer panel testing, establishment of sales quotas and territories, and promotional studies of premiums, coupons, sampling, deals, and so on.

The degree to which a company participates in any or all of these areas depends upon the type of business the company is engaged in, the size of the company, and the competitive environment. Whether or not to conduct a marketing research study is dependent on two key factors: (1) the cost of obtaining the information and (2) the risks and consequences of making a wrong decision. A marketing research study should be undertaken only if the value of the information is greater than the cost of gathering the information.

Department Organization

The most common organization structure is for the manager of marketing research to report in a staff capacity directly to the vice president of marketing or a senior marketing person. In some cases marketing research will report to corporate management or to the research-and-development department.

The organization structure under the manager of marketing research depends on whether the research department conducts its own research or uses field marketing research companies to conduct the projects. In either case, marketing research personnel have similar skills and backgrounds. Doctorate degrees are not necessary for either the manager or staff. Since most schools do not offer programs in marketing research, a broad educational base including marketing and business with emphasis on statistics is usually looked for in hiring. Other backgrounds that are desirable are economics, psychology, sociology, accounting, industrial engineering, or mathematics.

In addition, research personnel should have some of the following: creativity, good writing and oral communication skills, sales skills, leadership ability, administrative skills, and analytical abilities.

Research Design

Once the need for information has been identified, the first step is to identify and clearly define the specific objectives of the project. It is an excellent idea to put your objectives in writing.

A frequent mistake is made in the area of defining objectives. Once management has decided it will undertake a marketing research investigation, it broadens the objectives to include a diversity of informational needs. If there are too many information objectives, you will dilute the information gathered. It is better to have complete information as it relates to specific objectives than to have partial information as it relates to several objectives covering a number of different areas. The most important aspect of defining objectives is to keep them within well-defined parameters. If your primary reason for conducting the research is to develop new packaging, then stick to that area when developing your objectives.

When you begin to define objectives, ask yourself what action you will take with the information gathered. Costs will limit the extent of your research undertaking, so be certain to include those areas that are actionable. Recently, for example, psychographic research has become quite popular. Psychographic research is designed to psychologically describe your target audience—to define the prospect in terms of life style, buying habits, and so on. Before undertaking a costly psychographic study, you should ask yourself what action you would take if you found users of your product to be extroverted, narcissistic individuals who were audiophiles and drank imported wines on a regular basis. While this information could probably be used in the creative development of your advertising, it cannot be used very effectively to buy media or identify product problems.

Second, define your decision criteria before conducting a study in the field. What if 60 percent of the respondents like the product and 40 percent do not? Decide ahead of time what constitutes failure and success. It will make the analysis of your information much easier. Another important consideration is that you should prioritize even well-defined objectives. Marketing research is governed by time limits, the number of qualified people to work on a study, and costs. Know which information needs are most important in case one of those constraints becomes a factor in conducting your study.

Once you have written well-defined, prioritized, actionable objectives, be certain to review them with all persons who will be involved with the information. Get their agreement on objectives ahead of time, and you will avoid problems after the data are collected.

Secondary Data

After the objectives have been defined, the researcher should determine whether or not the information already exists. It could be available in company information or in published sources such as books, pamphlets, trade publications, or annual reports. A great deal of money can be saved by not duplicating someone else's study. You might also find that some of the information exists, but not everything you wanted to know. In this case, you can either shorten your study and cut costs or include additional informational objectives in your research.

It is important, however, to evaluate carefully any secondary information you have obtained. Be certain to determine the following: (1) How current is the information? (2) Who collected the data? (3) What was the purpose or objective of the research? (4) How were the data collected? (5) Who was included in the study? (6) How were the questions asked? (7) Is the report objective, that is, written without bias?

As mentioned earlier, there are two sources of secondary information: (1) internal company information, which includes sales records, invoices, and shipping statements, and (2) a variety of other information, including basic reference sources such as the library; trade associations; directories; federal, state, and local government; research organizations; and trade publications and articles.

Be certain to examine carefully these secondary sources. However, you may find that what you're looking for doesn't exist. Only in that case should you initiate primary research.

Basic Methods of Collecting Data

There are three basic methods of gathering information: personal interviews, telephone interviews, and a mail study.

Personal interviews. Information is gathered in a face-to-face situation. Respondents for a personal interview can be intercepted in a shopping center or central location, interviewed in their home, or interviewed through appointment at their place of business.

The personal-interview technique is generally favored for a number of reasons: (1) It allows you to use props or visual aids (such as ads) to aid the interviewee in answering questions. (2) It is easier to work with a respondent face to face when you have a difficult or long questionnaire. (3) It allows the interviewer to make personal observations as well as obtain structured information. (4) It is more flexible and enables the interviewer to pursue areas that seem to be of the greatest interest to the respondent. (5) There is usually a higher percentage of completed questions, because the interviewer is there to help explain what is wanted.

The primary disadvantage of the personal interview is cost, especially if a wide geographic area of sampling is desired.

Objectivity and sound training of the interviewer are essential. In a personal-interview situation, it is important that there be no interviewer bias operating, that is, that the interviewer not lead the respondent because of personal feelings on the subject. There is also a difference between individual interviewers in terms of how they interact with respondents and record information. Therefore, it is somewhat difficult to standardize information gathered.

Telephone surveys. Questioning for this type of study is done over the telephone. This type of study is best used in areas of well-defined information gathering, that is, where it is not necessary to use visual aids and the respondent clearly understands the subject discussed.

There are several advantages to a telephone study: It is the quickest method and is less expensive than personal interviews; it can reach a broader geographic area; and it is easier to recontact a respondent for follow-up information.

The single biggest problem is that you must limit the amount of time spent interviewing. Respondents are usually not willing to spend as much time being interviewed on the phone as they are in a personal interview. Also, telephone interviews are not as versatile as personal interviews, especially when visual aids are needed or questions are used that require long and complicated descriptions.

However, even with these disadvantages, telephone interviews have become the most popular technique because of their lower cost and their ability to reach a large geographic cross section of respondents.

Mail surveys. Mail surveys are used to broaden the base of information gathered or to supplement information acquired from personal interviews. They are most effective when they use questions that are highly structured and when the concepts are simple and well defined.

Questionnaires are sent through the mail. A letter explaining the study and the information needed from the respondent is usually included, as well as a self-addressed, stamped return envelope. Sometimes an incentive, such as 50¢ for a cup of coffee, is included.

The mail survey has the following advantages: You can reach a wide variety of respondents at relatively low costs; you can reach more remote places; and the respondent can remain anonymous and therefore may divulge more confidential information. A major problem in mail surveys is finding an up-to-date mailing list that zeroes in on your target audience. Also, returns may not be representative of the entire group you wish to survey. Usually, respondents who have stronger feelings, both positive and negative, respond in this type of study. In a mail survey, questions should be simple and the length of the questionnaire limited.

Marketing research studies allow you to gather information from persons who are *users* of your products or services. The major disadvantage of conducting your own survey is that you are limited by the willingness of respondents to help you. For example, some types of respondents, such as doctors or corporate executives, are difficult to get to, and once you have reached them, the amount of time they are willing to give is probably limited. Another basic disadvantage in conducting surveys is that sometimes people will not give you honest answers. Instead they will tell you what they think you want to hear.

Applications of Marketing Research

Identifying your market segment means determining that part or segment of the entire market that is key to your business. Most marketers are aware that not everyone is a potential prospect for buying their goods and services. The prospects may be defined in many ways—by their age, income, education, race, or where they live. Marketers are also aware that not everyone who uses their products or services uses them in equal proportion—some people are heavy users. In many product categories you will find that a minority percentage of the population consumes a majority of the products in the category. In other words, 30 percent might use 70 percent. Knowing this, a marketer can zero in on that all-important user (segment) in terms of items offered, advertising, and distribution of products/services. The result will be a more effective marketing program.

There are two basic approaches to market segmentation: segmentation by consumers or by products.

Consumer-characteristics segmentation. The most common way to define a consumer is in terms of demographic measurements. These include age, sex, size of family, income, education, size of city of residence, and section of country of residence. In recent years consumers have also been grouped by attitudes, life styles, interests, and the like. Studies in this area tend to be more sociological and psychological in nature. Market segmentation of consumers can, therefore, be done demographically or psychographically.

Product segmentation. One way to do this type of segmentation is to concentrate on different types of usage—that is, identifying heavy, light, and nonusers of a product or service. You can then analyze differences between these segments in terms of their demographics, psychographics, or the media they use. This is called the usage-rate approach.

Another way to segment the product is to identify consumers' attitudes toward and perceptions of different brands within a category. This is called the product or brand attribute approach to segmentation. It has become quite popular in recent years. Consumers determine their brand preferences by comparing various brands within a category. Each brand tends to have its own position within a market, and this approach takes into account not just the consumer's characteristics but how the consumer perceives different brands. This approach is considered especially helpful in new-product positioning (how you sell your product relative to competition).

Consumers' perceptions of attributes and benefits are desirable bases of segmenting a market because they presumably are the basis for a consumer choosing one brand over another.

Product Testing

The importance of products/services to a company is obvious, because the amount of money a company earns is ultimately dependent on the line of products it has to sell (product mix). The product mix of a company involves both items it currently sells and new products. We will differentiate between these two areas in the following discussion.

Testing of existing products. Marketing research as it relates to existing products can give a company the following types of information: (1) how your product is perceived by the consumer; (2) how your competition is perceived; (3) information that can help position your product; (4) information that can help you reformulate existing products; and (5) general information that can help your salespeople sell your products.

The first information that should be gathered about a product or service is usage information—how it is used, how often it is used, by whom it is used, when it is used, and what attributes it is perceived as having. The basic usage information is fairly simple to gather. Information relating to attributes is somewhat more complex.

The objective of obtaining information about a product's physical characteristics (attributes) is to be able to rank-order the attributes—to determine which characteristics are most or least important to your target audience. By obtaining this information for your product/service and your competitors', you can then determine where you fit in the mix of products that compete within your product category (the competitive mix). There are a number of methods for testing attributes, including paired comparison testing and monadic testing.

Paired comparison testing involves comparing two or more products against each other. Products are usually tested one after another (sequentially), and the order in which they are used is rotated to eliminate a bias (positioning bias) that may result from testing a product first or last. Typically, products are tested in twos. When choosing a competitor, you may choose the competitor that is usually the strongest brand compared to your own brand (forced pair analysis). Another way to choose a competitor is to use the brand usually used by the consumer. This is called relevant pair analysis.

Monadic testing is another method used in evaluating physical characteristics. With this technique, each respondent receives just one product. Different samples are used for each brand tested. When using a monadic testing procedure, it is extremely important to carefully match the groups of people (samples) that are testing each product. They should be carefully matched demographically in terms of product usage. Larger samples are usually used to minimize sampling error. When asked competitive questions in a monadic study, respondents are usually asked to compare the product they are testing to their usual brand or their "ideal" brand.

Specific questions used in either method are similar. The following is an explanation of various types of questions about product attributes. Not all of them are likely to be used in every study.

■ Open-ended questions about likes and dislikes are the most flexible but the least actionable. The reason is that it is more difficult to interpret meaning and quantify answers.

■ Triad questions offer respondents opposite alternatives (polarized positions) and a neutral position relating to specific attributes. An example of a triad question is:

The sauce is: ☐ too salty
                  ☐ just right
                  ☐ not salty enough

This type of questioning can easily be quantified, but it severely limits respondent expression.

- A third type of question is called semantic differential. This type of question gives respondents a bipolar scale on which to rate a product. Each scale consists of two opposing adjectives which are separated by a continuum divided, typically, into seven segments.

The sauce is: very salty □ □ □ □ □ □ □ not salty enough

Respondents are asked to check the segment that most closely reflects their position. This type of testing provides expanded percentage levels that can be quantified.

- Simple ranking of alternatives is another method frequently used. Respondents are asked to rank-order their preferences. This type of questioning provides a relative order but does not give a differential between alternatives.
- Purchase intent questions can be asked in a number of ways. Two that are most frequently used are the preference scale and the purchase allotment question. The preference scale is as follows:

Definitely would buy   □
Probably would buy   □
Definitely would not buy   □

In the purchase allotment question, respondents are asked for each x number of purchases how many would be the test product. The allotment technique gives you a relative degree of acceptance and anticipated repurchase intent.

The preceding list of different types of questions is not complete, but it includes the most popular techniques.

There are several general comments that should be made about product testing. First, make certain the questionnaire is complete. Be sure to include all aspects of the product itself and of using the product, including such elements as preparation, storage, serving, eating, aftereffects, clean-up, and purchasing (price, size, and so forth). Second, make sure the questionnaire is balanced—don't overload any one topic unless you have a specific need to do so. Third, make certain that topics included are actionable and will provide you with useful information for development. Finally, make certain to keep topic areas separated.

There are two other elements of a product that you may want to include in your testing. They are the packaging and the image of your product. Techniques for obtaining information about these areas are the same as for physical attributes.

Testing of new products. New products are extremely important to most companies. Fifteen percent of current sales volume is a result of new products introduced in the past five years. There is much written about the failure of new products, estimated to be as high as eight out of nine. Because of this marriage of importance and high risk, it is easy to understand why marketing research is such an important part of new-product development.

The following is a rather complete outline of procedural steps that may or may not be undertaken in the development of new products. Within each segment the role of marketing research can be seen.

Corporate/market analysis. Before engaging in the development of new products, a company should complete an analysis of its production and technological capabilities. It is also essential to outline categories of interest and define how these areas of interest relate to your present business and products. Once this is completed, several decisions should be made relative to your current business and new-product objectives. They involve answering the following questions: (1) What kind of investment is the company willing to make in terms of return, profit, plant, equipment, and marketing? (2) How will the product be distributed and sold? (3) In what kind of product life cycle are you interested (for example, fad versus long-term)? (4) Are there any seasonal or regional objectives? (5) What kind of sales potential are you looking for? (6) What are your current strengths or weaknesses in research and development, finance, production, marketing, and existing products?

Market information. The market you have defined as one of interest should then be examined. It should be looked at generally in terms of size, trends, seasonality, regionality, submarkets, distribution methods, regulations, and so on.

Second, a close examination of the competitive situation should be undertaken. This should include identification of major products and brands and their market share, product specifications, packaging, pricing, sales and distribution methods, advertising, and form of competition.

Then an examination of the consumer/customer should be made, including demographics, usage information, purchase information, and attitudinal information.

Only after these steps are completed should concept development begin. Basically, the concept(s) should be a translation of capabilities, objectives, and market and attitude information into a product *idea*. Each new-product idea should then be screened through marketing research (with the target audience) to obtain customers' reactions to it.

If reactions are favorable, the next stage would involve actual development of a product or product prototype. After products have been formulated, you may want to have additional consumer/customer input prior to product finalization.

If the company feels that the new product can meet goals and fulfill consumer needs, you can then move into the final stages of the process. This includes product positioning, name selection, packaging design and copy, pricing strategy, sales and profit goals, and overall marketing objectives.

A decision will also have to be made about whether or not to test-market the product. Whether or not test marketing is used, you will want to carefully evaluate on an ongoing basis what is happening to your new product in the marketplace.

Advertising Research

There are several ways to evaluate how well your advertising is performing.

Readership studies. These studies usually determine how many people saw your ad and, more specifically, to what extent they read or remembered the ad. There are several firms that specialize in this type of research. Obviously, you can conduct this research on your own as well.

Awareness, trial, and usage studies. This type of study is best used to compile trend information for a period of years. It measures the percentage of people who are aware of your brand; how many have tried the brand; how many have purchased it repeatedly; and with what frequency they use it. Obviously, the reason you advertise is to persuade more consumers to try your product and to remind those who have tried it to use it again. This type of study is simple and easy to administer. It should be done prior to advertising or before a change is made in media. This initial study is called a benchmark, and subsequent studies measure changes against the benchmark.

Recall studies. These tests are done to determine the extent to which the advertising, including theme lines, is remembered by the target audience. The one serious flaw of recall studies is that they do not measure motivation. A consumer may recall advertising and never purchase the product.

There are two types of recall tests: unaided and aided. In an unaided-recall situation, respondents are simply asked what brands or brand advertising in a category they recall. In aided questioning, respondents are read a list of brands and asked which they are aware of or have used.

The obvious advantage of unaided recall is that you are not leading respondents. The problem is that you may not obtain a sufficient number of respondents to give you the detailed information you need. Aided recall may tend to bias answers, especially toward less-known brands. Aiding a respondent too much may also cause him to guess or exaggerate. However, people do need to have their memories jogged, and aided recall can focus attention on the advertising being studied.

Market tests. Another way to measure advertising is to select two very similar markets and then put your advertising program into one market. You then track sales in each market and note any differences in performance.

Inquiry reports. Some advertising is designed to generate inquiries. Generally, the success of inquiry advertising is measured by the number of responses received. It is important for this type of advertising to carefully analyze those inquiries in terms of (1) number of inquiries obtained, source of the inquiry, and (3) action generated.

Sales Analysis

Sales control involves two key areas: sales analysis and sales forecasting. Sales analysis relates to your specific sales whereas market analysis relates to the market(s) in which you compete for business. Sales analysis can be undertaken in four key areas: (1) general sales, costs, and profit analysis; (2) customer analysis, including new versus old, size of orders, size of customers, frequency of purchase, and buying habits; (3) geographic analysis, including state or city, sales territory, individual salesman, product type, and types of customers; and (4) product analysis, including classification of products/product lines, packaging modes, and pricing analysis.

Sales forecasting is an especially difficult and technical function. The sales forecast is the basic guide for planning within a company. Forecasting may or may not be the responsibility of marketing research. More likely it will be the responsibility of the sales department. It is usually based upon past-trends analysis and involves complex statistical procedures that we will not go into in this general discussion of marketing research.

Market Analysis

One way to evaluate your marketing efforts is to determine your *share* of market. This is simply the percentage of business in a product category that belongs to your brand. You can look at your share either nationally or by city or territory. Besides using market share you can break out the information by type of customers, or you can look at channels of distribution, size of customer, or segments of business within a category. Market share represents a measurement at a specific point in time. You should track share on an ongoing basis, since it will provide you with valuable information about your and your competitors' place in the category. It can also provide you with information on emerging trends, new products, and so forth.

An analysis of individual markets can also help you to determine where to put your selling efforts and your advertising and promotion dollars.

In summary, this discussion of marketing research is meant to give you a general understanding of the importance of marketing research to a company, the applications of marketing research, and the various forms it takes. If you have further interest in this subject, there are several excellent texts that will provide you with detailed information on the subject. □ *Marlane L. Wolf*

PRODUCT PLANNING

All product-planning policies and decisions are directed toward a dual objective: anticipation of the consumer's or user's needs, and the incorporation of these needs in the products offered for sale. In order to attain this goal, it is necessary that clear and concise product objectives be set to determine the direction of policies and decisions. Product objectives direct product planning in certain directions related to the company's development of strategies, product policies, channels of distribution, type of selling, product scope, capacity utilization, and capital limitations.

As technology advances, the demand for new and improved products increases in order to meet its needs. Technological change results in more rapid product obsolescence; this compounds the pressure for innovation. Developing the capability to live with rapid change is becoming a major problem for many companies. The product-planning function is perhaps the most effective method developed thus far to meet the challenges of new-product demand, shorter product life, more complicated technology, improvement of existing products, and accelerating rate of product change.

Scope of Product Planning

Although companies interpret product planning differently, according to their own needs and facilities, product planning in general involves the following factors:

Recommendation of product scope, including determining which products belong in the line at present and in the future.

Analysis of customer needs, wants, and habits, and of the factors influencing
customers' choice of specific products.

Appraisal of products to determine the standing of a company's products in
relation to competition as viewed by the customer.

Determination of the product ideas worth investigating.

Development of product specifications to indicate what products should be like
and what they should do to meet customer requirements.

Definition of product appearance and design to determine visual appeal, style,
and value added through industrial design.

Specification of product timing to determine the most advantageous time to
introduce a new product or take some marketing action.

Product-line control policies for diversification, simplification, or elimination
of a line.

Formulation of pricing to achieve maximum volume, position, and profits.

Development of market and product information needed for advertising, promotion, sales, and service.

Product-Planning Strategies

To be fully successful, product planning must be an integrated process. There
are several other issues that influence the effectiveness of product planning.
These involve strategies of responsibility, assignment, scope, and emphasis.

Responsibility

Responsibility for product planning can be either centralized in one organization or divided between two organizational units—marketing and engineering. A
unified product-planning responsibility establishes single accountability for product successes or failures. It also streamlines the process, avoids costly duplication
of effort, and reduces the coordination requirements. On the other hand, division of product-planning responsibility forces tradeoffs and assures a check and
balance between the laboratory and the market. In addition, it enables product
planners to cope more effectively with the different managerial needs of changing markets and dynamic technology.

Direction

The product-planning function can be placed organizationally three separate
ways: assignment to marketing, to a technical organization, or independently in
general management. Placing product planning in marketing, as most consumer-
goods companies do, assures that the marketing concept and marketing orientation will direct product-planning activity. It also provides greater responsiveness
to customer needs and a sharper definition of new market requirements. Placing
product-planning responsibility in technical departments (research or engineering) permits tighter control and direction of development and engineering
projects. It also allows more effective incorporation of changing technologies into
improvements and innovations. Placing a product-planning staff independent of

marketing or technical functions balances conflicting viewpoints and risks and optimizes management decision. An independent product-planning group may involve top management more closely in key product decision, and it can manage complex marketing and technical choices more effectively. In effect, the decision as to where to place product-planning responsibility will be based on whether emphasis will be placed on market or customer needs, on choosing the right technological alternatives, or on product profitability.

Classification of Product Policies

When a manufacturer introduces an entirely new product, his initial strategy is simply growth. By effective merchandising and marketing he attempts to build volume as a means of achieving profit. The manufacturer's major policy is to establish primary demand for his new-product entry. If he is successful, competition soon follows, requiring a shift to a new strategy of maintaining selective demand for his brand. The manufacturer now relies on superior marketing techniques to feature product differentiation, broader distribution, and production economies of higher volume. As demand broadens and the product matures, he may find product diversification strategies more important. He can then provide additional related products for the original market segments. As his options expand, he frequently branches into unrelated products. Such strategies of product growth and diversification are highly developed in American consumer-goods fields, particularly in the food industry.

Closely attuned to product-planning policies is the product life cycle concept, which assumes that the life cycle of a product goes through five stages: introduction, growth, maturity, saturation, and decline. During a new-product introduction, sales start off modestly and start to increase in the growth stage. Sales continue to increase during the maturity stage and level off and start to decline at the saturation stage. During the decline stage, sales volume continues downward. New products have this characteristic pattern to their sales volume. Profit-margin curves also have a characteristic pattern; they tend to start descending while the sales curve is still rising. This suggests that product strategy is better planned around the profit curve than the sales curve. Sooner or later, competition enters the marketplace, making careful product planning necessary to maintain profit margins. Each industry has its own sales volume/profit pattern, but—as a generality—the closer a company is to consumer goods and the marketplace, the shorter is the cycle of its product. Conversely, the closer a product or service is to basic industry, the longer is the cycle.

Primary versus Selective Demand

Common sense, intuition, or market studies will reveal whether the principal marketing requirement is to establish new customers who have never tried the product or to emphasize product or brand differentiation. The ideal strategy is quite clear: endeavor to do both things simultaneously, and protect the flanks with an airtight patent or copyright. However, this strategy is seldom possible, and patent monopoly is a thing of the past.

Developing primary demand for new products. The policy of developing primary demand for new products often involves substantial economic risks and major obstacles. Classic examples of this point are color television and nylon. Four fundamental market situations present themselves when the marketer is following the policy of developing primary demand: (1) a new market for entirely new products with new uses; (2) a product new to the company but not new to its markets—essentially, a new product that is sold in markets not new to competitors; (3) a new product in a familiar market—essentially, a new product with uses similar to present products and sold in present markets or markets familiar to the company; and (4) new applications of established products or, similarly, new categories of customers for the same products and uses by virtue of fundamental changes in their buying power, leisure time, vocations, or avocations. Inherent risks, long lead times, and problems can be anticipated by following primary-demand strategy, and therefore careful consideration should be given to using this policy.

Expanding primary demand for established products. The development of markets for additional uses and applications is often a less costly and more rapid way of improving sales than simply introducing a new product. This strategy can be initiated at any stage of a product's life to extend or rejuvenate sales. An example of this strategy is a major computer manufacturer's market where there is continual marketing effort for new applications in new markets. It is feasible to follow this policy to prevent cyclical declines and to avoid the high investment and risk of new-product introductions. In addition, expanded volume enables use of excess plant capacity and absorption of overhead expenses.

Expanding selective demand for·established brands. More defensive than primary-demand development, the expansion of selective demand for established brands ultimately leads to reduced profits, higher prices, and proliferation of brands with little real product differentiation, as in the case of cigarettes and gasoline. The objectives of this policy are to capture larger market share and to establish and hold brand leadership in order to maintain strong shelf position with distributors and dealers. This policy permits entering competition later to avoid high initial costs of product development and introduction.

Diversification, Simplification, and Elimination

Certain types of product policies determine what product types and product-line scopes the company should offer. They are concerned with diversification of the product line and the related product-line policies of simplification and elimination.

Product diversification. Planned diversification offers business certain definite advantages: (1) higher return on investment, (2) enhanced market value of stock, (3) stability of sales and profits, (4) expansion of sales and profits, (5) maximum utilization of resources, (6) more efficient marketing, and (7) profitable use of opportunity. Product diversification can extend into related or unrelated products.

Related product diversification policy is followed when a company wants to fill out lines of related products needed by distributors and dealers and to take advantage of extra selling and distribution capacity. It also enables spreading overhead on R&D and manufacturing costs. Related product diversification takes advantage of new demand trends; it capitalizes on a family-brand "franchise" with consumers; and it results in supplementing static or declining volumes of a product line. This strategy is common in the food industry.

Unrelated product diversification is common in multiproduct companies, so-called conglomerates, which accelerate their rates of growth by stressing profitability and ROI as the main criteria of diversification. Followed extensively, this product policy often requires decentralization, which may lead to new difficulties with communication and control. However, unrelated product diversification can balance seasonal and cyclical gaps in a company's sales volume, and it can use idle capital. When used properly, this diversification policy capitalizes on outstanding management abilities and functional skills, allows the application of proprietary knowledge to new areas, and broadens opportunities for employees.

Product-line simplification. As product lines become more and more extensive, items may tend to duplicate one another, and older varieties become relatively obsolete. Thus there is opportunity for gains from line simplification. This policy is followed to eliminate unprofitable grades and variation, to reduce inventory expense, and to cull out slow movers. Line simplification emphasizes major product improvements and simplifies the manufacture and management of a product line.

Product elimination. A more extreme policy than simplification is the drastic pruning of major product types. This is done to eliminate unprofitable product lines, reduce dilution of management time, and free capital and facilities for new programs. In addition, product elimination allows concentration on prime talents and resources and specialization in prime markets.

Branding

Brand identification is a necessary policy for the producer who wishes to exercise maximum control over the demand for his products and to be able to compete on a nonprice basis. Most products that lend themselves to brand identification and differentiation are branded in the American market today. The decision to use or not to use brands depends on the ability of management to truly differentiate the product; and if this differentiation is to be helpful in creating brand recognition, it must be in terms of characteristics that are important to the consumer.

Brand Types

The four significant distinctions among types of brands are ownership of the brand, geographic coverage of the brand, the importance of the brand to its owner, and the number of products it covers. Brands may be owned by any manufacturer or wholesale or retail distributor. They may be sold nationally, regionally, sectionally, or citywide. Primary brands are those given major emphasis in advertising or those in which a greater portion of sales is made. Secondary or subsidiary brands may receive less emphasis or have lower quality. Individual brands cover one product, and family brands cover a group of products with like characteristics or products that appeal to particular market segments. National brands are generally sold by manufacturers or can refer to national distribution of a brand. Private brands are generally sold by distributors.

Objectives in Branding

Branding of goods has come to occupy a key position as the first step toward market control.

Control of demand. The assurance of a large and steady demand for a product facilitates planning and helps maintain a reasonable cost structure. By distinguishing one manufacturer's products from those of others through branding, other promotional activity becomes practicable. Branding individualizes a product, indicates its source of supply, and provides a connection between the manufacturer and the consumer.

Contact with market through servicing. Branding or other identification is a necessary condition for the administration of warranty, guarantee, or service policies. The fact of a warranty implies that there must be contact between the manufacturer and the consumer. The offer of warranties and service for promotional purposes is another means of securing and maintaining control over the market.

Greater independence in determining price. By branding, a manufacturer attempts to distinguish his products from others. He is then able to secure a quasi-independent status in pricing. Differences in product, unless readily apparent and substantial, generally do not affect price until they are brought to the attention of the buyer. However, when a buyer knows of the differences, a preference may result through which a price differential is established. The point to be made is that branding and advertising furnish the means by which a manufacturer can, at least in part, control price in his own interest.

Brand Coverage

Many products may be sold under one brand, or one product in one quality may be sold under many different brands. Moreover, in order to achieve quality differentiation, different qualities of a product may be sold under different brands. Brands may be developed for specific geographic sectors or human sectors—age or nationality, for example.

Family brands. Family brands cover a group of products more or less closely connected in type or quality. The main objective in establishing family brands is to connect them in the minds of consumers so that one product will help sell another. The family brand establishes a threshold in the market for any product that bears it, even though the product is new and untried. A major advantage in family brands is that promotional costs are incurred for only one brand. Carryover of goodwill from each product and lower promotional costs are achieved by using family brands, but no one product receives as much promotional effort as an individual product. As a result, a family brand acts as a leveler, for it implies that all products under the brand are of equal quality and distinctiveness. Items are included in family brands for the following reasons: because they are closely associated in use, because they appeal to the same buying motives, because they are distinctive as a group but not individually, because they are of the same general quality, or because they will cause little difficulty in maintaining standardization.

Multiple brands. Multiple branding implies that the manufacturer is competing with himself, and there are times when this makes sense. Often, it is necessary to serve the market by offering different price lines and more than one quality, with differentiation through secondary brands. Usually, it is not desirable to place more than one quality of product under the same brand, especially if the difference is substantial. Companies give a simple justification for multiple branding where the markets are extremely large and widespread and where competition is actively pursuing the same business. They hope to expand primary demand for the type of product and increase the company's share of market, and thus spread management overhead and use excessive plant capacity. Multiple branding also stimulates internal competition in market development, takes advantage of newer technologies, and offers customers more choices favorable to the company.

Private brands. Private brands are owned and controlled by middlemen rather than manufacturers. Private-label items have contributed major volume for many years in the food and drug chains, mail-order firms, and voluntary food wholesalers. The decision to produce private brands may be affected by several factors. Commodity-type products may gain increased volume, and additional plant capacity may be used. Orders for private brands may offset declining demand for name brands and help realize lower per-unit sales and distribution expenses. In addition, private labels reach new customers through multiple distribution channels. □ *David B. Uman*

PRODUCT DEVELOPMENT

Product development involves product design, which establishes the esthetics of the product, and product engineering, which ensures both the proper functioning of the product and the ability to manufacture the product feasibly. The product development process includes prototype development and both performance and consumer testing. The product that is the output of this process can be totally new or some modification of an existing product.

It is important to note that even with the overall average failure rate of new products at about 35 percent, most successful companies that do a good marketing job have a good chance of product success.

The objective of the product development effort is to develop and maintain a viable product mix that reflects market needs and satisfies the objectives of the corporate business plan. An effective product development program must be able to accomplish the following: (1) react to changing market trends; (2) create and satisfy customer needs; (3) hold or increase market share; (4) maximize use of production and distribution outlets; (5) diversify product lines; and (6) advance technological capabilities.

Product Life Cycle

As with all things, there is a beginning and an end to every product. Theodore Levitt described this process as the product life cycle. Levitt stated that all products have a beginning, which is the introduction or launch stage of the product into the market, and an end, which is the decline of product sales, with growth and maturity stages occurring in between.

When products decline in the life cycle, new products must be available to replace them. Successful new products need to be available for introduction into a company's product mix. Existing products should also be scrutinized with the idea of extending their life cycle. Extension of a life cycle can be accomplished by communicating new uses for a product or altering some of its characteristics. The stages of the product life cycle are outlined below.

Stage 1: market development.   This is the launch stage of a product in the market. Demand is usually not realized at this stage and must be created. Sales are generally low and price is high. The product may not be proved technically. Competition is scarce, as many competitors wait for some market acceptance and attempt to improve on their ability to compete if future entry in the market becomes necessary.

Stage 2: market growth.   Demand accelerates, and market size increases. Competition stiffens as copies and improved versions of the product enter the market. Brand differentiation develops, and the originator puts more effort into seeking customer preference of his brand. Lower profit margins are accepted as distribution pipelines fill rapidly.

Stage 3: market maturity.   This is most evident by the sign of market saturation. Price competition is intense, and sales growth is marginal or nil. Holding market share by holding distribution outlets becomes necessary. Product differences, delivery time, and price become critical factors in holding market share.

Stage 4: market decline.   The product no longer has appeal to the customer. Sales drop throughout the industry. Mergers and buy-outs are common. Death of the product is near.

Scope of New Products

New products can take a number of forms and have varying scope. In general, the scope of most new products fits into the following categories: (1) a completely new product for the producer and the industry; (2) a new product for the producer but not for the industry; and (3) a variation of an existing product by its present producer. The scope of new products has specific impact on the risk and opportunity a company will have in the market and the impact on the company's character. For example, a company may choose to develop a completely new product. The television set, for example, when first introduced, carried a high degree of risk and a great deal of opportunity. The company introducing this type of product experiences major changes in corporate character. A second area may be the launch of a product new to the company but not new to the industry. A broadcasting company launching a new magazine will experience moderate risk, moderate opportunity, and little impact on the company character as a whole. A third product concept is the launch of an existing product with some fundamental changes in that product. An example would be the launch of a fat-free milk by a company in the dairy industry. Risk would be lower than in our other two cases, and opportunity will be moderate. The overall impact on the existing company is of less consequence than in the first two examples.

Sources of New Product Ideas

The marketplace. Information about the marketplace is available through any distribution network. Salespeople, sales managers, marketing personnel, dealers, and distributors are all vital sources. Direct contact with the end user is invaluable. Buyers' needs, market trends, competitive position, and company strengths and weaknesses can all be evaluated from these sources.

External influences. Monitoring of social, political, environmental, judicial, and economic influences produces information showing specific trends in these areas. These trends will offer clear insight into the future environment affecting a business.

Company personnel. Employees can produce intuitive ideas in the new-product area. When this resource is called upon, internal communication among personnel may be improved and a feeling of pride by employees may ensue.

R&D personnel. A fertile source of new product ideas and an area where information from outside sources can be developed. Key research personnel who are in touch with corporate objectives and outside trends are important.

New-Product Development Process

The initial stages of a new-product development program must incorporate recognizable support by top management and open communication between the functional areas committed to the program. These areas, including marketing, research and development, finance, legal, manufacturing, and additional support, must take a role in the project, whether it be active or advisory. The product development program is made up of two separate functions: management and execution. Management is concerned with the elements of planning, coordination, communicating, and reporting. Execution is delegated by management to the support areas, and is a process that keeps in line with the strategies outlined by the project manager.

Once the overall company strategy for the new-product development program is established and communicated, the following steps take place (see Figure 6-11):

Idea inception. This involves the identification of a product that will meet company objectives. The product concept is generated from product-planning sessions that incorporate input from the sources of product ideas previously discussed.

Product definition. This involves the identification of product specifications, benefits, and value. It is the point at which an idea shapes into a product. At this point in the process, steps 3 through 6 carry on concurrently.

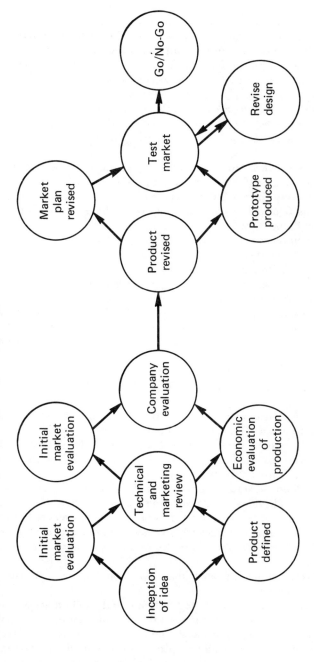

Figure 6-11. PERT chart for marketing and product design.

Technical review. This involves the analysis of the technical aspects of the product. Is the company technically capable of producing the product? What are costs of production, lead time, and development time, and how might the production of the item affect production of other items in the product mix?

Market evaluation. This phase concerns itself with whether a market exists for the product. Demographics of the customer, available market share, market trends, and opportunity areas are studied. A primary market plan is created.

Economic evaluation. ROI of product, estimated price, volume, added value, external business climate, and value added to product mix are some aspects to be evaluated.

Company evaluation. How does this product relate to the company's business? What is the capacity of the company to produce and make the product? How will the product concept affect the company?

Reevaluate the product, comparing new insight into the product to the objectives of the program.

Prototype production.

Redefine the market plan.

Test-market the product and measure results.

Launch the product, scrap it, or reevaluate and modify it.

Throughout this process, control, coordination, and communication are key elements in achieving a successful new-product development program. A system for evaluation of the steps in this process must be established and adhered to.

$\square$ **Michael Chinnici**

PRICING STRATEGY

Developing product pricing strategy is one of the most challenging aspects of the marketing function. The military definition of strategy is "the action of planning and directing operations; the maneuvering of forces into the most advantageous positions prior to actual engagement with the enemy." Tactics is "the management of those forces in battle."

The development and implementation of a strategy and tactics are the essence of marketing. They deal with developing the answers to the basic question, How do we get to where we want to be? Developing the answers to this all-important question does not require magic, but rather a pragmatic approach using creative thinking, expertise in evaluating tradeoffs, good judgment, intuition, and a little bit of luck.

It has been said that if strategy is the essence of marketing, pricing is the quintessence of strategy.

The key to sound pricing strategy is found in the following statement, which is almost axiomatic: Product pricing is a function of what the market will bear for the product benefits offered and should have no relationship to the manufacturing cost. If the market will not bear product pricing levels that exceed the costs of both manufacture and promotion plus a margin of profit, the product is usually not economically viable. In a free market, there is no limit on either the upper levels of pricing or profitability other than what the consumer is willing to pay for a product.

Establishing product price points relative to what the market will bear requires examination of a number of factors; among these are (1) nature of the market, (2) competitive product offerings, (3) design and quality of the product, (4) product positioning in the market relative to competition, and (5) life cycle stage of the product. These factors help establish basic pricing parameters, which interface with cost factors generated by manufacturing costs, marketing mix required (advertising, packaging, promotion), and selling efforts. Product pricing strategy and specific tactics are developed from the analysis of these important inputs.

Mechanics of Pricing

The mechanics of pricing in its simplest form are to first establish the total cost of the product or service, including the cost to produce it, all the fixed and variable overheads, and the costs to promote it, and to add to this the margin of profit desired. This yields the selling price for that product. When we use the term product, we mean both those whose benefits take a physical form and those whose benefits take the form of services.

The retail selling price is what the consumer pays for the product. If the producer sells directly to the consumer, the producer selling price is also the retail selling price. In most markets it is not practical for the producer to sell directly to the consumer. To get the product from the producer to the consumer, a distribution system is used that usually involves one or more distributors or jobbers and a retail selling establishment. Each element in the distribution system must mark up the price of the product.

Pricing structures and strategies depend to a large degree on the company and the industry in which it operates. As an example, the pricing of capital goods is quite different from consumer or service industry pricing. Although there are no universal pricing formulas or strategies, there are general concepts that can be adapted to fit specific needs.

Pricing Strategies

The core pricing strategy establishes the basic pricing philosophy. Core strategy may follow one of these approaches: (1) Price low to keep out competition and maintain market share. (2) Be a follower; let the competition set prices. If you have a product that is no more than just comparable, just meet that price. (3) Be lower than the competition; price so that your product is a predetermined percentage under the market leader. (4) Price to what the market will bear. Develop a product that has definitive benefits that are distinctive, assess their value to the market, and price accordingly.

The strategy of pricing to what the market will bear can be the most productive from a profitability standpoint. This policy, when coupled with noncommodity-type products—meaning those with major product differentiation features—can give pricing flexibility, which can be the key to maintaining profitability in inflationary economies.

Pricing matrix. The development of a pricing matrix that lists all competitive products in the marketplace with their most up-to-date price points can prove to be a vital aid in the development of pricing strategies.

Strategic pricing. With existing product it's important to periodically examine price/volume relationships in order to determine if products are currently priced in keeping with sales opportunities.

Demand curves. Traditional theory indicates that a negatively sloped demand curve exists: as price rises, demand decreases. It is important to realize that this theory is valid only for certain types of products, in particular agricultural commodities and products that lack major differentiation from others available on the market.

Recent findings indicate additional dimensions to the pricing of products, including such factors as the psychological aspects affecting consumer demand. Price-consciousness and price-sensitivity vary according to the nature of the product and the psychographics of the consumer. With many products that give high ego satisfaction and certain benefits that are hard to compare and quantify, high price can indicate high quality and give the product a snob appeal that has a positive effect on sales volume.

These psychological effects of pricing can generate demand curves for many products that are not negatively sloped—that is, higher selling prices increase rather than decrease consumer demand for such products and can give the marketer a strategic advantage. Perfumes, fashion products, jewelry, and luxury automobiles are some products that can exhibit this type of demand curve.

Market share. Market share is a critical element in developing the pricing strategy. Pricing is a major determinant of market share, and market share is a major determinant of pricing flexibility. In theory, the more dominant share of market achieved, the more unit volume is generated resulting in manufacturing efficiencies that enable the producer to offer profitable products at lower prices than the competition, which doesn't have the unit volume to achieve the same production efficiency.

Experience curve. The experience curve, publicized by the Boston Consulting Group, tells us that market share is vital to increased profits. It is based on the concept that product costs decline by a constant percentage each time volume doubles. A classic example is Ford Motor Company in its early days. During its initial production period, the price of the Model T was cut from about $5,000 to $3,000, and by 1923 the price was $900—reflecting an 85 percent experience-curve slope. During this time span, wages tripled, the working day was reduced from ten to eight hours, and one of the nation's largest industrial complexes, River Rouge, was created entirely from retained earnings.

PIMS (Profit Impact of Marketing Strategies). Another convincing argument for big market share comes from PIMS, a study undertaken by the Marketing Science Institute at the Harvard Business School. In the study, 37 factors bearing on profit performance in different industries are analyzed through data contributed by 57 corporations. Analysis of market—ratio of dollar sales by a company to total sales of all competitors—shows the effect of dominant share on pretax

ROI. On an average, an increase of 10 percent in market share is accompanied by an increase of about 5 percent in ROI. Companies that enjoy a strong competitive position in their primary markets tend to be highly profitable.

Although production efficiency is a big plus, influences like *market leadership, advertising concentration, technical superiority,* and *service availability* are other factors that have a positive effect on share of market.

With new products, high market share should ideally be achieved by the end of the market growth stage, since initial per-unit profits are usually negative because sales volume is low and only starts to build during the introductory stage of the product life cycle. At the point that high market share is reached, unit profits boom as output increases and production costs dramatically decrease. This presents a challenge to the market leader, since those profits generated by the high market share both attract competitors and can be used to ultimately destroy competitors. Since the leader sets the pricing standard for his market, his ability to produce a profitable product at the lowest cost drives out competition and enables the leader to maintain his market share.

The relationship of market share to profitability generally holds until the product becomes obsolete or pricing and promotional support costs needed to hold high volume reach a level beyond what production efficiency can achieve.

It should be noted that high unit volume is not the only way to ensure profitability. There are many products that have low market share and are highly profitable. Since the products or the markets are specialized and command better-than-average margins, specialized products can be desirable components of the producer's product mix.

Consumer research.   Consumer research is an important tool to be used in evaluating the price/value relationship for many products. The research used can be qualitative (such as individual interviews and focus group sessions in which attitudes about products are examined as they relate to the values placed on the product benefits) or quantitative, such as market sales testing and specialized price sensitivity tests.

It is important, particularly in inflationary economies, to regularly evaluate product pricing as it relates to demand, since it is necessary to achieve maximum pricing levels in order to maintain profitability.

Legal Aspects of Pricing

Even in a free market economy, there are legal restrictions on what is considered to be unfair pricing practices that discriminate against certain elements in the distribution system and ultimately might prove harmful to consumers by increasing the legitimate price they have to pay for a product or service. The marketer should be aware of these regulations and avail himself of legal counsel for his proper guidance. The following is a brief description of these regulations.

Clayton Act (1914).   Designed to prevent substantial lessening of competition and creation of monopolies, this law also covers mergers and interlocking directorates and provides for treble damages for violations.

Robinson-Patman Act (1936). Aimed at preventing price discrimination, this law applies to commodities only, and the seller must be engaged in interstate commerce. It has provisions covering cost justification and meeting competition defenses, brokerage, advertising allowances, furnishing extra services, and so on.

Sherman Antitrust Act (1890). In essence, this law declares illegal every contract, combination, or conspiracy in restraint of trade or commerce and all monopolies or attempts to monopolize trade. It also provides the government with both civil and criminal sanctions to employ against violators, and grants the victims of such practices the right to recover their damages threefold.

Federal Trade Commission Act (1914). This legislation makes unfair methods of competition in interstate commerce unlawful. In its nature, it is preventive legislation and seeks to preserve competition as far as possible by supervisory action of the Federal Trade Commission. It is particularly aimed at misrepresentation of materials, ingredients, nature of manufacture, and origin of product; false advertising; trade restraints; and lottery-type giveaways as sales inducements.

It should be remembered that it is illegal for the producer to fix retail selling prices. He may only suggest retail selling prices, but any measure taken to maintain the suggested retail price is in violation of fair trade legislation.

□ *David J. Freiman*

MARKETING COMMUNICATIONS

The remaining decades of the twentieth century will be a period of increasing sophistication and will place greater demands on all levels of business. These demands will go beyond sales profit into such qualitative areas as employee relations, management of human resources, and fully satisfying consumer wants and desires. In this more sophisticated and precise time, many of the "frills" of marketing will be challenged. Marginal brands and inefficient and ineffective systems will disappear. On the other hand, the tried and true principles of marketing communications will become even more important, and be further enhanced by new, more sophisticated techniques.

As these new communications needs and techniques are examined, it is important not to get carried away with them. The basic rudimentary needs and importance of communications in the marketing mix will still be there and even increase.

As we go deeper into the 1980s and beyond, one age-old adage will still hold true: nothing moves in business until somebody sells something. In order for a sale to be made, some form of communication to a customer must be made. The form of the communication may change, techniques may improve, and its role and degree of importance in the marketing mix will vary from product to product, category to category, year to year, and brand to brand. But the need to communicate key consumer selling points in order to generate a sale will always be there—whether one uses sky writing, billboards, or some new type of cable broadcast. Marketing Intercontinental, a marketing consulting firm, uses a very

Figure 6-12. Marketing and advertising communication model.

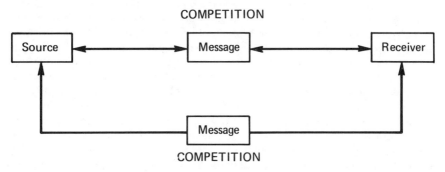

interesting definition of marketing that vividly illustrates this need for a customer focus: "Marketing is the practice of satisfying customer needs and desires. Profitability is the measure of how well it is done."

A Simple Model Is the Key

At the root of all effective marketing and advertising communications is a very simple model (Figure 6-12), which should constantly be used. It very clearly and vividly illustrates the key elements that must be addressed to develop effective advertising. Very simply: Know your product or service well, fully understand your potential customer, be totally aware of the competitive environment, and have a very specific idea of the desired response. All these should shape the message. All too often seasoned professionals and well-trained executives lose sight of this model and make severe mistakes. Either omissions or errors in judgment about one or more of these elements can usually be found at the root of advertising failures. Recognition of and attentiveness to *all* these elements are usually at the root of successful advertising programs. In order for an advertising campaign to be totally successful, all these elements must work together. They are interdependent and their individual importance varies, but they must come together for a successful communication that breaks through the clutter of the competitive marketplace. Techniques may change and tools may grow in sophistication, but an in-depth knowledge of and sensitivity to this model are always critical.

The Value of an Idea

Also, in the final analysis, marketing communications, despite all the latest disciplines and techniques, still remains more of an art than a science. It has come to be an art/science that employs many scientific tools but still depends on creativity and judgment. New media vehicles and better research techniques are essential, but they will never replace a truly great idea. One simple strong idea that can uniquely position a product or indelibly implant a selling benefit in the consumer's mind can sometimes be more useful and valuable than all the research in the world. Advertising, then, evolves from a process of disciplined creativity. Of course, anyone seriously involved in advertising and marketing communications must be knowledgeable about research and fully use these disciplines to develop effective communication. Research and systems should be tools, not crutches. Equally important, however, is the ability and conviction to disregard research or proceed without it when a great creative idea comes along. A well-known marketing consultant, Loren Smith, put it very succinctly: "Probably the biggest enemy of a great idea is lots of good ideas." It takes sound, confident judgment and a lot of guts to proceed with a truly innovative idea that may not be totally proved, particularly in the face of other more traditional options with research backup. The exciting thing, though, is that each of us has the capacity to develop that creative advertising idea that can change or fix a brand, alter the course of an industry, launch a new product, influence consumer trends, and even save lives. This potential is in all of us, and it is this potential and ability that make the advertising function an exciting and worthwhile but sometimes frustrating one.

Defining the Marketing Communications Program

Virtually every communication that occurs between the manufacturer of a product or service and the buyers of that product/service is a marketing communication. It can take the form of sales presentations, sales promotion, merchandising, public relations, or advertising. This specific discussion deals with advertising, but the principles and techniques that are applied to the advertising communication are applicable to these other disciplines as well. These principles should be viewed as guidelines that help direct all communications with the consumer, and then be adapted to suit the specific needs of a given discipline.

The Role of the Communications Program

The first and perhaps most important part of any sound effective communications program, whether it be advertising, public relations, or sales promotion, is to define its role and value. The task is to clearly and precisely assess the role that each specific element of the marketing mix will play in the overall marketing and sales success of a given product or service. Regarding advertising, this does not mean the definition of advertising objectives and strategies. These are also very important but should come after the role of advertising is defined. The objective of this exercise is to quantify and clearly delineate advertising's role in the profitable marketing of a product versus other key marketing elements. Will it be the driving force that leads the promotion and sales efforts with both consumer and trade? Will it have a backup or support function to some other element of the marketing mix? By enforcing this discipline with advertising and every element in the marketing mix, a strong sense of priorities is established. This clearly directs specific functional managers and company management toward the proper allocation of time and funds. While this may sound simple, many times this is probably one of the most difficult areas for managers to quantify and define, and sometimes the most overlooked. A helpful way to get at this definition of roles is to ask the question: What would happen if a product or service couldn't be advertised, or if a budget were cut in half? What would happen if a sales promotion or other merchandising effort had to be withdrawn?

Advertising's Role

Defining the role of advertising is probably more crucial and more difficult than defining the roles of the other communication elements of the marketing mix. Usually, advertising receives a substantial amount of funds, sufficient to affect bottom-line profit directly. Very often advertising is the only representation or "window" that a company might have with the ultimate consumer. Unfortunately, however, the role of advertising is not understood or quantified, and as a result it does not receive the "proper" amount of time and attention. Many times, even though advertising should play a minor role in a given product's or service's marketing mix, it receives an undue amount of attention and funding. Since it is exciting and visible, key managers at all levels sometimes misallocate their time for and attention to it. On the other hand, there are many instances where advertising plays a very significant role in the marketing mix but, because it is misunderstood or subjectively intimidating, gets delegated downward too far. The way to avoid this problem is to define roles and, on the basis of these roles, assign the proper time, attention, and funding priorities for advertising and all other elements of the marketing mix.

Defining the Marketing Mix

The marketing mix of a given product or service can vary not only in its content but also in the degree of importance of each individual element in the mix. The following is a concise list of the elements in the marketing mix against which advertising's role must be evaluated and properly positioned.

The product mix. This should include a very clear definition of the product or service that is currently marketed and a projection of future changes, additions, or alterations to the product or service.

Pricing. The role of pricing in the marketing mix, and how it influences consumer perception and competitive positioning, should be clearly defined. This analysis should be conducted at all levels of the distribution chain.

Distribution. Defining the specific channels of distribution and their importance to the ultimate marketing of the product or service is critical. Distribution channels should be evaluated very carefully and objectively with a precise definition of "value added" and impact of each factor.

Personal selling. The role of the sales force and personal selling should be examined so that its importance for and impact upon the ultimate sale of the product or service can be defined. Only after this is accomplished can the proper support tools be developed.

Advertising. The role advertising will play, the dollars allocated, the specific mix of trade and consumer advertising all need to be reviewed relative to other marketing elements. It is particularly important to examine these issues in light of the competition.

Sales promotion. The role sales promotion will play at all trade levels and how it will specifically relate to the advertising must be evaluated. Included in this element of the mix should be a clear definition of the role of display and exposure at the point of ultimate sale to the consumer. Equally important are the amount and type of trade promotional funds that must be employed to secure support.

Packaging. Packaging can play a very important role both at the trade level and at the consumer level. Packaging is often one of the most underestimated communications tools in the marketing mix. It often is the final billboard at point of purchase and can be a major sales tool.

Public relations. "Marketing" public relations has become a newly discovered business-building tool. It can be a major support element to advertising as well.

Physical handling and warehousing. The role of physical handling, warehousing, and transportation and how they affect the ultimate delivery of the product or service should be defined and understood.

These are the basic elements of the marketing mix that largely come under the control of the marketer. To properly develop an effective advertising program for a given product or service, the marketing mix must be clearly understood. This analysis must take place for major competition as well. The elements of the mix just reviewed generally come under the control of the marketer. However, there are additional elements of the marketing mix that are equally important, but strangely enough do not come under the direct control of the marketer.

External Factors Affecting the Marketing Mix

These external factors affecting the marketing mix play a very heavy role in the eventual success or failure of any product or service. Even though they do not come under the direct control of a specific marketer, these elements must be carefully studied and kept up to date. A marketer must have his hand on the pulse of these four basic issues constantly to develop effective marketing and communications programs.

Consumers' buying behavior. What motivates the consumers to purchase, their purchasing habits, and the environment in which a product or service is viewed all directly affect the marketing effort. The marketer must develop products or services that clearly reflect consumers' needs and desires. In a free, open, competitive environment, the marketer cannot effectively dictate consumer trends and preferences.

The trade's buying behavior. This, too, is an area that can directly affect marketing success or failure. Distribution and exposure to the ultimate consumer are key. Sometimes maintaining adequate inventory levels, for example, can play a major role in the financial success of the product. One only has to look at recent history and how the cost of money and financing has affected retailer and wholesaler attitudes toward inventory levels, display, and promotion activity to gauge the impact and importance of this marketing element.

Competitors' position or behavior. The marketer must always be closely attuned to all competitive developments and, wherever possible, have contingency plans to either defend against competitive thrusts or mount offensive plans to take advantage of competitive weaknesses. The moves of competitors are not always predictable. The range of possible competitive options can be "game-planned" and catalogued for each competitor in the marketplace. Then, one's ability to effectively react to competitive moves can sometimes make the difference between success or failure. One only has to look at the airline industry over the last few years with its discount structures, couponing, and route changes to see how competitive moves could dramatically affect sales, profit, and market share.

The government's behavior. The government probably exercises a greater control over the marketing of products than it ever has. While the current environment calls for some relaxing of these controls, the presence of government and its dramatic impact on marketers will always be a factor to contend with. One only has to look at such industries as cigarettes, alcoholic beverages, health care, toys, and airlines to see how the factor of government behavior can weigh heavily on the marketing future of a product or service.

Advertising in the Context of the Marketing Plan

Once the role of advertising has been adequately defined and each internal and external element of the marketing mix has been clearly enumerated, the next step in developing an advertising campaign is to position the advertising plan in the context of an overall marketing plan. The preparation and details of a marketing plan will not be reviewed in depth here. However, it is important to understand what a marketing plan is and to determine how the advertising plan fits into the marketing plan.

The marketing plan provides the total framework for managing a product or service in a given fiscal year. It should be the document that provides direction for all contributing elements of the marketing mix and the yardstick by which produce or service performance for that year is measured. It should include (1) volume and financial objectives (planned versus current year); (2) situation analysis; (3) brief review of trends and significant developments in the product category; (4) competitive review by brand (business position, media spending, copy review, and pricing and promotion); (5) major problems and opportunities; (6) market objectives (nonfinancial); (7) marketing strategies; (8) tactical plans (individual sections containing statements of objectives, strategies, plan details, and rationale for advertising, promotion/merchandising, distribution/pricing, research and testing, and public relations); and (9) budget summary.

Remember that a marketing plan is a living document and basically is out of date the minute it is written. The marketing plan should be totally flexible and adaptable to the needs of the marketplace to be effective.

The development of an advertising campaign or program can take many forms. It can vary in length, intensity, and detail from product to product and service to service. A successful campaign can burst on the scene from one simple creative spark emanated from an idea generated by a copywriter, consumer, or president of a company, or it can be the result of a disciplined, carefully planned approach out of which campaign and creative ideas flow and then are tested and proved.

Managing the creative process and the specific steps involved in developing an advertising campaign can sometimes be subjective and unpredictable. It has been the subject of many books and articles. Advertising agencies' successes and failures have been based on it, and it is subject to many different styles and points of view. While management of the creative process will not be dealt with in depth, creative management must be understood and respected to effectively deal with the advertising process. It follows very basic steps (see Figure 6-13), and it is important to remember that in certain stages these steps may overlap and become interdependent upon each other. Nevertheless, they can be looked at as discrete, individual disciplines that logically follow from each other and tie directly back to the communication model discussed earlier.

Step 1: Get to Know the Product

Fully understand and appreciate the product or service being marketed. Anyone involved in the advertising of a particular product or service must unequivocally become the expert about that product or service. No stone should remain unturned. The analysis and review that go into developing an understanding of, respect for, and sensitivity to what makes a particular product or service have its own identity in a competitive marketplace are absolutely critical. Basic to this analysis should be the standard review of all the specifications of a product or service, placed against competition. Also, an objective assessment of the company's strength or leverage for a particular product or service must be made.

While one should become an expert and intimate with the product or service being marketed, objectivity and a sense of competitive reality must also be maintained. If the product or service does not have competitive superiority and/or

Figure 6-13. Steps in the advertising-development process.

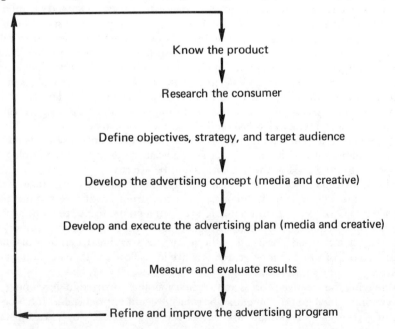

Know the product

Research the consumer

Define objectives, strategy, and target audience

Develop the advertising concept (media and creative)

Develop and execute the advertising plan (media and creative)

Measure and evaluate results

Refine and improve the advertising program

cannot totally fulfill consumer expectations and desires, this must be recognized. Advertising cannot be the cure-all or panacea for deficiencies in a product or service. In fact, the misuse of advertising in this regard can sometimes be harmful and destructive. The need for objectivity and realistic assessment of product strengths and weaknesses was best expressed by Doyle, Dane and Bernbach, one of the most creative agencies in the history of advertising. Doyle, Dane and Bernbach summed it up in one simple sentence, "Great advertising can only make a bad product worse." If one remembers that simple admonition, errors in judgment or advertising that overpromises can be minimized.

Step 2: Get to Know the Consumer

Market the product or service the consumer really wants, not what the marketer thinks the consumer wants or what can be manufactured most efficiently. The greatest product in the world will not be successful unless the consumer is willing to pay a fair price for that product or service. Before a product can be advertised to the consumer, the marketer must have a clear indication not only of *who* the potential consumer will be but also of *why* that person will be a potential consumer. In consumer research, the "who" is determined through demographic information gathering, whereas the "why" is discovered through psychographic research.

Even if a company does not have a major market-research budget to conduct massive amounts of consumer research, the marketer can make some assumptions about these key facts and work with judgment. This segment of the advertising-development process analyzes the consumer and then attempts to place the product against consumer needs and benefits. Sometimes a full and thorough consumer analysis may alter product development and totally change the course of a brand's or service's evolution. The product and service technology to be marketed must reflect what the consumer wants and desires. This is true for packaged-goods products, industrial products, or services. For virtually any product that is marketed, the customer ultimately dictates what he or she will purchase. The manufacturer or marketer that is most attentive to these signals will ultimately win out over competition, provided the company resources and technology are there to back it up.

Step 3: Set Objectives and Strategies and Define the Target Audience

Valid objectives and strategies or properly defined target audiences cannot be written or clearly laid out until a thorough analysis and understanding of both the consumer and the product are achieved. This step should occur before any creative or media explorations are undertaken. It must be very thoughtfully and painstakingly completed. The objectives and strategies established in this step become the road map and guidelines upon which all activity must be based. These objectives and strategies also represent the yardstick against which all communications activity must be judged.

This stage is ultimately the most important stage in the development of an advertising campaign. In many respects, it could be the most difficult stage as well. Of course, developing the ultimate creative idea is equally as challenging and arduous and, in some ways, more difficult. The process of defining objectives, strategies, and target audience requires special professional skills. Of necessity, one must narrow down alternatives, eliminate options, and pick the best and most effective way to go. It largely is a deductive process that requires the marketer to make critical judgments and interpretations of facts and data.

Ultimately it is the advertising executive most adept in making these critical judgments who will develop the most effective strategies and unique positionings for a product or service. Precisely written strategies are extremely important. Every word must be carefully considered, since each word can have a specific bearing on the development of a concept or the execution of an idea.

A well-written strategy is essential to good advertising because it forces a discipline and focuses the attention of both the advertiser and the advertising agency. The consumer is the ultimate judge of an advertisement's effectiveness. However, before exposure to the consumer, it is the objectives and the strategy which should judge the quality of the advertising idea. They should be the yardstick by which all creative work is measured. In very simple terms, the following is what should be included in the definition of a target audience and the elements of an advertising strategy.

Defining the target audience.   Through analysis of all available consumer data for a given product or service (and its competitors), the target-audience statement attempts to define *prime prospects* for a product or service. While it considers all potential consumers, it narrows this consumer group down to those who are most likely to purchase the product or service and yield the most business. They are defined in two ways: demographically (by age, sex, income, region, purchase versus usage, frequency of usage, and so on) and psychographically (why they use certain products, their preferred brand images, wants, desires, and the like).

Setting creative objectives and strategy.   The creative objectives define the specific goal of the advertising. The strategy is the means to achieve that goal. Their content and format can vary substantially from organization to organization, but in essence a good objectives and strategy statement contains the following: (1) to whom to sell—target audience; (2) how to sell—generically, competitively; (3) what to sell—benefit(s) plus supporting information; and (4) way of selling—totality of advertising and guidelines for executing it. These elements must be there in as precise and concise a form as possible in order to have a sound, workable advertising plan.

Just as great advertising ideas are more difficult to develop than mediocre ones, great strategies are much more difficult to write than weak ones. Strong on-target strategies involve the critical, difficult tasks of making decisions and narrowing alternatives. Before reviewing the elements of sound objectives, strategies, and target-audience statements, it would be worthwhile to characterize some of the elements of a bad strategy.

First, a bad strategy tries to talk to all consumers rather than select prime customers. Second, it puts no limitations on the kind of creative effort that can be mounted and tends to be vague, general, and all-inclusive. Third, it provides a laundry list of all the possible, positive attributes that can be given for purchasing a product, instead of selecting the very best reasons. In effect, it tries to become everything to everyone, and in so doing totally misses its mark.

The following is an example of a bad strategy for an imaginary product competing in the wine category. The brand in question happens to be a low-calorie wine. Here is the type of strategy one *should not* write.

Target audience: all adults over the age of 18.
Brand X copy objectives are:
1. To develop a consumer preference for the wine among the following wine consumer groups, in order of priority:
    Current Brand X heavy users.
    Non-Brand X users who use both low-calorie and regular wines together.
    Non-brand users who use only low-calorie wines.
    All regular wine consumers.
2. To convince all non-brand users and reassure current users that:
    Brand X has taste and flavor characteristics superior to those of other low-calorie wines.
    Brand X is universally liked and accepted for all wine-drinking occasions and provides the optimum wine-drinking experience.

It becomes obvious that this strategy tries to do too much and, in effect, provides little or no guidance and would generate ineffective advertising. On the other hand, a good, well-written strategy forces both the advertiser and the agency and, therefore, the consumer to make a decision about a product or service. It identifies this decision as precisely and positively as possible. Rather than speak to everyone, it selects its prime customers. It selects the area in which the product or service will compete, and it decides on the key benefit and the selling idea. It is sharp, selective, and totally single-minded, and it deliberately limits the creative man's area of opportunity to where the sales potential is best.

Here is an example of a well-written strategy for Brand Y, a product competing in the category of fortified drinks for children. This particular imaginary product is a fruit drink fortified with the protein of soybeans.

Target audience: mothers age 18-45 with children age 2-12.
Brand Y copy objectives are:
1. To convince these mothers that a serving of Brand Y once a day will provide their children with all the nourishment of a full meal.
2. To convince these mothers that their children will enjoy drinking this form of protein nourishment because of the product's exceptional, all-natural fruit-flavor taste.

In essence, then, a good strategy should give those who create the advertising maximum freedom to use their creative talents and insights, yet provide the discipline to make their work pertinent and relevant to the particular challenges the product or service offers. Given the importance of this process, strategy development must be a total partnership between the advertiser and the advertising agency. There is a simple exercise that demonstrates the importance of developing objectives and strategies and their impact on the actual advertising. Spend an afternoon or evening reading a magazine or watching television and take each piece of advertising you see (print ad or commercial) and attempt to write the specific objectives and strategies under which that advertising was written. If a simple single-minded strategy statement cannot be written, chances are it wasn't done prior to developing the advertising. It is also highly likely that it would not be an effective communication.

Step 4: Develop the Advertising Concept

It is difficult to pinpoint when and how an advertising idea begins and emerges. Ideally, after the target audience and objectives and strategy are defined, the advertising concept, which positions the product, is then defined. An advertising idea or concept should encompass not only the creative but also media elements. That is, it should represent a total package. The core and heart of every communications plan is the overall positioning and marketing posture of a brand. The brand positioning must define exactly what a product or service will stand for in the mind of the consumer. It is the key element around which products or services build their consumer and customer franchises.

Brand positioning is a delicate balancing act. Marketers must constantly balance the consumers' wants and desires with corporate objectives. If one permits an imbalance between these two, the marketing equilibrium is disrupted. If customer needs and consumer wants dictate marketing programs that are excessive, corporate goals will not be achieved. If excessive profit is pursued and insufficient product support results, consumer franchises can be lost.

It sounds basic, but all too often very sophisticated marketers, with all the marketing tools and techniques, lose sight of this balance, and brands and companies fail. A well-prepared and faithfully executed marketing communications concept that develops a strong brand position prevents this imbalance.

The advertising concept should form the basis for all advertising and communications elements. It should be simple, direct, and memorable and fulfill the objectives and strategy. Perhaps a way to illustrate this would be to use an example of a well-known product in an advertising campaign and attempt to break it down into its target audience, objectives and strategy, and advertising concept. The product is Charmin toilet tissue, with Mr. Whipple and "Please Don't Squeeze the Charmin!" The basic *target audience* for Charmin toilet tissue is women, who are primary purchasers of toilet tissue, with a priority on women in average middle-income households with children and in the 25-to-49-year age bracket. The *objective* of the Charmin advertising would be to convince the target consumer that Charmin is the softest toilet tissue she can buy.

Next, the *strategy* would be to convince women that Charmin is the softest tissue by convincingly demonstrating its superior softness and describing that softness in a unique way that is proprietary to the Charmin brand. The advertising *concept* that emerges from this strategy is that Charmin toilet tissue is so soft that women find it irresistible and must squeeze it. The *execution* of that concept is the whole character and interaction of Mr. Whipple with his famous admonition, "Ladies, please don't squeeze the Charmin!" and the copy line of "squeezably soft." Again, whether the concept came before the idea of Mr. Whipple can be known only to the people on the creative team that developed the campaign. However, in analyzing that advertising and in attempting to develop advertising in a deductive manner, one can see that the *concept* of the advertising is critical to the execution of the strategy and the fulfillment of the objectives. Once that concept is defined, all further activity must be directed toward enhancing the communication thrust of that concept, creatively and in media selection.

The media plan is as much an integral part of the advertising concept as is the creative idea. The media plan basically defines the vehicles which will deliver the advertising message to the ultimate consumer. The ultimate delivery takes place in two basic stages: the development of the plan and the execution of the plan. Media planning is a very complex, technical subject. To be understood and covered fully, it should be reviewed in great detail and is usually the subject of separate courses, seminars, and books. However, the major purpose in discussing it here is to underline the importance of the link between the media plan and the overall advertising message. Where and how advertising is scheduled is sometimes just as important as what is scheduled. The overall objective of any media plan is to deliver the advertising message as effectively and efficiently as possible to the target audience. There are three operative concepts in media. The first is effectiveness, which means the maximum *impact* on the consumer. The second is efficiency, which means delivering the message to the greatest number of consumers at the lowest cost. The third is target audience, which means that the advertising message must be focused on the prime prospects and the key target groups.

In order for the media plan to be developed effectively, these key elements must be in place. First and foremost, the target audience must be well defined. Second, the concept of the creative message must be defined within the context of the overall advertising program. Third, a specific media budget must be provided. Fourth, guidelines as to seasonality of spending should be set forth. Fifth, geographic spending needs and requirements should be spelled out.

The media planner then takes all this input and develops the outline of a media plan and strategy that will accomplish the objectives within the budget. This plan is then placed in careful synchrony with the overall creative plan, and the advertising program emerges. The next critical stage is the execution of both the media plan and the creative plan to make sure that they effectively deliver the plan and reflect the latest conditions in the marketplace.

Step 5: Execute the Concept and the Plan

Once the conceptual positioning for a brand has been established, both creatively and in media, it is necessary to develop and execute the final plan. The execution of the creative plan takes the form of final production, that is, filming of the actual television commercial, shooting and engraving of the actual print ad, and so on. It is in the execution of the creative concept that specialness and extraordinary work can emerge. Sound strategies and concepts are essential; even brilliant executions cannot correct incorrect strategies and/or poorly defined concepts. However, it is extremely important that as much care and creativity be taken in the execution of an idea as in strategy and concept development. Such things as selection of the photographer, the television production house, the director, actors, actresses, and models are very critical. If the execution of the idea does not dramatically and faithfully live up to the concept, the ultimate communication to the consumer will not be as strong as desired.

The same is also true in the execution of the media plan. After the plan has been developed, it is essential that the actual purchases in the magazines or specific television or radio programs be true to the plan and effectively reach the target audience. Many times, however, factors occur in the marketplace that necessitate changes from the original media plan. For example, network television might be sold out or too expensive at a particular time, or the outdoor billboards in the marketplace might be sold out. Nevertheless, even though these things might occur, the plan must be flexible enough to accommodate not only the negative possibilities but also the positive opportunities that might emerge. An extraordinary efficient buy in a magazine might become available that was not available at the time the original plan was constructed. The advertising agency and the client must be prepared to take advantage of these opportunities if they occur.

Step 6: Measure and Evaluate Results

Every marketing communications program must have a set of objectives against which it is developed. It is equally important that a program for measuring the effectiveness of these efforts be in place. If there is no true business and profitability evaluation of a program, a program's economic viability cannot be proved. Measuring efforts in marketing communications, particularly advertising, take three basic forms: (1) measuring the effect of a specific piece of communication before running the program, (2) measuring consumer reaction to the program after it has run, and (3) measuring actual sales in the marketplace. The ideal program of measurement encompasses all three, but this is not always possible. A company must decide for itself which form of measurement to use, and this is usually dictated by the nature of the business, budgets, and marketing expertise.

Pretesting advertising communications. The purpose of this type of testing is to get consumer reaction to advertising before it is run. It can be accomplished in rough or finished form. It can be an exposure of a commercial or a print ad to a small group of consumers in focus groups, which is qualitative to quantitative testing in simulated media environment. Testing a print ad usually takes the form of a portfolio test. In the testing, sample ads are actually tipped into magazines and consumers are tested for recall, comprehension, and persuasion. The same takes place in television, where the consumer is exposed to a television commercial either on the air or in a simulated on-air environment.

Various testing techniques exist for each medium, and each has its pros and cons. The main purpose of this testing is to determine consumer reaction to advertising before it goes into the marketplace and before media dollars are expended. Each company and advertising agency has points of view about which technique is the most effective.

Testing consumer reaction to advertising. This usually takes place in test markets but sometimes can also be gathered in simulated market situations called lab tests. These usually take the form of consumer attitude and usage studies. The primary purpose of this type of research is to measure the awareness levels generated by communications programs, the attitudes developed by consumers, and the levels of trial or purchase of the service or product. In addition to obtaining all this information about the "test" product or service, performances of competitive products or services are also measured to determine total impact on the consumer. As with advertising testing, many different techniques and suppliers are available, and the research can be costly. However, it is a very important measure of the effectiveness of a program for its target audience. It is almost mandatory when actual sales data cannot be gathered.

Actual sales movement. Of course, actual sales of a product or service represent the ultimate measure of a program's success. However, it must be remembered that in the competitive marketplace many things can affect sales that may go beyond the actual communications program put in place in the marketplace. This is all the more reason to conduct consumer attitude and awareness tests.

For example, unforeseen competitive reactions, economic conditions, or government regulations could have an effect on the actual sales of the product. Sometimes a communications program can fulfill all the objectives that were set for it but not generate the planned sales levels because of these "external" factors. However, it is highly recommended that a measurement of sales at the consumer level be undertaken as an important measure of the success of any communications effort.

Many times products or services compete in categories for which syndicated services such as Nielsen or Audits & Surveys can be purchased to read actual retail movement. In other cases where this is not available, custom retail audits may be purchased. Also, sometimes it is possible to have the company's sales force or its distributor's or broker's sales force read actual sales movement. Whatever system is used, it is important that it be kept in a selling area as specifically defined as possible so that the true measure of the effectiveness of the program in a given marketplace can be read.

Step 7: Refine the Program

As soon as a communications program is put in the marketplace, the communications executive should begin refining and fine-tuning the entire effort. Personal judgment, sales force reaction, trade reaction, and consumer reaction, as well as all the measurements, are all important inputs into this process. However, the consumer research program outlined is a key ingredient in the refinement and fine-tuning of communications programs. Also, once a communications program is launched, competitors usually react. Sometimes they react in a very direct way, sometimes indirectly. It is important to keep monitoring these competitive moves and shifts and to adapt the communications program accordingly. It is very important to note here that refinement and fine-tuning do not necessarily mean wholesale change. Probably one of the most important rules to keep in mind in communications is to change as little as possible. The best approach is one that maintains consistency and develops a long-term program that has a long-term positive effect on the consumer. Frequent and multiple changes in communications programs only tend to confuse the consumer and work against creating a lasting impact and position for a product or service. When refinements and changes are made, they should be evolutionary and make the program better. Revolutionary changes that present the ultimate customers with totally different points of view should be made only after serious consideration. It is recognized, however, that sometimes, due to extreme conditions in the marketplace or total ineffectiveness of the program, major changes are required. However, they must be reviewed very carefully.

The Marketing Environment—What Will It Be Like?

The marketing environment of the future will be a very exciting, challenging, and rewarding arena in which to compete. The next decade or two should be a period of dramatic and accelerated change. Companies and individuals that can anticipate and manage those changes in their overall business practice should survive and flourish. The same type of change and flexibility will be required in marketing and communications. Therefore, long-term strategic planning, flexibility, and the speed and quality of decision making will be very important keys to success in tomorrow's marketing world.

The Past and the Present

In planning for the future it is helpful to review the past and take a snapshot of the current environment. Although this may not always be totally predictive of the future, it sometimes is the only experience base from which to operate. Over the past few decades, the marketing and advertising communication profession has undergone some very important changes. For most industries, each period can be characterized by a prevailing point of view or philosophy that dominated the industry, and the communications industry has been very good at putting labels on itself, such as (1) the "Fabulous Fifties"—a decade of marketing and new-product proliferation, marketing expansion, and development of sophisticated marketing techniques; (2) the "Soaring Sixties"—a period of creative revolution during which the value of an idea and executional style were emphasized and qualitative research took on added dimension and importance; (3) the "Seeking Seventies"—a decade of research into positioning, characterized by the filling of marketing niches and gaps, smart product positioning, and a return to tougher, more hard-sell advertising, and (4) the "Enlightened Eighties" (as we would label it)—a period of dichotomy, characterized by a reasonable learning from the past coupled with an upheaval in media with the new and emerging technologies. Communications will keep its hard sell but also emphasize style and creativity.

The Future

Table 6-3 summarizes some basic trends and developments that should emerge in the next few decades and affect the practice of marketing communications. Some are continuations of trends, while others are new developments that are likely to emerge. They represent the best collection of opinions and predictions

Table 6-3. Predictions of basic trends affecting marketing communications.

Trend	Effect
MARKETING	
Increasing importance of middle-age group (45–65)	More "youthful" outlook.
Death of in-market test marketing due to • Competitive retaliations • Long lead periods • Competitive preemptions on a national scale • Rise in simulated testing	Increasing defensive reactions to test marketing. Lack of predictability of market tests. Need for alternatives to test marketing. Better lab testing techniques.
Growth of "extrinsic" marketing—reliance on trends and developments in other industries to spawn marketing innovations in others (e.g., microwave cookery and the need for new nonaluminum containers for frozen foods).	Product/technology breakthroughs are less prevalent. Need to hitchhike on trends and market to them. Microwave ovens and the food industry.
Changing social values	Fitness/nutrition becoming more important. Distrust of institutions. Quality of life seen as more important. Increasing importance of self-fulfillment.
Ever-increasing energy costs	Price increases. Travel environment in turmoil. Shrinking food-service business. Shrinking automobile market.
Smaller families/later marriages	Shift in marketing value per household. More discretionary income. Increasing importance of single-household market.
More working women	Changes in purchase/consumption patterns. More income per household. Advertising-target changes.
Electronic revolution—teleshopping	Distribution upheaval. Packaging less important. Advertising more important.

Table 6-3. *Continued.*

Trend	Effect
ADVERTISING ENVIRONMENT	
More sophisticated creative testing techniques (persuasion and effectiveness measurements)	More competitive advertising arena. Greater competition for creative talent. Greater reliance on research.
Overbearing legal restrictions on advertising content	Seeking of new, less regulated media. More factually oriented messages. Less new-product proliferation.
Increasing media clutter—new media types will be sought	Complete upheaval in all media due to cable television. More segmentation of audience delivery by all media. Innovative commercial and sponsorship forms.
Greater restrictions on certain product categories' use of general advertising (children's products, potential health hazards, etc.) and move to more selective use of advertising.	Increasing importance of distribution and public relations. Search for new media types.
ADVERTISING AGENCIES	
More agency acquisitions (big getting bigger)	Less available choice. Relaxing of conflict policies by clients. Disappearance of medium-size agencies.
Better finance management (fee take-over commission system)	More stability in agencies and agency-client relationships.
More decentralization (branch-office autonomy)	Growth of regional offices. Less dependence on New York and Chicago.
Less available talent, particularly account management	Greater client reliance on own marketing departments More fragmented use of consultants.
Hot creative agencies not limited to small shops	General uplifting of all agencies' creative products.
More sophisticated use of agencies by both consumer and industrial clients	General upgrading of industry advertising. Increased competition among advertising agencies.

Table 6-3. *Continued.*

Trend	Effect
MEDIA	
Television broadcast media to change dramatically as a result of cable television	Broadcast syndication growing in importance. Barter to become more effective and better managed. Television stations' rates and programming face potential turmoil due to satellites. Cable television expected to make serious inroads. All media rates will continue to increase, but at slower rates.

of key industry leaders and trade publications. For the sake of clarity and simplicity, they have been organized and catalogued into four basic areas—marketing, the advertising environment, the media, and advertising agencies—and only the major developments are cited.

Not all these exact developments may come to pass as predicted, but one can be certain that the majority of them will take place and have a dramatic impact on communications in the next few decades. This underscores the need for marketing and communications executives to be sensitive to change and plan for it, then make decisions quickly but intelligently.

In addition, new media types and different use of current media will emerge in the next few decades. These new media will be largely driven by the video revolution, which includes cable television, satellite transmission, cassettes, and video disks. The consumer will have many more alternatives on his viewing menu, and most likely the advertiser will also have many more alternatives by which to advertise. However, this will not stop at traditional media as we know them today. Already in the works are 24-hour TV music programs, home shopping, interactive cable whereby immediate viewer response can be achieved, and video text, whereby the consumer can see his daily newspaper or favorite magazine on one of the cable outlets. In addition, prerecorded disks and tapes will be available, which will allow an advertiser to selectively place not only his message, but entire shows that will not only have entertainment value but also carry commercial selling appeal.

This subject is very complicated and important and cannot be covered in great depth here. However, the major advertising agencies such as Benton & Bowles and Ted Bates have issued detailed papers on cable, and anyone interested in this subject should contact them for the data.

This wiring of America will create great turmoil in the communications media —many will rush to fill the gaps, and mistakes will be made. However, there is no doubt that cable technology will lead the communications industry in the next decades.

Role of the Client in an Agency

To maintain the most effective relationship, and usually to develop the most effective advertising, a client and the advertising agency should operate as partners. Many times there are problems between agencies and clients and account shifts occur, and usually there are valid reasons for these moves. However, these client/agency relationship problems can be minimized and ineffective advertising can be avoided if both the client and the agency keep one thing in mind. They are both there to effectively sell a product or service, and the product or service should be the master they *both* serve. If this is kept in mind, self-centered, ego-oriented mistakes and problems can be avoided.

In this relationship, both the agency and the client have some very distinctive roles to play. The client must provide the agency with proper business direction, business goals, and objectives for the advertising. The agency must define and recommend all the elements of the advertising program and participate in the marketing to the extent the client desires. This process is a two-way street, and the client and the agency must cooperate fully. Ultimately, however, it is the client's responsibility to make the decision and approve the advertising, then stick to that decision and support the agency and the advertising. It is the agency's duty to provide the client with objective business input and evaluation, recommend the most effective and efficient creative and media programs, and, where possible, back those programs up with research and document the results. Ultimately, it is the advertising product and its sales effectiveness which make an advertising agency great and the client happy and successful. Many times research is not available to make these decisions; then it is up to the agency to provide the client with its best creative and marketing judgment and stand by those decisions.

It is not easy to be a smart, aggressive, and effective client. Many times a client has a great deal more input and leverage over the eventual effectiveness of advertising than it realizes. The role is more than a simple approval process. The client along with the agency makes critical decisions and contributions to an advertising program every step of the way. Again, as stated earlier, probably the most important area for solid client input is in the development of creative objectives and strategies. The goals and standards should give the agency direction but not restrict its creativity. If the agency and the client are functioning properly as a team, disagreements and controversy should be minimum. The key is honest and direct communication, a system of feedback, evaluation, and, when appropriate, rewards.

Selection and Evaluation of Advertising Agencies

Changing or hiring an advertising agency is a very big and important decision. The decision not only affects companies' relationships and people but also very directly affects the bottom line of a company. Advertising dollars are direct bottom-line expenses and should be viewed by all levels of management as a major business expense. Therefore, selecting the agency that is responsible for the placement of these advertising dollars should be viewed as a major business decision. This, combined with the fact that advertising for many companies determines their total public or corporate image, makes the advertising-agency decision all the more critical. Also, where change in an advertising agency is involved, the movement of an account can have a very grave impact on the health of that agency and the people who work for it. Therefore, realizing the magnitude and importance of the decision, when it comes down to changing agencies, the simplest and most basic rule is: *Do not change agencies unless it is absolutely essential to do so.* Many times the disruption in both the company's operations and individual brand or product activities is very great, and an agency change should not be taken lightly.

Also, even after an exhaustive and thorough selection process, the new agency that is selected sometimes turns out to be no better than the agency that was just released. There is a risk, and management must realize this before moves are made.

How to Avoid Agency Changes

Before reviewing how to select an agency, it would be helpful to briefly discuss some steps that could be taken to minimize the need to change. Very simply, the key to maintaining a solid client–agency relationship is to have a constant, honest, and open system of communication and evaluation. There are no basic formats for these evaluations; each company and agency must adapt them to the operations of its own individual organization. However, it is recommended that they be conducted formally twice a year and that the top management of both the client and the agency be involved in these evaluations.

The Four A's, ANA, and American Marketing Association have evaluation forms that can be used, but it is important here to review the basic purpose of these evaluations. They are (1) to inform the agency of the objectives of the efforts and their performance expectations at all levels; (2) to have a clear understanding of the method and criteria of evaluation that will be used; (3) to provide feedback on the performance of the agency in general and its specific personnel against the objectives; (4) to provide for an early-warning system to correct problems before they turn into major, terminal disagreements; and (5) to provide a forum for the advertising agency to let the client know whether there are any weak spots or areas that should be fixed within the client organization.

However, no matter how formal and thorough an evaluation system is used it is quite possible that agency changes result. In fact, it is inevitable in case of incompatibility of the company, consistently poor performance on the part of the agency, changes in management, changes in client needs, and the like. Again, however, if agency changes do have to be made, the magnitude and impact of that decision must be fully comprehended, and the proper amount of time and effort must be devoted to making the selection of the new agency as thorough and positive as possible.

How to Select an Advertising Agency

As with evaluations, the exact selection process will vary from company to company and will, in some part, depend on the clients' needs, sophistication of marketing personnel, and availability of time. The following is the basic approach recommended; it can be adapted to individual needs:

▪ *Define your needs very specifically.* A very specific and definitive list of criteria should be developed, and you should outline all the agency's requirements and expectations. This list should be as long or as detailed as possible and must be agreed to by all parties involved before selection begins. One may wish to share these criteria with the agency and have it address them in future presentations. Figure 6-14 shows a sample list of criteria.

▪ *Determine the type of agency required.* A client seeking an agency must have a very clear indication of its own organization's philosophy and point of view re-

Figure 6-14. Sample agency selection criteria for a packaged-goods manufacturing company.

Outstanding creative product in *all* media (strategically and executionally).

Stability of top management, a steady record of growth and financial stability, and a history of longevity and growth with its clients.

A management and operational style compatible with the company's.

Sensitivity to the needs of franchise dealers for actual agency contact, as well as the company's operational needs.

Strong general marketing capabilities, particularly in strategic thinking and long-term planning.

Heavy packaged-goods experience with a particular expertise on supermarket marketing.

Deep involvement of senior management in the company's business, with an ability to provide counsel beyond individual-brand assignment.

Strong day-to-day account management that can work closely with a lean brand management group to provide leadership in some areas and be available as a general backup for brand groups.

Very strong media department with a particular expertise and strength in broadcast and print.

In-depth research capabilities and a capacity to provide counseling, guidance, and interpretation in all aspects of marketing and product research.

Good sense of budget control and a willingness to work on a fee basis, if required.

A strong New York presence.

garding marketing and advertising. It is important that the agency selected have similar philosophies and points of view or the relationship may not be a lasting one.

■ *Search available information to determine preliminary agency list.* After criteria and qualifications have been established, secondary resources can be screened to develop a preliminary list of agency candidates. This is available through the American Association of National Advertisers (ANA), the American Marketing Association (AMA), American Association of Advertising Agencies (Four A's), and also such publications as *Advertising Age* and a new service called Advertising Agency Register. By screening factual data, client lists, billing, size, and so on, a preliminary list of agencies can be established.

■ *Determine the exact selection process that will be carried out.* This should include deadlines by which decisions must be made, estimates of the time that will be required at all levels of company management, budgets for the search, the exact process the agency will have to go through, and the guidelines that management will use to select the agency.

■ *Set up policy for future operations.* Once the agency has been selected, the policies and principles that will govern the relationship with the agency must be spelled out to the agency, and a continuing system of review and feedback must be put into place.

With this broad process in mind, here is a recommended "ideal" selection process:

■ Set criteria and objectives and determine the basic kind of agency that will be required.

■ Screen secondary resources on the basis of the criteria that have been set. Secondary resources should be screened to turn up no more than 15 preliminary choices.

■ Narrow the selection to eight to ten. This can be done using the agencies' annual reports, preliminary reference checks, reviews of their work, and so on.

■ Forward a questionnaire to each agency and request that a reel or portfolio of creative work be sent back with the questionnaire. Also include some questions about written case histories and success stories. Again, each questionnaire must be tailored to the needs and criteria that have been outlined by the client. Many excellent questionnaires are available from the sources listed above.

■ Select five preliminary finalists on the basis of the review of the questionnaire material.

■ Have a preliminary meeting with the top management of each of the five agencies.

■ Narrow the selection to three on the basis of these initial meetings and ask that speculative assignments be addressed by each finalist. These need not be creative assignments, and they can focus on marketing, media promotion, or both. However, it is important that the agency be provided with adequate input to complete the assignments, a reasonable timetable, and fair compensation for its out-of-pocket costs.

■ Evaluate the agencies on the basis of the way they approached the assignment, as well as the quality of their work. It must be underlined here that the basic evaluation criteria may not necessarily apply only to a specific idea or a specific media plan proposal. Selection should be based on the quality of thinking that went into the work and the quality of the people who have done the work. Many times agencies are awarded business even though they do not present a firm proposal of winning creative approach.

- Make the final selection and set up policies for the relationship.

Sometimes companies have such very specific and tight criteria on agency selection that it might not be necessary to go through all these steps, and perhaps even speculative presentations might not be called for. The selection process put forth here is not meant to be the only one. The process used must be tailored to the needs of the advertiser and the amount of time that is available to spend on actual selection.

Very often client–agency relationships are expressed in marital terms. With that in mind, here are a few summary guidelines.

- Realize that sometimes divorce is more expensive than marriage, and that sometimes your new mate is no better than your first. It costs money to change agencies, and you have to be prepared for a loss in momentum. Also, even after the most elaborate screening process, there is still a risk that you won't find a better solution. If you just change for the sake of it, you avoid defining the real problem, which could be in your own organization.

- Before you marry anyone else, meet the parents before you meet the girl. Meet the management and ownership of the agency. Spend time with them and discuss their business objectives and philosophy, as well as their operational point of view. As in any organization, the direction in an agency comes from the top.

- After you meet the girl, resist instant infatuations. Don't get instantly attached to one person or to one great campaign. First impressions are not always lasting impressions.

- Spend as much time with your prospective bride as possible. Have the agency work on a speculative assignment on your business, but make sure you pay the agency for it.

- Get married, but negotiate a marital contract. Don't automatically assume it has to be a 15 percent commission arrangement. Try to negotiate a financial package that will return a fair, but not exorbitant, profit to the agency, and that will allow you to receive the depth of attention and service you require. This might mean a fee lower or higher than the normal 15 percent commission.

- Go away for a second honeymoon every three months. Have constant ongoing evaluations with your agency to spot problems before they arise.

□ *Hank Wasiak*

Marketing Public Relations

What has been known by communications specialists for some time as product publicity has evolved today into a sophisticated discipline called "marketing public relations." While publicity is still one step in the process, public relations applied in a marketing context can make a total marketing effort more effective. What makes PR attractive to marketing professionals is its ability to maximize consumer awareness, achieve greater credibility, and provide cost efficiency.

Marketing public relations has emerged in the past decade to become one of the fastest-growing segments·in the public relations field today. Its rising growth and stature are due in large part to its ability to enhance and extend advertising and other marketing efforts for products, services, and organizations.

PR specialists and savvy marketers find similarities in developing and implementing consumer advertising and marketing PR campaigns. However, they also recognize that marketing PR serves a distinct and unique function that cannot be accomplished or duplicated with traditional advertising and promotion strategies.

In its evolution from simple product publicity, marketing public relations steps far beyond simply distributing news releases or holding press conferences. It does this by adopting several basic principles that make it similar to advertising in its approach.

Similarities to Advertising

Because it seeks to create customers for a product, service, or company, just as advertising does, marketing PR supports the sales function most effectively when it (1) is based on sound research; (2) has clearly defined, measurable objectives; and (3) is aimed at specific target audiences.

Evaluation of the results is no less important to a marketing PR plan than it is to an advertising campaign. But measuring PR's direct impact on sales can be more elusive. It is difficult to single out the results that PR achieves when it works in concert with several other marketing tools. Also, measuring PR's impact through pre- and post-attitude studies is usually too expensive.

In spite of these limitations, marketing PR does create greater visibility and sharper image in contrast to the competition, just as advertising seeks to do. This is most often measured in terms of publicity results generated by the media. Admittedly, this is not the most sophisticated approach to measuring PR's impact, but it is less costly and can be singly applied to PR even while other marketing tools may be working at the same time.

Since research and evaluation have become important elements in marketing PR's design and function, another significant similarity to advertising is gaining recognition: PR's effectiveness in achieving long-term benefits and continued exposure. Whereas traditional publicity is often employed in a "one-shot" approach to introducing new products or promoting established ones, marketing PR is a sustaining function that builds over the years to meet marketing objectives indicated by research or determined by the client.

Differences from Advertising

Beyond the similarities to advertising, marketing PR is a unique self-supporting function. It has its own communication tools and techniques not found in advertising and other promotion activities, such as media tours, press conferences, media events, news releases, feature stories, photo features, broadcast public-service announcements, feature films, editorial deskside briefings, and press kits.

Aside from these specialized tools, what distinguishes marketing PR most is its ability to build credibility, exposure, and newsworthiness by orchestrating any one or all of these tools to gain media coverage. Unlike paid advertising and promotional materials that are bought and controlled, a successfully placed news release or a well-covered media event that appears on a TV news program is not "paid for" or "controlled" in the traditional marketing sense—nor is it a form of "free advertising."

Although a marketing PR effort may be carefully planned by PR practitioners, the editor or broadcaster has the final say about what is said or not said about a particular product, service, or company. This lack of control over what gets printed or broadcast is a risk factor not associated with advertising. This requires the PR specialist not only to know what can *and* cannot be accomplished, but also to communicate this to the client and the advertising agency.

The more newsworthy or interesting a PR-generated plan, the better the chances of gaining media support and exposure. In advertising, the client and the agency decide what is interesting and how much exposure the message should receive in which media. With marketing PR, editors and broadcasters make those decisions on the basis of information the PR practitioner supplies. This requires the public relations person to "think like an editor" and scrutinize all materials and activities with a journalistic sense. And this is a crucial factor to incorporate into the initial PR planning process in order to gain the most effective media support during implementation.

Information published by a newspaper or magazine editor, or reported by a broadcast commentator, results in a degree of credibility with consumers that is not accomplished through advertising alone. While both public relations and advertising seek to inform and influence consumers, advertising's vested interests are obvious. In contrast, PR employs a subtle approach and builds credibility with consumers by generating third-party endorsement through editors and broadcasters. The effect is that consumers perceive information in magazines, newspapers, television, and radio as being reported by "impartial" editors and broadcasters. Through an effective marketing PR plan, these opinion leaders create a snowball effect through convincing word-of-mouth exposure. This kind of media exposure helps create positive consumer attitudes toward a product, service, or company, and is the marketing PR expert's greatest challenge and reward.

Whatever techniques (media tours, feature stories, TV film clips, and so on) the PR practitioner employs in a marketing PR plan, they should convey a public-service value that demonstrates some inherent benefit to the consumer and/or community to gain media support. "Hype" or commercialism in place of news or human-interest value creates a negative impression with the media and jeopardizes their support.

Whereas the purpose of advertising is to sell with obvious intent, PR's role in a marketing plan is a unique soft sell that is persuasive and effective in generating sales and influencing consumer attitudes. In avoiding advertising's direct approach, marketing PR achieves visibility that is natural and subtle with consumers. Through third-party endorsement, it positions a product or service to demonstrate a benefit to potential customers at the same time that it helps establish favorable attitudes. This positioning enhances not only a product's credibility, but a company's too.

As a working partner with advertising, marketing PR bridges the credibility gap and generates greater exposure in several ways. It complements advertising to introduce new products to a large audience in an exciting and memorable way. PR builds credibility with potential customers through third-party endorsements that illuminate key advertising copy points through in-depth editorial coverage. It generates trade support for a product that is beginning to build distribution or for which the company is trying to maintain distribution. Along with advertising, PR can focus on a regional or test market or one segment of a broad audience. It offers immediacy in implementation and early feedback, which can help refine marketing strategy, especially for new products in test markets. Often the PR person is the first to hear, through reports from media contacts, if a product benefit is misunderstood by consumers. And PR does all this at a very favorable cost, as will be explained later.

This is not to suggest that marketing PR should replace any or all of the other marketing tools that are traditional companions of advertising. What it does advocate is taking advantage of the beneficial synergism that results when advertising and public relations work together. This opportunity should not be overlooked by marketing specialists. Marketing PR adds a new and vital dimension, and is most effective when integrated into a marketing plan along with advertising aimed at the same predetermined objectives and target audiences.

While marketing PR can be used to promote a service or a company, it is most often employed to promote products, especially new ones. A new product has an inherent "newsworthiness," which by itself creates interest with the media. Publicity that is published or broadcast about a new product extends the reach to key audiences who are also important to advertising and promotion efforts. Marketing PR succeeds in creating greater impact, visibility, and credibility for the product.

But marketing PR is not limited to promoting new products. It can also generate fresh consumer enthusiasm and understanding for established products. It gives consumers a reason to buy one product rather than others even where performance and price differences may not be competitive factors.

Cost-efficiency is another good reason to employ marketing PR for mature as well as new products. Marketing PR is an excellent use of incremental dollars once the base advertising level is reached. Whereas an increase of several hundred thousand dollars will only marginally improve frequency and reach in an advertising budget, this same dollar amount, put into an effective public relations program, can greatly increase both frequency and reach. Also, PR can support "secondary" products that might not warrant significant advertising budgets, and can expand reach to peripheral audiences that might not be economically reached through advertising.

Case Example

One example of how marketing PR makes a compatible working partner with advertising is a program created by Grey Advertising for Kikkoman in 1980 and 1981. Since 1975, Kikkoman has grown from third to first place as the soy sauce brand leader in the United States. This was achieved by positioning Kikkoman Soy Sauce as an all-purpose recipe ingredient, not limited to Oriental cooking.

While this strategy gained success with consumers on the East and West Coasts, where creative attitudes about food prevail, the company experienced resistance in the Midwest. This was attributed to more conservative attitudes on food preparation and three factors uncovered by Grey's market research: (1) association with Oriental cooking only, (2) lack of recipes calling for soy sauce, and (3) ignorance of how to use soy sauce as an all-purpose ingredient.

To overcome these obstacles in the Midwest, Grey developed a PR plan designed to achieve the same objectives assigned to advertising: (1) increase consumer awareness of Kikkoman brand name and (2) increase consumer understanding of product benefits not limited to Oriental cuisine. To accomplish this, Grey designed a PR program that used a Kikkoman spokesperson to increase brand awareness and encourage product usage by demonstrating non-Oriental recipes. A major market media tour became the primary platform and communication vehicle to generate consumer awareness of Kikkoman Soy Sauce all-purpose uses.

The media tour featured Kikkoman's TV-commercial spokesman Merle Ellis, who is nationally recognized as "The Butcher" through his newspaper column and syndicated television program. Having gained wide appeal and credibility as a food expert, The Butcher's endorsement of Kikkoman Soy Sauce enhanced both the advertising and public relations campaign thrusts. Through appearances on local television and radio programs and interviews with food-page editors, Ellis gained high visibility for Kikkoman Soy Sauce as an all-purpose recipe ingredient not limited to Oriental cooking.

The media tour proved to be a very effective marketing-support public relations venture for Kikkoman in 1980. Working with a "Cross Country Cookin'" theme, The Butcher appeared on television talk shows in 12 Midwest markets and demonstrated recipes native to American regions, using Kikkoman Soy Sauce. These recipes were further highlighted in feature articles by newspaper food editors gleaned from interviews with Ellis, who emphasized soy sauce's versatility in non-Oriental recipes. That first year, the media tour generated 2.3 million gross impressions.

On the basis of this success, in 1981 Grey continued with the media tour concept, kept the same marketing objectives, but introduced a timely and newsworthy theme: "More for Your Money." Using economy-oriented information and recipes and The Butcher's expertise to help consumers save money at the meat counter again made the media receptive to interviews with Ellis.

In 1981, the tour was expanded into 16 Midwest markets and included an interview on a nationally syndicated television program that reached an additional 100 markets across the country. In all interviews, The Butcher positioned Kikkoman Soy Sauce as an all-purpose recipe ingredient that makes recipes using less expensive cuts of meat taste delicious. The second media tour gained greater visibility for Kikkoman Soy Sauce by more than doubling total gross impressions to 4.9 million (target audience impressions for adults 18–49 only).

The Kikkoman story vividly demonstrates how public relations in a marketing context makes an excellent partner with advertising in achieving the same objectives. It is a cost-efficient approach to gaining and increasing exposure to and impact on important target audiences. It generates favorable third-party endorsement, which in turn builds credibility. And, as the Kikkoman program shows, it can be tailored to overcome obstacles to influencing specific "problem" audiences. Working along with advertising, public relations builds a momentum in creating long-term benefits for products and companies alike. As this realization spreads, marketing public relations has a very bright future indeed.

□ *Carol Crawford*

Sales Promotion

For the purposes of this discussion, sales promotion consists of a wide range of supporting sales activities that supplement personal selling and advertising. It fills the gaps in marketing campaigns. It is a kind of follow-through process that picks up many loose ends and helps tie the components into a tight fabric.

The major concerns of sales promotion are dealer assistance and direct consumer stimulation. Sales-promotion activities also extend into the manufacturer's marketing department, complementing the training, equipping, and motivating of company salesmen and "merchandising the advertising."

Dealer Promotion

To an increasing degree, manufacturers have attempted to promote their products by building up their own brands, reputations, and followings. Mass production makes necessary mass distribution, and to this end increasingly large budgets are set aside for advertising and product identification.

The result has been to make the retailer more and more dependent on the manufacturer. This builds up the manufacturer's position in the market, but at the same time it increases retailers' demands for service. The retailer expects the products to move off the floor with minimum effort. Increasingly, store traffic and sales have become the manufacturer's responsibility. Should an item not move satisfactorily, the dealer is sure to blame the manufacturer, because it is his product and his image which seem to be deficient. Branded and heavily promoted lines cannot easily release themselves from this responsibility. The result has been a continuous proliferation of manufacturer-sponsored dealer services.

Self-service and sales promotion.   For various reasons, personal-service selling has been declining. It has become inordinately expensive as salaries have risen. Any technique that would minimize individual solicitation and yet consummate sales would be to the advantage of manufacturer and retailer alike. Intensive brand development by manufacturer advertising presells consumers and decreases the need for personal contact. At the same time, new generations of consumers have become accustomed to self-service purchasing. The present generation of consumers accepts and often prefers this mode of shopping, especially when the price reflects the cut in service.

Where once it was thought that minimum-service distribution was acceptable only for low-priced, repetitively purchased items, it is now recognized that this method is also acceptable for higher-priced products such as clothing and major appliances. With even larger items, such as automobiles and tract houses, personal selling has been minimized and often is limited to negotiating the price and taking the order.

Impulse buying has been growing in importance. Studies have indicated that more than two out of three shoppers make up their minds in the store. If this trend is considered together with diminishing personal contact at the retail level, the need for manufacturer-oriented promotional impact at the point of sale becomes obvious. It becomes the manufacturer's concern not only to lead prospects to the retailer but also to help him complete the sale, and in order to do so, a host of promotional tactics have been developed: cooperative advertising programs, point-of-sale display, and a variety of more specialized traffic-building devices.

Cooperative advertising. Whereas manufacturer advertising tends to educate the consumer regarding a product, dealer advertising tends to lead the customer to the store where the item can be purchased. In this sense dealer advertising fills a promotional gap. Not the least important advantage of such a program is that it activates particular dealer interest in the line.

Cooperative advertising arrangements vary, but almost all of them call for the manufacturer to compensate the dealer partially or fully for his promotional efforts in the manufacturer's behalf. The typical contract reimburses the retailer for advertising the manufacturer's product, up to an agreed-upon percent of dealer purchases. At the low end, manufacturers will allow a credit of 2 to 3 percent of purchases. This may range as high as 10 percent when products carry a wide profit margin or when the manufacturer wishes to introduce a new kind of product.

Additional benefits may accrue to the manufacturer from such a program because retailers are able to buy local advertising at significantly lower prices than the manufacturer can. This differential may be as much as 50 percent. Unfortunately, retail billing processes often leave much to be desired, and the anticipated savings may never be realized. Nevertheless, the manufacturer's product receives vital support at the point of sale. This must be achieved in one way or another.

Point-of-sale display. Once traffic has been generated by advertising, it is important to attract attention and to activate the selling process. In-store display is the tool used for this purpose. Competition is intense, and the battle for display opportunities is fierce. The dealer's problems must be studied carefully. His interests are vital. Consequently, displays must be designed that will fit the needs of the dealer. The physical aspects of display are best left to professionals.

How effective are displays? The answer is astonishing to the uninitiated. Increases in sales of 300 to 500 percent are common, and increases in volume of 500 to 1,000 percent are not unusual. A serious concern of the manufacturer is the extent to which residual sales effect can be expected from his display. He would like to know how many people will continue buying after the display is gone and for how long, and what this will mean in terms of extra income. Such analysis is important, because it is usually necessary to compensate the retailer in order to be permitted to install a display. Obviously, if this cost is not more than compensated for by increased volume, it is not worth the effort.

To gain an objective picture of the value of displays, they may be pretested. Field studies can be set up that will measure display impact fairly accurately. It is customary to select a number of test stores and to measure sales in those which have received the display against those in which there has been no change. Careful sales records are kept for a period prior to the installation of any displays, then during the actual display period, and then after the displays are removed, to measure the residual effect. The test scores may be rotated and the studies performed again. Many variations are possible. This procedure is far superior to guesses based upon experience.

Traffic-building devices.   Dealer advertising is a potent traffic builder, and many other successful devices have been developed, such as fashion shows, unusual demonstrations, and special exhibits. Demonstrators are effective traffic builders. Special services—beauty clinics, product-repair services, and instruction programs, for example—are successful. The range of promotion ideas is limited only by the creativity of the marketing person.

Consumer Promotion

The intensive efforts of consumer-products manufacturers to presell the consumer have led to the refinement of direct consumer promotion techniques. Such consumer promotions use sampling, premiums, consumer contests, and other more specialized devices.

Sampling.   The more expensive the product, the more important is sampling. Whereas the consumer may be induced to buy an inexpensive item without pretesting, it is unlikely that he will buy a higher-priced item without prior trial. There is a tendency to think of sampling as something applicable only to the marketing of inexpensive, repetitively purchased products, but that is not the case. People do not usually purchase a radio or a suit or an automobile without at least trying out a sample of the product. They listen to the radio, try on the suit, test-drive the automobile preparatory to making up their minds.

In marketing industrial products, sampling is extremely important. Raw materials are pretested before substantial commitments are made. Office machines are often left with potential customers for extensive periods of time. Machinery is carefully studied under actual operating conditions and then purchased on a guarantee of satisfaction.

Consumer sampling techniques have been carefully refined and have undergone rapid growth. Couponing, through mail and printed media, has mushroomed to gigantic proportions. Many problems have arisen from the abuse of coupons, but their sales impact is so great that they are bound to become even more important.

Related tactics include in-store coupons, refund offers, discount sales, and bonus packs; these are commonly tied in with trade deals in which the manufacturer offers special values to the dealer if he will cooperate in extra display or other promotion tactics designed to implement the sampling program.

Premiums.   A premium is something extra offered to induce a prospect to buy. For many consumers the additional value makes the all-important difference in the purchase decision. When this offer can be made at little or no cost to the manufacturer and at the same time give significant benefit to the purchaser, the promotion tactic may have great value.

Of greatest interest is the self-liquidating premium, which makes it possible to achieve this dual objective. With these premiums the consumer is offered a good value at a price that seems very low to him but is high enough to cover the distributor's expenses. Consumers have responded by the millions to successful premium promotions.

Industrial products have successfully used the premium tactic in promotion. In situations where items are used by employees, suitable premiums can help generate considerate extra volume. For example, office workers look favorably on premiums tied in to the use of supplies. Working men like to accumulate premium coupons that come with products they use—hardware, for example—and thus build up strong preferences for those particular brands. Women are notorious coupon savers. Children, on the other hand, respond best to immediately available premiums.

Services also may be promoted by using premiums. Banks and personal-finance firms have found premiums to be attractive business builders.

Contests. People like to compete, especially when it does not seem to cost them anything. Contests sponsored by manufacturers offer them such an opportunity. Entry usually seems free, because the contestant need only submit as proof of purchase the wrapper that he would normally throw away. In many instances the contestant need not even purchase the product.

Contests are of special value to the manufacturer because they tend to force contestants to think favorably about his products. The contest often requires the respondent to say or do something favorable about the manufacturer's product. Even in the "sweepstakes" contest, in which the entrant need only enter his name and address, he is bound to develop interest in the manufacturer's product. The impact is almost assuredly far stronger than the transitory attention received by advertising in the usual media.

There are problems in contest operation, however. No one likes to lose. Every entrant secretly hopes to win, and there is disappointment in failing to win. Abuse from disgruntled losers is not uncommon, and even the honesty of the manufacturer may be impugned. Despite these drawbacks, contests are effective for promoting many kinds of products or services.

Contests are also very effective for motivating sales personnel and dealers. The classic device for generating excitement among manufacturer or dealer salespeople is to run a contest. It pulls salespeople out of the doldrums and gives management a platform from which to create new excitement. The contest may be used to focus on any one or a combination of problems: it may be designed to open up new accounts, to sell a slow-moving line, to fight off competition, or simply to expand sales. It can be tailored exactly to fit a specialized marketing problem at a particular time. In many firms the staff looks forward to contests. This is especially true when salespeople's families are informed of the program and invited to help in selecting prizes.

Internal Sales Promotion

In addition to developing internal motivational programs such as sales contests, promotion work encompasses such projects as preparing salespeople's manuals, advertising portfolios, catalogs, house organs, brochures, and other direct advertising material. Some of this work may be done by the advertising agency, but much of it is considered an internal house activity. The range of such services will naturally be tailored to the needs and marketing program of the individual firm. □ *Alfred Gross*

SALES MANAGEMENT

Sales management is concerned with the development of the people who are responsible for selling and servicing the company's products or services, or both, in such a manner as to produce steadily increasing sales and profits. Good sales management can make people of ordinary ability achieve extraordinary performance—and do so willingly.

Organization and Objectives

Sales management is at the middle-management level. The sales manager reports to a higher executive (the president in a smaller company; the vice president of marketing in a larger one). The general sales manager, in turn, may have reporting to him or her one or two lower echelons of sales management (regional or area sales managers and district sales managers). Finally, there is the sales force itself, or dealers or distributors. In addition, sales management is often accountable for the efficient operation of sales offices, both at headquarters and in the field, and in some companies the branch warehouse also falls under sales management control. In each case, the manager has the right to know—indeed, must know—from his superior exactly what is expected of him. These expectations, clearly stated and reduced to writing, become the objectives around which the sales manager plans his work. Only when he knows what is expected of him and accepts the full responsibility within his area of authority is it possible for him to function effectively. As middle manager he must then assign some part of each of his objectives to those under him, making sure that they accept and understand the assignment and carry it out.

Sales management's primary concern is the development of people. The first step is to determine personnel needs. With his objectives before him, the manager should know what staff he must have to achieve them. The second step is to determine present strengths and weaknesses of the staff and the gaps in personnel. Present sales personnel should be classified as (1) capable of development and therefore to be retained and developed; (2) not capable of development, in which case they should be marked for replacement; (3) long-term employees who cannot exceed their present level of performance, which is adequate (thus, they are not capable of development, but do not deserve to be terminated: most companies cannot afford to have many sales personnel in this category). Now the sales manager knows what additional manpower must be secured, and he can set about achieving this goal. Inherent in this operation is the development of job descriptions for all jobs under his jurisdiction.

Cost Control

The sales management function requires the expenditure of considerable sums of money: for compensation, for employee expenses, for office expenses, possibly for warehouse operations, and for special expenses incurred by contests, customer entertainment, and the like. Top management may allocate funds to the sales manager for these purposes or may ask the manager to prepare a request based upon his own estimates. In either case he must know how much money he has at his disposal, and it is his responsibility to see that he and his people operate within the amount allowed.

Planning

Planning revolves around the achievement of the objectives that the manager has received and accepted from his immediate superior. It is his responsibility to develop a plan of action, the net result of which is the attainment of the agreed-upon objectives. The plan covers the responsibilities that he will perform personally and other responsibilities that he will delegate to those under him. For instance, the general sales manager may delegate responsibility for a specific volume of business to each of his regional sales managers; they in turn will delegate responsibility for a specific volume to each of their district sales managers, who will do the same with each of their salespeople.

The sales manager may also delegate some of his responsibilities to his office manager and to his warehouse manager. In any case, the sales manager is responsible to his superiors for the attainment of the objectives; he cannot place blame for failure on his subordinates. The sales manager's chief job is to help all those to whom he has delegated responsibility achieve their commitments and to help them get their subordinates to fulfill their commitments in turn. How he carries out this function is his own choice, but do it he must. It will be done largely through work in the field and, to some extent, by means of conferences with each key person under him. This, then, is the plan of action: delegate responsibility to key people and work with them to help them achieve the objectives on which they and the sales manager have agreed.

Carrying Out the Plan

Involved in carrying out plans are several key matters that must be understood. First, it is impossible to help a person unless the kind of help he requires is known. Second, the only way to know with certainty what help a person requires is to observe him in the actual performance of his job. Observation cannot be replaced with paper reports, figures, oral explanations, or even written explanations. The manager must see his subordinate perform in order to know his strengths and weaknesses and to be clear as to the areas where his subordinate needs help. Third, the manager must plan his time so that he is able to do the development job that is the key to his successful performance. He must beware of allowing desk work to overwhelm him and thus "excuse" him from necessary work in the field. The sales manager, whatever his rank, should spend most of his time in the field with those under his immediate supervision and with certain very important accounts, together with the salesmen responsible for those accounts.

The key word in pressing forward to effective results is "continuity." Each field contact must be related to the one that preceded it and the one that will follow it, and all of them should be related to the attainment of the objectives. Contacts with personnel under the sales manager's supervision should be carefully planned in advance through correspondence or long-distance telephone calls and should be planned with the person to be contacted. The sales manager's subordinates should feel that they are being helped, not policed, and should be aided in so concrete a manner that they welcome his coming. The manager should work to develop a team spirit; it will appear when the subordinate discusses his affairs as "our territory (or district)" and "our problem" rather than "my territory" and "my problem." When the subordinate feels that he and his manager are working together toward the attainment of common objectives, the management job is being well done.

Appraisal and Counseling

Every employee would be less apprehensive and more comfortable in his job if he knew how his superior felt about his performance; and every supervisor has the responsibility to know how each person under him is doing. Intuitively, every manager is continually appraising those under him; it is an ongoing act. Informal appraisal is valuable, provided it is done in a sound manner, without prejudice and with complete objectivity; but this is a tall order. Some time should be set aside regularly—perhaps once a week—for informal appraisal of subordinates. The appraisal should be against agreed-upon objectives, not against factors that have never been agreed upon between the manager and his subordinate. It is a good idea for the manager to set aside a period when he is to be with the subordinate for counseling him with respect to his progress or lack of it. This may be done in an informal setting—perhaps over luncheon—and occupy no more than 30 minutes. (It may, however, require a much longer period.)

It is sound practice to make a formal appraisal of each subordinate at least once a year and to require lower managers to do the same for their subordinates. Such appraisals are often set up by top management, and the forms are provided by headquarters. The results of the appraisal are frequently discussed by the manager with his own immediate superior before he reviews the results with the subordinate. The appraisal is then discussed at length with the subordinate. The success of such a counseling interview depends largely upon whether or not the subordinate recognizes that the primary purpose of the appraisal and the counseling interview is to improve his performance, not to criticize or find fault.

The end result of a successful counseling interview is agreement between the manager and his subordinate on steps to be taken to improve the subordinate's performance. Although in some cases this kind of interview also ends in some determination with regard to compensation, it is generally considered better to discuss compensation at another time and devote this entire interview to performance.

The manager may be compared to a doctor, and the appraisal may be compared to the diagnosis, while the counseling may be compared to the discussion of the diagnosis with the patient. The appraisal is valueless unless followed by counseling. The results should never be permitted to "gather dust"; they should be used as an active tool for the development of the subordinate. One caution: Personal traits are better left unmentioned unless they affect the job performance of the subordinate or the image of the company in the area in which the subordinate operates.

Motivation

Motivation of his subordinates is one of the manager's most important responsibilities. It means that he must inspire his people to want to do better—to want to grow and develop. Where motivation is concerned, the manager must concentrate his thinking on the person and for the time being forget about sales, quotas, policies, and so on. For instance, if he learns that the subordinate feels a need for recognition within his community, the manager may be able to motivate him by having an article about him or some accomplishment of his published in a local paper. Or he may motivate a man by showing him how to plan his work better so that he is relieved of tension and pressure that have been making him irritable at home and inefficient in his work.

Motivation is achieved, first, when the manager manifests to his subordinate his complete confidence in him. The sales manager is not a policeman or a social worker but a manager, and he is not continually "breathing down the neck" of his subordinate. Second, motivation is achieved when the subordinate is given real responsibility. The assignment often involves risk on the part of the sales manager; but experience indicates that when responsibility is given to a deserving person, he or she seldom fails to come through. It is worth the risk to build good people. Third, a person is motivated when he achieves success in some area and receives the congratulations of his superior. Success breeds success, and when the manager can help those under his management to do well in some one area, they gain confidence in their ability to achieve in other areas. Fourth, a man is motivated when he receives recognition in his job and in his private life. The manager should be alert to opportunities to give recognition to those under him and to give them some feeling of importance. Fifth, motivation exists when a man feels that he is "on the team" and when his boss asks his opinion and advice on various matters or otherwise indicates that he values the subordinate's judgment. Sixth, motivation is achieved when the manager and his subordinate have agreed upon objectives so that the subordinate knows what it is he is expected to do and knows that his manager is trying to help him.

Many companies have found that sales contests are strong motivating forces. However, contests at best are never substitutes for good sales management. If used, they should be planned by specialists, and care should be taken that the objectives of the contest are compatible with the overall objectives of the development of the subordinates.

Territory Design

A territory is a collection of a number of large and small accounts with a total potential buying power of a company's products or services large enough to warrant assigning a salesman, dealer, or distributor to go after the business. "Territory" is not a geographic term: territorial coverage means account coverage, not geographic coverage.

In most organizations, approximately 20 percent of the accounts in any territory make up about 80 percent of the total potential business available; it is therefore highly important that those 20 percent are sold and developed—and, of course, that they are identified and followed by sales management. Even companies that sell to supermarkets and retail stores find it desirable for their salesmen to give more time and attention to the larger accounts. Accounts are sold chiefly by "service," which in this sense means all the acts of a company and its salesmen that indicate their concern and interest in the customer and his problems. The more important accounts are sold by giving them a degree of service superior to the service they would receive elsewhere; and in order to do this, the salesman gives somewhat less service to the smaller accounts.

Sales management, in looking at a territory, must isolate the key or important accounts and locate them on a map. They are usually found in clusters, and zones of a territory can be built around them. Territory coverage is planned around an adequate coverage of these important accounts, and the smaller accounts located around and near the larger accounts are called upon less frequently, as time and convenience permit, depending upon their relative importance. Sales management has the responsibility of setting up territories in this manner and of supervising the coverage of the territories so as to ensure that the business of the most important accounts is secured. In many instances sales management is involved with an important account through making calls with the salesman, obtaining contact with higher echelons that the salesman cannot reach, advising the salesman on strategy, and overcoming obstacles that the salesman encounters. The sales manager cannot keep his eye on every potential customer, but he must be alert to the progress being made with the accounts that compose the greater portion of the potential of a territory.

Compensation

A compensation plan must start with top management, for only top management can determine how many pennies out of every sales dollar are available for the functions that come under the jurisdiction of the sales manager. The sales manager can then deploy these funds to pay the salesmen, dealers, and distributors, the office personnel, and perhaps the warehouse people at branches. How much he pays the salespeople depends generally upon a number of factors, such as industry custom, the kind and amount of work to be performed, and the going market price for sales personnel of the kind desired.

Special situations may call for differences in treatment, as in the case of a salesman who is expected to make sales only after long effort (selling bridges, for example), while a salesman in another line may be expected to obtain several orders every day. With some few exceptions it is generally felt that the best compensation plans have some built-in incentives; that is, they offer a drawing account against commissions, or a salary and commission, or a salary and bonus, rather than a straight salary with annual review for increases. Each company must determine the plan most likely to satisfy its employees and provide a sound base for their development. Generally speaking, the best kind of compensation is the simplest and the easiest to understand. If the plan is based on too many different kinds of performance, it is likely to be confusing to salespeople and more likely to breed discontent.

Communications

Someone has said that if the job of a sales manager were to be defined by a single word, that word would be "communicator." The sales management job has been compared to that of the switchboard operator through whom important calls are passing from the top of an organization to the marketplace (salesmen, dealers, distributors, customers), and vice versa. If the line is not plugged in, someone may be talking while no one is listening. Certainly, top management cannot do its job well without a thorough knowledge of what is going on out in the field: what customers think of the product or service, price, terms, service, and delivery; what the competitive situation is; what the morale situation of the sales organization is, and how the sales force feels about company policies, compensation, and the products it must sell; what improvements should be made in products, and what new products should be developed; which products are becoming obsolete. All this kind of information must flow upward to top management through the sales management team.

It is through this same team that salesmen and dealers and distributors are given important communications from top management: compensation plans and fringe benefits are explained clearly so that they are accepted; product knowledge is given to the field; policies are explained to personnel and to customers so that the policies are clear and are accepted; the company philosophy and basic purposes are explained clearly; and the company image is presented in a favorable light to those in the market. It is the responsibility of sales management to perform this communication job continually and with great diligence; no person deserves a place on the sales management team if he or she fails to perform this function diligently.

One word perhaps needs to be said about "washing dirty linen in public." The sales manager must understand to whom to go when he is dissatisfied—certainly not to those under his supervision. The sales manager must be the champion of the company when he is in the field and the champion of his men when he is at headquarters; then he is a good communicator and an effective manager.

The Control Function

It is expected that the sales manager will be in control at all times and will see to it that the entire job is performed properly—the responsibilities that he has delegated to others as well as those he has been given. He must constantly ask himself: How is each territory going? Where are the weak spots, and what must be done to correct weak situations? Are there any weak spots in distribution? How about product mix? How about all classes of trade being sold?

The manager knows what he must control by consulting his job description, the objectives that his superior set with him, the objectives that he set up with each of his key subordinates, and the statistical material available to him. He is in control when he sees and reacts quickly to any signal that tells him a job is not being done or is not being done correctly or effectively.

The manager must set up some system that enables him to maintain control. It should be a very simple system, much like the traffic lights at an important intersection in a large city—a green light to say that all is well and everything can move forward, or a red light to say that traffic is stopped. There are many ways in which a sales manager can exercise control, but the method he works out for himself must tell him, at least once a week, where the lights are green and where they are red.

Controls need to be of two kinds: (1) controls that enable the sales manager to be sure he is performing on time all the responsibilities that he has undertaken and accepted, and (2) controls that give him the picture of the situation with respect to all responsibilities he has delegated to those under his supervision.

Sales Meetings

Almost every sales manager feels it necessary, for a variety of reasons, to bring his men together periodically. These meetings are time-consuming and costly. The men who attend are often out of production for at least a day before the meeting and a day afterward. It is therefore imperative that there be a very good reason for holding a sales meeting and that the meeting itself be well planned and its purpose clearly defined. One thing is clear: no sales meeting may be used to take the place of the field sales manager's direct work with his people out in the marketplace.

A sales meeting may encompass an entire sales organization or a large section of a sales organization, or it may be a small district sales meeting with only six or seven salespeople attending. The large sales meeting can do no more than stimulate salesmen, "pep them up," establish a good company feeling, and give salesmen an opportunity to meet people they have been reading about in house organs and/or corresponding with all through the year. Such meetings are very costly, and they seem to be on the decline. They are held no more frequently than once a year—in many companies, every five years.

Much more valuable and helpful is the smaller district or regional meeting with no more than 30 or 35 people attending, and preferably even fewer. Such meetings, carefully planned by the sales manager, are valuable for considering regional sales problems, giving product information, discussing and explaining policies, discussing dissatisfactions, and exchanging experiences and sales techniques among the people attending. The most successful meeting of this nature is one where the manager makes the salespeople feel that it is their own meeting. He chairs the meeting, keeps it rolling, involves those who are not eager to participate, quiets those who try to take over the meeting, keeps the meeting on its time schedule, moderates—and, otherwise, keeps quiet. The manager does not lecture, does not tell what to do, does not "throw his weight." No agreement should be forced; it is the discussion that is important. These meetings are informal; they are often used when sales districts or regions are so compact that salesmen can lose no more than a single day from the field in attending, although they can be employed effectively even when salespeople must fly to attend them.

Sales management is increasingly finding a selling tool of great value in carefully planned meetings of customers and prospects in important centers. Such meetings need expert help, headquarters planning, careful use of the time of those attending, and subject matter of strong interest to those attending. The ways in which they may be conducted depend upon the kind of product and how it is used and the need for providing important information to many people in a short time. The local salespeople must participate; such meetings provide excellent opportunities for them to be with their customers and prospects and to improve their relationships with them.

Distributors and Dealers

The chief job of sales management is to develop the people for whom it is responsible. This is just as important where selling is done through dealers and distributors as it is where selling uses a direct sales force. The dealer or distributor needs much more than a call from a company representative. He needs all of the same kind of help that a direct salesman requires. The fact that he may have other lines than those of the company should make no difference. Show him how to operate more effectively and efficiently, and his results will improve, with most of the benefits accruing to the company that has worked with him helpfully.

Performance Criteria for Sales Managers

The sales manager is performing his job well when he has a plan of action for himself and for each of his key people; when he knows that his plan is being carried out and that each of his people wants to carry it out; when he knows how well he is doing with regard to every task assigned to him; when he knows the next step that he and each of his key people must take to achieve their objectives; when he constantly strives to improve his own performance and that of his organization; and when his people realize that they are doing a better job because of the help he has given them. □ *Ronald Brown*

Independent Sales Representatives

Independent sales representatives, or manufacturer's representatives, are individuals or organizations that perform the selling function for a manufacturer on a commission. The use of "reps" is helpful to small businesses that cannot afford the fixed cost of a sales force and to businesses dealing in either diverse product lines or multichannel distribution of products where duplication of staff selling function is not warranted economically. Reps specialize in select markets, and the cost of sales is spread over the various product lines that they carry.

The three major challenges in managing the efforts of independent sales representatives are in their initial selection, ensuring that the proper selling efforts are being expended, and communicating updated product and marketing input.

A large housewares manufacturer recently wanted to gain distribution with the individual gourmet specialty shops. It was not feasible to use the manufacturer's national sales force, since the salespeople's time was fully occupied calling on distributors and large retail chains. The manufacturer hired independent representatives who specialized in calling on this trade. Since there was no one national rep group, several were hired on a geographic basis. This housewares manufacturer now enjoys additional distribution and sales at a cost of about 5 percent, which is the commission paid the reps.

This illustration is a good example of how independent sales representatives can be used in conjunction with a company-employed sales staff.

□ *David J. Freiman*

NATIONAL-ACCOUNT MARKETING

Most companies find that a large portion of their business comes from their largest customers. Frequently, the purchases of these valued customers are essential to the survival of the supplier firm. For this reason, they are often singled out for the special treatment that large-volume purchasers warrant.

In smaller companies these important accounts are sometimes handled by the suppliers' top executives. In others, they receive the service of the best salespeople. Often this assignment is a reward for superior sales performance.

The complexity of many of these valued customers has increased in recent years, with a trend toward more and more mergers and acquisitions. The servicing of these accounts by the regular sales force or as additional duties for top executives has become burdensome or ineffective. Not infrequently, the larger customer will request one sales- and service-oriented individual to represent all the supplier's relationships with the customer.

In response to this demand for specializing, a new kind of sales executive developed. Instead of servicing the historic geographic sales territory, his responsibility is to the whole customer corporate entity. He represents his customer to his company, as well as the reverse. He is required to operate at the interface of the two companies, seeking the best interests of both.

From this situation, the concept of national-account marketing emerges. Companies that adopt the technique identify these large customers as "national accounts."

An official definition of a national account was established by the National Account Marketing Association (NAMA) of New York City in 1973: "A national account is a customer that has substantial overall potential and that buys for, directs, or influences from a central purchasing office several units that are geographically dispersed in more than one sales territory."

This broad definition must be modified to suit the particular requirements of each supplier who becomes involved in the national-account concept.

Another general definition of a national account is: "A national account is a company with multiple locations and large volume potential, one in which a general office controls stocking of merchandise and selling of specific products by branches, and preferably one to which billing is made to a central billing point."

There are and should be many definitions of national accounts, each set up to suit particular situations of a specific company. Some variables to be considered in framing the specific definition are (1) minimum sales/profit potential of the account; (2) degree of centralization of purchasing within the customer company; (3) geographic dispersement of service required; (4) desire of the customer for national-account status; and (5) prestige acquired in supplying a "big name" account.

The definition developed for one company would involve a description of all the variables, but would not necessarily coincide with the definition another company might develop. Likewise, the definition one company may adopt one year may not be the one that is valid a few years later. Each, however, should be the best current appraisal of at least the variables mentioned.

The national-account manager's importance has increased as changes have occurred in the marketplace. Some notable changes are the decentralization of manufacturing plants, the centralization of purchasing influences, system selling, and contract purchasing.

This discussion will develop further details concerning the activities of successful national-account marketing programs. It will emphasize the role of the national-account manager and his relationships to others in his own company as well as his national account(s).*

Professional Purchasing and National Accounts

In recent years there have been major changes in the purchasing function. The net result has been the development of truly professional people in the procurement activity of most large corporations—the companies typically served by a national-account manager.

Recognition by top management of the importance of purchasing's contribution has led to the promotion of many purchasing people who are capable, well educated, and broad-gauged in their comprehension of intercompany relationships with suppliers. Information systems developed through the extensive use of data processing provide current statistics on market intelligence and inventory control to permit the buyer to arrive at professional purchasing decisions. Because of its increased importance to the corporation, the purchasing decision continues to move upward in the corporate structure.

---

* While the term "national account" is used almost universally, marketers sometimes refer to a key account, target account, special account, major account, or corporate account. These terms have very similar meanings, although some companies prefer more restrictive definitions for a key, target, major, special, or corporate account. For purposes of this chapter, we will consider the term national account to be interchangeable with the others.

These changes in customer corporate purchasing have led to the need for professional counterparts on the supply side—the national-account manager. Indeed, many national-account programs have been started because the customer demanded it to interact with his professional procurement executives.

This requires that the national-account function have the full support of its top management. If not, the customer will question the capability of the national-account function to fulfill the role of properly representing the customer's wants and needs to the supplier.

Today's professional corporate purchasing executive has the right to expect the same professionalism on the part of the national-account manager. He asks for and needs a counterpart who maintains the confidence of all supplier personnel involved in the relationship. He wants a manager who will provide few surprises, who knows the market conditions of the buyer as well as the seller, who can readily find answers to puzzling questions, and who can be at ease with lower echelons as well as top brass.

The corporate purchasing person wants a lot. He deserves it, and if the national-account manager is properly qualified, motivated, and supported, he will provide it.

There are times when the top decision maker is someone other than the top purchasing executive. If he is a buyer or a notch or two below the top person, the national-account manager must relate to him in the same easy way he would to a top executive. It is, however, the principal thrust of the national-account marketing program to relate to the decision maker, whoever that may be. More often than not it will be the top purchasing executive.

The National-Account Manager

The person who heads a national-account program must possess a variety of capabilities and characteristics. He will probably have been a successful salesman or marketing specialist. He will be equipped with a broad knowledge of the business in which he is involved. He will possess the unusual combination of enthusiasm and objectivity. He must instinctively cultivate credibility. He should be forceful yet diplomatic. He will relate properly with many levels of management. He is salesman, diplomat, and ombudsman in his relationships with the people in his national account and with the people in his own company.

If he is to accomplish the mission of managing his national account, he will develop an account plan designed to accomplish goals established with his superiors and others in the supplying company who will work with him to accomplish the plan.

His department will report to a ranking marketing or sales executive who is anxious to support the national-account manager's activities at top-management levels. Unless he has line responsibility, the people in his own company who work with him on his national account will be in a staff relationship. For this reason, he will have to achieve their cooperation through a carefully executed communication program. This will be designed to encourage the progress of the action plan and to create among the people involved a sensitivity to his national account. If the program is successful, his people will respond to their counterparts in the national account exactly as the national-account manager would respond if he were the one doing the communicating.

To succeed, the national-account manager continually sells his program to his people, primarily inside and outside salespeople working on the account, and to top management. He is all the while selling the benefits of his plan to the people of his national account.

A good portion of this activity is his role as representative of his national account to his own company—a most important diplomatic assignment. As an interpreter of customer wants, he must know not only his own business strategy but that of his customer as well.

Some say that credibility is the characteristic most important to all successful national-account managers. Credibility projection is basic to the character of some people. If credibility comes naturally to the national-account manager, he needs only to cherish and nurture it. If it is less easily discerned in a national-account manager, he must cultivate it and strengthen it so that it becomes a highly visible characteristic.

How do you accomplish this? Some experienced managers will maintain that this is impossible without the cooperation and support of the various people inside his own company whose activities interact within the supplier–customer relationship. They say the road to success comes from a strategy of strengthening the "internal sell."

Two basic aspects of credibility are reliability and responsiveness. A national-account manager can reinforce and cultivate credibility if he is responsive and reliable. If a national-account manager strengthens his internal sell, his ability to supply diverse expertise for the different needs of his customers, he will gain the reputation of being responsive. If the national-account manager, working with his counterparts at the account, brings into focus fragmented activities and knowledge, he will avoid bringing surprises to his customer and will be considered reliable.

The strategy of structuring for the internal sell must include the following:

Focus. The national-account manager must be a highly visible focal point for the customer, always available and easy to do business with. He minimizes aggravation to customers and cuts through red tape. It must be readily apparent that he has the real and perceived authority to accomplish things.

Continuity. The program must feature continuous dialog between the customer and the manager's top decision makers, with the national-account manager as the focal point. This also provides a vehicle for identifying the changing attitudes and needs of the customer.

Reinforcement. The national-account manager must validate the program proposals that result from his internal-sell strategy. There must be continuous emphasis on customer benefits in terms of increased return on investment and cash flow.

Expertise. The key to being responsive is the national-account manager's ability to supply various degrees of expertise to different levels of the customer's organization.

The strategy of emphasizing the internal sell will increase the national-account manager's responsiveness and reliability, leading to an enhancement of his credibility.

To create an atmosphere of intercompany confidence, the national-account manager will foster the development of top-level relationships between the two executive suites. This is often accomplished through "home and home" executive meetings. These are carefully planned and executed programs designed to inform the national account of the capabilities and accomplishments of the supplier company as well as to review the needs and wants of the customer. The national-account manager must also be sensitive to the need for keeping his top executives' confidence in the validity of his planned program.

The Account Plan

To many executives, the national-account plan is a very important element in any national-account relationship. Other basics play their part in the success of the function. Nevertheless, the appropriateness of the plan and the skill of its execution are the essence of the national-account concept.

In the beginning, a new national-account function goes through all the basics to develop its first account plan. Once a marketing organization has made the determination to go ahead, something needs to be done to get the program under way. Usually one follows well-documented procedures to define a national account, establish policy, agree to goals and objectives, write position descriptions, and structure and staff the department.

When all these basics have been accomplished, the national-account function is in place and ready to do something.

Ranking Accounts

A plan is needed for each specific account that will be serviced by the national-account function. It must match the needs and wants of the prospect with the capabilities and desires of the selling organization. A review of the corporate and/or division goals will establish primary markets and priority products to be considered. Market research will determine which accounts dominate or are likely to dominate particular markets. It will also indicate the types of distribution to which these accounts are accustomed and whether or not they are familiar with the national-account approach. The most important national-account prospects will be determined.

With marketing research information of this type on hand, account analysis on specific accounts is conducted. It condenses all the knowledge at hand about each of the accounts to evaluate them against each other and rank them in priority.

Once this ranking through account analysis has been established, account research is begun on the top one, two, or three prospects.

Researching the Account

The goal of account research is to enlarge on the detail and validate the information already collected about the account. It is this that will permit the identification of specific opportunities.

Field calls on the account can divulge what "fit" the seller's products and services have with the current and projected needs of the prospect. Volume and geography of the consumption of these products are overlaid on the volume and geography of the production and distribution of the products by the seller and his competition.

In some organizations, individuals seeking this information are provided with special forms to be filled out at key locations. The results are tabulated and expanded. Overall statistics are solicited. Product specification information is acquired and related to the qualitative features of the seller's products. Comparisons are made to determine compatibility between user requirements and vendor capabilities. Information on compliance of current sources is sought.

The prospect's position in his market is investigated. What is his track record?

What can be learned about the prospect's policies and people? How does he acquire each of his products? Does the corporate office develop specifications? Can local plants requisition a specific vendor's products? Does the corporate office have contracts against which the plants must (or may) buy? What are the policies, *de facto* and *de jure*, that apply to this procurement? What changes might be proposed by the vendor to the buyer to improve the effectiveness? Would the proposal of such changes provide opportunities for the seller? And benefits to the buyer?

Who are the people who determine these policies and procedures? What are their positions and relationships? How does each make his decisions?

What about competition? Who is now providing for these needs? How well do they do the job? What are the suppliers' strengths and weaknesses relative to policies, products, and people?

Identifying Opportunities

The whole purpose of researching the account is to be able to develop enough knowledge for the identification of one or more opportunities on which the account plan is to be built. The goal is established by the identified opportunity. The plan specifies how it is going to be accomplished.

The opportunity involves action on the part of the seller that will result in a favorable reaction on the part of the buyer. Just as the account plan is the heart of the national-account effort, the identification of the opportunity is the essence of the plan.

Opportunity is "a favorable juncture of circumstances, a good chance for advancement or progress." With respect to the national-account manager, his opportunity might be the benefits involving exchanges of goods and services. It is the account plan which develops the understanding of the mutual opportunity by those who will be involved.

Some national-account managers, in their search for opportunities around which to build an account plan, look for problems that are plaguing the prospect. The investigation of and proposed solution to the problem is the account manager's plan that will result in mutual benefits.

Potential profit improvement for the customer is always an attractive opportunity for the account manager. This might be a change in payment terms, or the introduction of a new product or process that cuts costs. It might involve changes in inventory concepts to improve cash flow (consignment or warehouse programs). Shipping changes to cut freight or other distribution costs are another possibility (your trucks or customer fleet). These avenues and others could provide profit improvement for the customer resulting from the national-account manager's knowledge and management of his account.

These pursuits involve the management of change. Not all take kindly to suggestions for changing the way things are done. Resistance to change is not unusual. It must be reckoned with, and the national-account manager will learn how to deal with it.

One way for the account manager to overcome this resistance to change is to single out and cultivate key customer personnel with more ambition and flexibility than most. Working with such people to introduce profit-improvement suggestions in their own goals or objectives gives them the opportunities for success and glory they are seeking. The account manager creates a hero and at the same time implements his own account plan.

Developing the Plan

Once the opportunity has been decided upon, a book of information collected by account research is published and distributed to the individuals in the selling organization who will be responsible for the execution of the plan. Included in the book will be an organization chart showing the national-account department's relationship with others, the objectives of the department, the position descriptions of the individuals who will be involved, and a national-account manual. Organization charts of the prospect and position descriptions of its key individuals will be included.

A review of the history of the prospect's business and other relationships will also be given. His usage of different products will be charted and forecast for the future. Competitive sales coverage is outlined. Information such as annual reports and other financial data is provided.

The goals of the plan are established and reviewed with the individuals who will be responsible for its execution. A step-by-step outline of what is to be done is written, the personnel involved are familiarized with these goals, and agreement on them and a schedule for their achievement are obtained.

Some method of keeping regular check on accomplishments is established. Progress is checked quarterly, monthly, or weekly. Finally, a mechanism is established to alter the plan as circumstances change. When all the foregoing has been accomplished, the execution of the account plan begins.

Developing Good Relationships

To be successful with this plan, the national-account manager must be effective in the coordination of several different relationships, each perhaps involving several different individuals. Some of these are in line relationships with the national-account manager, but more often than not the coordination must be accomplished from a staff position.

The coordination is mandatory. The national-account manager uses diplo-

macy, cajoling, persuasion, and other motivation in the pursuit of these important coordination activities. Frequently, it is his effectiveness in this area or the
lack of it that determines the success or failure of the account plan.

The foremost relationship to be coordinated is the interface of the personnel
of the national-account manager's company and the personnel of the national account involved. The account manager must make the proper moves to ensure
that all intercompany exchanges are directed at achieving the account plan's goal.
To accomplish this complicated coordination successfully, the national-account
manager must have a knowledge of all intercompany communications.

Second, but of nearly equal importance, is the coordination of people in his
own company insofar as they are involved in the execution of the plan. It means
coordinating production and engineering people, quality control, and customer
service. This is the "internal sell," and it is often this element of coordination
which proves the most difficult for the national-account manager.

It requires continued conversations, constant rededication to the goal, reevaluation of accomplishments and progress, and reinspiration by the national-account manager for all individuals.

The national-account manager must develop a relationship with the managers
concerned that permits him to go to them to enlist their aid in solving internal
problems as they arise. He and his account plan must be accepted by these managers so that when trouble occurs, he can ask for and expect support.

The success of an account plan depends on the selection of an appropriate opportunity on which to base the plan, and the skill of the national-account manager who is responsible for its accomplishments.

The National-Account Manager in Action

In developing the account plan the national-account manager must coordinate
the activities of many people in his company. In doing this, his goal is not only to
represent his company to his national account but, perhaps more important, to
represent his national account to his company. His aim is to establish with his
working counterparts at his national account a rapport, a confidence in his integrity and capability. They must be so impressed with his ability to encourage his
company to accomplish the things his customer wants that they think of him as
their ambassador or ombudsman. They want to feel secure that he is providing
them with the best mix of his company products and services that is available.
They learn to trust him not to confront them with surprises.

In many ways, his is a diplomatic role. He must know and be respected by every
individual of influence in his national account. All must feel that he is providing
the highest quality of account management expertise.

If his contacts at the account have the proper confidence in him—and they will
if he is doing his job properly—he will have supportive customer emissaries at
many levels to whom he can turn to help him solve problems when they arise.

Sometimes he has problems with his own management and salespeople (or
others in his company) that he alone can resolve. The internal sell anticipates
these problems and solves them through various communications.

Communications

Familiar communications, such as call reports, monthly statistical reports, and quarterly summaries of progress, are basics for the national-account manager who is interested in other aspects of communications as well. Some of these are communications from the vendor company to the business community, and some are internal. Some are originated by the national-account manager, and some are written or prepared by others but should be monitored to some extent by the national-account manager.

The manager should have an internal communications plan of his or her own, with specific personal goals established. It may include attendance at sales meetings, product-planning meetings, quality-control meetings, and executive-management meetings. At such meetings, emphasizing the successes of the national-account program will help reinforce its support.

The national-account manager may convene a meeting of all the people in his company who are concerned with a specific national account. They may have other duties as well. It is solely because their activities bear on their relationship with one specific national account that they are called on to attend this kind of meeting. The purpose may be to introduce a program, policy, price, or product. It may be to discuss a problem or to develop new approaches. The important point is that all of the national-account manager's people who are called on to deal with one national account are expected to attend. Typically, the national-account manager will have some regular written communication vehicle to the people involved. A meeting is called only when regular communication methods are not adequate.

The manager may publish a national-account bulletin for internal use that praises national-account supporters in line sales, production, or other areas for their participation in a successful program. He or she never overlooks an opportunity to communicate appreciation to others for the help they are giving the national-account program. Some other problems requiring the national-account manager's coordination are personality conflicts involving the national account; gaps in coverage of the national account; price, service, and quality problems; and product-line changes.

The national-account manager will make a regular yearly, quarterly, or monthly review of the relationship between the two companies. If this is done right, it will be a review of progress toward mutual goals that have been established by the national-account manager and his customer counterpart at the beginning of the period. Frequently, this will involve bringing in one or more individuals from the manager's company to inform the customer headquarters people of an unusually successful program that has been completed at an outlying plant or location.

The national-account manager's presence and personality must be such that in an interview with the lowest buyer involved, the buyer feels comfortable with the account manager (and vice versa). Moreover, the manager must be comfortable with the customer CEO, and vice versa. And he must have a low-key, yet effective, continuing program of reminding his customer contacts of the benefits that his company is providing through his intercession.

Corporate-Capabilities Presentation

A major tool with which the national-account manager must be familiar is the corporate-capabilities presentation. Basically, this is a communications bridge designed by the vendor to educate certain key customers or prospect personnel concerning benefits the vendor company is capable of providing. It is frequently used as a springboard to expand the relationship between the two companies.

Most commonly, a corporate-capabilities presentation is proposed by the national-account manager of the vendor company to enhance his or her own position. The purchaser may suggest such a presentation. It may feel it can use what the supplier offers better if its own people are more familiar with what the vendor can accomplish.

First and foremost, the purpose of the presentation should be identified and agreed to by those who will be responsible for the development and execution of the presentation. The whole program should be geared to accomplishing that purpose.

Before evaluating alternative proposals for the presentation, one should review and analyze the people who are expected to make up the customer attendance roster, from the standpoint of their knowledge of the subject and personal as well as business interests. Consideration of both the interest of those attending and the purpose of the presentation should provide guidelines for the elements of the program. It should assist in selecting the proper atmosphere, setting, content, and timing of the presentation, and it will result in a properly programmed business discussion. Frequently, to make the relationship more personal, entertainment will be included as well. A number of successful national-account managers play golf or tennis or go fishing or hunting. A lot of customers like the same entertainment.

Done with good taste and proper planning, these executive meetings can materially improve the national-account manager's stature with his account—and with his own executives as well.

Consultants

The time may come when the national-account manager wants to consider a consultant to help with something the manager or his organization does not have the time or ability to learn for itself.

The national-account manager will want to know two things: where to look for consultants and how to evaluate them before signing them up. *Branford's Directory of Marketing Research Agencies and Management Consultants in the U.S. and the World* is a possibility. The National Account Marketing Association in New York City would be able to recommend consultants. Other marketing and management associations might be helpful.

Getting the right firm for the job is more difficult than some think. There is no grading system or scorecard for consultants. The only way to find out about a consultant's ability is to ask around and work up a list of two or three that seem to get favorable comments. Don't sign up a firm without meeting the people.

In interviewing consultants, it is important that you feel comfortable with them. You have to work together and must be compatible. It pays to shop, as long as you look for something besides price. There is a shortage of good small research outfits. Obviously, the big ones would do a good job, but they are also high-priced. There are some good smaller ones, but you have to look around and seek them out.

Associations

The national-account manager will want to keep up with the latest successful trends in his specialized management sphere. To do so, he will read what is available about national accounts and attend appropriate meetings and workshops.

The national-account executive is fortunate to have one association, the National Account Marketing Association, devoted entirely to the furtherance of the exact job he or she is trying to do. The primary objective of NAMA is to provide an educational forum for national-account managers. Headquartered in New York, NAMA has other chapters in Pittsburgh, Chicago, Atlanta, Houston, and the West Coast. All these offer seminars and workshops on national accounts. The highlight of the year is the annual meeting, which provides the finest national-account educational sessions available.

A counterpart to NAMA is the National Association of Purchasing Management in New York City. There are also the American Management Associations, The Conference Board, and the Sales Executive Club, as well as industry associations. These provide in one measure or another educational programs for the national-account manager to help him do his job better.

Summary and Conclusions

Our discussion of national-account management has been concerned with the need for proper definition of national accounts, the place of national-account management in the organization structure, an appropriate account plan, and other activities of the national-account manager.

Coordination of various plans and programs has been discussed. The need for effective communications has been emphasized. The benefits of consultants and association membership have been outlined.

Finally, it must be repeated that it is a requirement of the national-account manager to ably represent to his own organization the account for which he is responsible, as well as the reverse. He also maintains the confidence of his company's field salespeople and inside people, and cultivates support from top management. How well he accomplishes these requirements will provide the ultimate measure of his success.

The bottom line, and let's not forget it, is: Does your management feel that the national-account program provides a satisfactory return on the investment your company is making to support it? There are presently several people working to develop responsible measurements of national-account contribution. So far, no measurement is completely valid. At this point, the value of the contribution made by the national-account function is ultimately founded, with some help from specific measurements, on the confidence top management has in the program.

A national-account manager's primary requirement is to keep the confidence and support of his management, his customer, and his people.

□ *Valentine B. Chamberlain III*

MANAGING SALES AND MARKETING PEOPLE

The marketing and sales organizations of a company are the teams that ultimately decide the company's destiny. It is the marketing and sales professionals who have the most direct impact on the corporate bottom line. Consequently, the analytical and creative abilities of the marketing people, together with the persuasion skills of the sales force, must be evaluated, assessed, and nurtured with insight and professionalism.

Given the competitive character of industry today and the challenges inherent in the management of human resources, it is incumbent upon companies to build and maintain happy and productive sales and marketing departments. As technology becomes increasingly sophisticated, companies must be aware that the most valuable resource in industry is still the human resource.

Recruiting

Many different resources can and should be used simultaneously in the quest for the best sales and marketing people—resources that are commonly used, but rarely in tandem. Too often a hiring executive will rely on one source of talent rather than explore several.

Yet diverse resources ultimately not only offer a more liberal choice of qualified candidates, but often provide the hiring manager with valuable feedback on a candidate from several different sources with different points of view. The best candidates are likely to surface more than once, and a good deal of information on candidates who may be *less* than desirable for the job is likely to emerge in the process as well.

As time and budget allow, sales and marketing people may be found in a combination of the following ways:

Networking

Based on the premise that "people lead to people," networking can be used to find the right people for the right jobs. The networking process involves the recommendation of qualified others who know or have done business with the reference source. The method is older than advertising, and one in which everyone likes to participate, because it is reciprocal: a recommendation offered today may well mean a responsive reply on the other end tomorrow. It is the cheapest, and perhaps the most valuable, tool for talent scouting.

Through compatible companies. Networking may be developed among peers in the same or compatible companies, as long as the other companies are not directly competitive but market and sell their products or services in a similar manner. It is not so important that salespeople or marketing experts have sold a similar product; it is crucial that they have used the same techniques in their marketing and selling experience, no matter what product they have been selling.

Through customers. The hiring manager should speak to customers and find out which sales and marketing people of other companies that they deal with are doing the best job of servicing their account. The marketing and sales areas turn over with greater frequency than, for example, R&D, and customers are in an excellent position to both spot the best people and learn quickly of a good person who, for some reason, wants or needs to make a change. People who buy are often the best judge of people who sell.

Through associations. The networking component of trade associations and professional societies provides just one more reason to belong to them; in fact, membership in these groups is largely related to their networking value. Associations and societies provide an excellent climate for keeping current on most fields—and on the people in them.

Through suppliers. Suppliers, consultants, and vendors should also be on the list of resources to tap. Public relations, marketing, and advertising agencies are invaluable resources for identifying talent, and as consultants they are more than happy to refer good sales and marketing people to their client companies. Obviously, any supplier on the company's books wants to accommodate its best customers.

Newspaper and Trade Advertisements

When advertising for a sales or marketing person who is middle-management or higher, the display section of newspapers, trade magazines, and journals should be used. If newspaper space is purchased, it is most often the Sunday issue that is consulted, not only by people who are "looking" but also by people who want to stay abreast of their industry or learn what the competition is doing.

The ad should be signed with the corporate logo and symbol. A blind box number should not be used unless the advertiser is just "going fishing" and the number of responses doesn't count. Even if a potential candidate is in the job market, he or she may be advisedly reticent about responding to blind box advertisements that just might have been placed by their current employer. And as long as a company is paying a premium price for display space, it might as well enjoy the visibility, which subliminally says, "We're doing well. We need good people." It's good public relations for the company.

When a job opening is confidential, the company has the option of holding back its signature on the ad; however, the replies will be sparser than to ads that are signed, and at this point, the company should probably choose to invest in the formal executive search process—a guarantee of confidentiality.

Employment Agencies

Agencies are a good resource when they are used as a device to recruit individuals earning approximately $30,000 and less. The company pays an agency fee for a placement only if one of the agency's candidates is actually hired, so companies needn't be too circumspect in eliciting their help. If the assignment is canceled or postponed, the company has not incurred any expense.

Like any other vendor or supplier, an employment agency should be scrutinized before its services are sought. The hiring manager should see and get to know the employment agency and the counselor who will be servicing the account. A relationship that is nurtured and developed will reap the best dividends.

A job order should not be placed with many agencies but limited to one or two. Like any vendor, an agency is most valuable to a valued client. It will offer priority service to its best customers.

Executive Search Firms

When a company is seeking a specialized sales or marketing professional who will earn $30,000 or more, the most thorough, direct, and time-saving source of talented and experienced people is the executive search process.

Unlike employment agencies, which work on an "if/come" (contingency) basis, executive search firms charge a fee that is payable during the process—not at the end when a hire is effected. So the use of a search firm requires a commitment by the company using it, not only of time but of considerable dollars—generally amounting today to one-third of the salary package to be earned by the individual. Clearly, then, the executive search firm must be chosen with care, and the search process must be a partnership between the firm chosen and the corporate executives who will be involved in the selection of its new member.

The process is a demanding one; however, the internal executives' time is ultimately better spent in assessing and evaluating a small number of eminently qualified candidates than in recruiting and finding them.

Executive search can provide excellent results, provided that the companies using it are willing to be unyieldingly honest about themselves and their needs; detailed yet realistic about their specifications (which may change with the complexion of the marketplace); in agreement among their key executives about the individual sought; and willing to involve the search firm in every step of the process—from beginning to end.

Selecting Marketing Professionals

The marketing person should possess both keen analytic skills and creativity, a unique combination of qualities in the corporate hierarchy. These qualities may be difficult to evaluate in candidates, and the hiring manager should be educated about what to look for in a marketing person and how best to arrive at the information necessary in the selection process.

It is analytic skills, coupled with the understanding of statistics, that enable the marketing team to develop new products or markets, change or enlarge upon a product, or penetrate or expand the marketplace.

Insightful questioning is the keystone of an effective interview. The manner in which a candidate answers questions is just as important as the content of the answers in determining his analytic skills. Some of the questions that may prove helpful are:

What has been your biggest marketing problem since taking your current assignment? How did you attack it? How did you solve it?

What was your most difficult marketing decision to date?

What was your biggest marketing blunder? How much was budgeted on this program? Why didn't it work? How would you redevelop it?

How would you construct your career differently if you could?

The nonscientific or creative skills of the adept marketing person distinguish him from other members of the management team. These are the more amorphous aptitudes that enable the marketing professional to be both an innovator and a visionary. During the interview, the hiring manager might ask:

What was your most imaginative marketing program to date? What made it successful? How did you "sell it" to management?

If you could change anything at your present company, what would you change? How might the change be effected?

What was your role in the development of a product of which you are proudest?

How did you go about penetrating a formerly impenetrable market?

The marketing team is among the most outward-directed groups in a company. Internally, it relates to decision makers in the engineering, R&D, manufacturing, and sales departments, and often behaves as liaison between them. Outside the corporate setting, the marketing people relate directly with customers or vendors, with whom they may negotiate price or solve problems and create solutions. Consequently, marketing executives must possess highly developed interpersonal skills and be able to perceive both themselves and others realistically.

Personality characteristics that may be desirable in marketing people are described by the following adjectives: persuasive, verbal, aggressive, initiating, ambitious, articulate, tenacious, outgoing, responsible, sharp, quick-witted, perceptive, innovative, inquisitive, imaginative, logical.

To assess correct self-perception and interpersonal skills, the hiring manager might ask:

How would you describe yourself? How would your boss describe you? How would your peers describe you? How would your subordinates describe you?

If you weren't to be considered for your boss's job, what would the reasons be?

If you were to hire an individual for your boss's job, what would you look for?

What was your biggest blunder in dealing with a customer? How did you rectify it?

What do you look for in hiring an individual? How many people have you fired? Why did you fire them?

How many marketing people have you trained who were promoted?

What should we realistically be able to expect from you?

What will be written on your tombstone?

Another index of the marketing professional's suitability to the company is his career achievements in relation to the goals that he has set for himself. The hiring manager can establish the potential of the person to achieve corporate goals by determining how successful the individual has been in fulfilling his own. The resulting data will further enable the company to appropriately match its own personality and pacing with that of its candidates.

Is the individual's judgment of his own success appropriate, and is his degree of success sufficient for this position? What have the candidate's choices been—from educational to job choices—and what processes has he used to arrive at those choices?

In answering these questions, the candidate will offer considerable information about how he perceives himself, the degree of accuracy he possesses, his pacing, and his ability to live by the goals he sets for himself.

Selecting Field Salespeople

The selection of field salespeople is a time-consuming and costly process, and one which warrants considerable effort on the part of a company if the best people are to be found and the money is to be well spent. Because the company will be making the investment of time in defining appropriate candidates and training those ultimately chosen, the company must ask the right questions—both of itself and of its candidates—to assure results that count on the bottom line.

Customers lose their confidence in a company when exposed to frequent change in field salespeople because of careless selection. Another risk factor in cavalier selection is the irretrievable loss of money spent in salaries for field representatives who don't ever make the grade.

An inherent principle of cost-effective hiring, particularly meaningful in the selection of field salespeople, is the matching of company and staff dispositions. The hiring manager must evaluate his own management style long before he questions his applicants, and he should take a careful and objective "inventory" of his company's texture—its objectives, patterns, and pacing—so that he can best match the company's personality to that of its field sales force. Obviously, a salesperson accustomed to an environment in which decisions are made quickly and orders given on the spot will be frustrated and impatient in a sales setting where decisions take weeks or months.

At first, the hiring manager should be introspective. How aggressive is the company? What is its growth pattern to date, and how quickly does it expect to expand? In what direction? Who are its customers; are they three-piece suiters or shop foremen? What are the company's "tone" and structure; does it have an entrepreneurial or a corporate flavor? Does the company offer opportunity or stability, challenge or routine? Does the company value planning and reporting, or does it tackle problems as they arise?

The hiring manager may find direction in analyzing past hiring successes and failures. What personality types does he work best with? Is there a pattern to the success of the last ten company hires? Is it the field salespersons' knowledge of the company's industry or product? Are there specific personality traits that "work" best in the department and the company?

The focus can then move away from the company, outward. Because field salespeople will not generally stay on their first job, a person with two to five years of experience is a better candidate than a recent college graduate. And an astute company will be less concerned with the product candidates have sold than the marketplace in which they have sold it. It is most often knowledge of the customer, not of the product, that suggests strong candidates.

At the interview stage, provocative questioning can shortcut costly efforts in hiring field salespeople. Here are some examples:

> How has your territory grown? How much of the growth was due to inflation? Did a new customer move there, or did you generate the additional sales?
> What was your toughest sale? How did you close it?
> What is the sale of which you are proudest?
> What was your greatest error in judgment?
> What are the accounts that you lost, and why did you lose them?
> Why do you like being a salesperson?
> What makes you a better salesperson than others?
> How did you rank with your former company? What might you have done to position yourself to be #1? How will you get to be #1 here?
> Why weren't you promoted?
> What did you do to effect larger sales in your last job? What didn't you do that you might have done?
> To your mind, what constitutes a successful day? Week? Month? Year?
> What part of the sales process do you like most? What part do you like least?
> What is your five-year career goal? Ten-year goal? Twenty-year goal?

When hiring field representatives, a company should beware of the trap of hiring individuals because they're available; make sure their long-term goals are compatible with the goals of the company. Overhiring always means loss.

In checking references, a company will find valuable information on candidates not only from former employers but from their former customers. It is in this arena that the company can verify sales figures or go beyond sometimes misleading ones. What are the customers' perceptions of the salesperson? Have they been satisfied with the salesperson's performance, responsiveness, and originality in the sales environment?

When the company spends the time, effort, and money involved in asking itself, its candidates, and the marketplace thoughtful questions that prompt complete and accurate answers, the result will unfailingly be felt on the bottom line.

Eliminating Turnover

The marketing executive is a key individual, responsible at once for generating, designing, and implementing projects that can capture a hefty share of the market and catapult corporate profits in the process. The loss of the marketing person not only represents a loss of time and money but also can result in the disruption of the company's timing and pacing in its marketing programs and marketplace. Consequently, the company must carefully plan a strategy to eliminate turnover in its marketing department.

Success depends upon the company's ability to assess, to motivate, and to reward.

The company has hopefully recruited, evaluated, and selected its marketing people wisely, and established a marketing team that is reflective of the company's objectives and corporate personality. Unlike a marriage, in which dissimilar personalities may complement each other, a company and its marketing staff should be dispositionally alike if an enduring relationship is to ensue.

Paramount to winning the allegiance of its marketing people is the company's commitment to allotting a sufficient budget to keep the marketing team challenged. The marketing function is a creative one, and the marketing person must be given money enough to be imaginative in developing new products, new markets, new applications, or new methods for increased penetration in existing markets. Nowhere is there better indication of a company's commitment to an aggressive marketing program than on the appropriate budget line, and a company that has hired marketing executives with keen analytic, strategic, and tactical skills without providing the budget to permit the use of them is sabotaging itself.

Ambitious marketing executives know that to secure their future, they must make significant contributions to the corporate bottom line. They want to be able to show that they have brought the company from point A to point B in a carefully charted manner and in a predetermined amount of time. It is the company's responsibility to provide an atmosphere in which innovation is valued and projects are encouraged that require forethought and planning. Putting out brushfires is a short-term daily task of the marketing department, but provides little motivation for the marketing executive who is skilled in long-range planning and business development.

The marketing function can often be a critical career path to a high-level job, and if the marketing executive perceives himself properly, he knows it. Corporate visibility is thus a priority to the astute marketing professional, who wants to know that his contributions not only will be felt at the top levels of the company but will be visible as his own. A career-minded marketing executive who is given recognition is generally motivated to be perceived as a competent manager— bringing his people along as he grows, and developing their careers to keep pace with his.

Marketing is an art, not a science, and can often be seen as an amorphous, unrealistic, or idealistic practice. The company can help combat this perception by listening to its marketing people and creating an attentive, receptive environment. A veritable corporate octopus, interfacing daily with the manufacturing, engineering, R&D, accounting, and sales departments, the marketing executive can effectively influence all of them, and a company must encourage those in decision-making positions in other departments to be attuned to his or her ideas. The free-flowing exchange of ideas between marketing and other departments often is a catalyst for new product ideas.

How can the company reward its marketing executives? Rewards come in the form of salary, incentive programs, benefits, bonuses, profit sharing, and opportunities for upward mobility. The less obvious rewards are just as significant. The marketing executive will thrive on praise and recognition, since by the nature of his work, he is often less able to track his successes than, for example, the sales executive. Internal employee publications are excellent vehicles for such messages, as are internal memoranda from his superiors and awards.

Support of the marketing executive's continuing education at marketing courses, meetings, and seminars, as well as membership in professional associations, helps greatly in telling the marketing executive that he is a valuable part of the management team.

Ultimately, a company's time and effort expended in the quest for the loyalty and devotion of its marketing executives are an investment in its own health and profitability.

The Exit Interview

The corporate "divorce" is never a pleasant experience, either for the company or for the employee leaving it; but it can be a valuable experience for both if useful information is its by-product. The exit interview is the vehicle for such information. When the employee has resigned, the company stands to gain most from the exit interview. When the employee has been fired, it is the employee who benefits most.

The meeting should be conducted by the personnel department if such a department exists within the organization. If not, the person's immediate supervisor should conduct the exit interview on behalf of the company. In either case it is incumbent upon the company representative to maintain an aura of objectivity throughout the exit interview so that the exchange of information is not tainted with name-calling or defensiveness of any kind, and the resulting information is fodder for evaluation and possible change.

When the employee has resigned, the company may want to ask the following questions during the exit interview:

General questions
What could we have done to make your time here more fruitful for you?
What could we have done to keep you from seeking opportunity elsewhere?
How might we have challenged you better?
How might we have increased your learning experience?
To what measure is the money factor responsible for your leaving? Opportunity? Geography? Challenge?

Marketing-oriented questions
What is the relationship, if any, between your allotted budget and your decision to leave?
What is the relationship, if any, between the nature of your projects and your decision to leave?
What is the relationship, if any, between the pace of the company and your decision to leave?
In your view, is our sense of urgency appropriate to our follow-through?

Sales-oriented questions

Does the product or service that you are selling relate to your desire to leave?

How did the assignment of your territory affect your decision to leave? Have we "stretched" you too much? Have we cut back on your territory often?

How does the selling environment relate to your decision to leave? Is it too slow? Too fast-track?

When the employee has been let go, the exit interview provides the opportunity for him or her to understand why the relationship didn't work from the employer's point of view. It may also provide counseling for the employee about what to pursue next: what, in the employer's view, the person should seek in the next job that will capitalize on his or her strengths.

The company representative should first review the employee's strengths—those qualities that have been valuable to the company and may be the tools on which to build in the next position. When the person's weaknesses are discussed, the interviewer may want to cite them stressing the reasons that the company was not a good environment for the person, rather than positioning the person as out of step with the corporate culture. (The company can afford to be positive at this juncture.)

The interviewer may want to illustrate the reason why the employee is more suitable for a position where he or she may have a line rather than a staff role, or be an individual contributor rather than a team player. If the person was not dispositionally suited to the corporate culture, the interviewer will want to suggest alternative environments. Perhaps the person would be better suited to a smaller organization or a larger one, or a firm that is more entrepreneurial than "buttoned down."

Both the interviewer and the interviewee should remember that although they are together in a perhaps difficult situation today, they may be colleagues tomorrow. Both should behave accordingly and make the exit interview as helpful an experience as possible.   □ *Lynn Gilbert and Janet Tweed*

CHANNELS OF DISTRIBUTION

Distribution strategy essentially involves two decision areas. The first centers on the selection of distribution channels and the determination of channel strategy; the second is concerned with physical distribution.

Nature of Channel Decisions

Channel-selection decisions receive major focus in this discussion. However, they interact with physical distribution strategy, and both relate to overall marketing strategy.

Channel Concepts

A marketing channel has been defined as "a group of firms organized as a loose coalition for the purpose of exploiting joint opportunity in the market."

This concept of a channel as a loose coalition implies that the marketing executive is confronted with recurring problems in coordinating channel activities.

The usual definition views a trade channel as the combination of institutions through which goods pass while en route from a producer to the next seller or ultimate consumer. The segment of the trade channel identified with a particular middleman often assumes his name; thus the reference to "wholesale channels" and "retail channels." When a producer talks of using alternative channels, it is often referring to the use of different types of middlemen. In this context, channel selection is a matter of choosing appropriate middlemen to move goods closer to the ultimate consumer.

Channels of distribution can also be viewed as organizational structures through which goods move from producer to consumer. These structures are composed of a variety of middleman-type operations. There are merchant middlemen who take title to goods as they perform marketing services. There are functional middlemen such as brokers and agents who perform distribution services without ownership. Various middleman functions are often integrated into one organization. Vertical integration comes into existence when two or more successive stages of production and/or distribution are under a common management control. Horizontal integration combines various products that might use the same channel of distribution.

Some of the more common channels of distribution are as follows: (1) manufacturer's direct sale to consumer; (2) manufacturer to retailer to consumer; (3) manufacturer to wholesaler (or jobber) to retailer to consumer; (4) manufacturer to chain store to consumer; (5) manufacturer to broker to wholesaler to retailer to consumer; (6) manufacturer to industrial distributor to user; and (7) manufacturer to government agency.

Channel decisions are made to some degree by all members of the channel. Producers choose among alternative channels; middlemen decide which market segments they want to reach; and ultimate consumers choose the retail stores they patronize.

Economic Role of Channels

Marketing channels represent a composite of activities essential to the efficient distribution of goods. A widespread belief is that the shorter the channel, the lower the costs of distribution and the lower the prices paid by consumers. Some firms advertise "Direct from factory to you," and place emphasis on the elimination of the middleman. Such claims may or may not be true. The test is not the length of the trade channel but whether the set of activities associated with marketing of the goods is performed in an efficient manner. More effective distribution may result from using not one, but perhaps two or three middlemen.

Manufactured goods are generally produced by mass-production methods at locations involving minimum transportation cost to gain economies of scale. Such a situation is frequently accompanied by widely scattered consumption. Middlemen can serve as the low-cost mechanism to distribute these goods because of transactional efficiency; that is, the economy of handling a number of different products results in fewer buyer-seller contacts than would be the case if all producers sold direct.

The economic function of coordinating production and consumption copes with time, distance, and the diversity of products produced in volume at concentrated points. This function is performed for most commodities by buyer-seller contact at successive stages of intermediate distribution. Middlemen survive in the channel by performing this buyer-seller contact efficiently.

Another important economic function performed by resellers in the channel is called the intermediate sort. The intermediate sort involves four activities: (1) assembling over a period of time, in a single place, similar commodities that meet standard specifications for the assortment; (2) assembling over a period of time, in a single place, dissimilar supplies in accordance with some pattern determined by demand; (3) "breaking bulk" or dividing a large homogeneous lot into smaller lots; and (4) breaking the assortment into various types of goods for resale. Middlemen who are specialists can usually perform the intermediate sort with maximum effectiveness. In any event, in a competitive situation only the efficient trade channels survive.

Basic Alternatives

The market executive has three basic alternatives with respect to overall channel strategy: (1) exclusive distribution; (2) selective distribution; and (3) intensive distribution.

Exclusive distribution exists when a single product outlet has an exclusive franchise in a well-defined territory. Products that require specialized efforts and large investments in facilities and inventories are ordinarily marketed through exclusive dealers.

Selective distribution involves careful selection of a limited number of dealers to represent the manufacturer in a given market. Shopping goods, especially women's and men's clothing, are ordinarily marketed through selected dealers.

Intensive distribution is a policy of marketing products in many different types of outlets and in as many outlets as possible. Products such as razor blades, sold in almost every drug store, supermarket, and hardware store, are intensively distributed. These manufacturers believe that general availability is the key to greater sales volume. Most products of low unit value and high frequency of purchase require intensive distribution.

Overall channel strategy can be viewed as a continuum with exclusive distribution at one end and intensive distribution at the other. The marketing executive's decision is to select the intensity of distribution that is in harmony with the nature of his product line and his company's objectives.

Other Alternatives

Managements of competitive firms often choose different distribution channels. Relevant decision factors are the peculiar nature of the product, sales volume that will support a particular physical distribution alternative, brand image in the marketplace, and the firm's long-term marketing goal.

Control of the distribution channel is a continuous battle. Mass retailers control the channels for many products with purchasing power and extensive use of private brands. In some instances national wholesalers are more powerful than either their suppliers or their customers. In other instances manufacturers control —especially manufacturers that do heavy advertising and offer franchises coveted by middlemen. The market institution that controls the channel of distribution is sometimes referred to as the channel commander or the channel captain.

If a producer is also a channel commander, it has the alternatives of choosing middlemen or selling direct. By using a middleman, the producer delegates certain marketing responsibilities. Transferring marketing responsibilities depends upon the producer's ability to evaluate who can best perform these services. Further, the producer's decision regarding the use of middlemen will influence the kind of sales organization it maintains and its merchandising and promotional activity.

Once a system of distribution using middlemen is in effect, the producer may come to think of the middlemen as being a part of its total marketing organization. However, the earlier definition of the channel as a loose coalition comes to mind, and the marketing executive must continually strive for close coordination of company marketing programs and middlemen efforts.

□ *Kenneth U. Flood and Donald L. Shawver*

The Role of the Jobber or Wholesaler

The jobber forms the link between the manufacturer and the retailer in two-stage distribution systems. The role of the jobber is to buy goods from the manufacturer, warehouse those goods, distribute them to retailers, and, in some instances, maintain adequate inventories at point of sale. In some industries, the distributor is expected, in addition to his other duties, to price-mark merchandise and sometimes provide special packaging.

The costs of providing all these services are considerable and in many industries require a jobber markup in the 20 percent range. There are many that see the role of the jobber diminishing with the advent of the large multistore retailer that has the distribution facilities and financing to effect the savings by buying directly from the manufacturer.

This trend would leave the jobber with smaller retailers to service. Small retailers can be less profitable, since they present credit and slow collection problems and represent an increasing cost for servicing in our inflationary environment. Decreasing profits have caused many jobbers to merge for efficiency or, in some instances recently, to go out of business.

The manufacturer who has relied on jobber distribution in the past may have to look at other methods of distribution to reach the retailer, such as using the company sales force, mail, telephone solicitation, and independent sales representatives.

Electronic Retailing

The 1980s will see some major changes in the distribution of products to the end user, particularly in consumer products. The rapidly rising costs of prime retailing real estate and the trend toward self-service that is the result of lack of trained sales help and high labor costs encourage a change in the method of selling for many types of consumer products.

Electronic retailing is a new approach to selling, in which product lines and competitive product-benefit information are displayed electronically to the consumer on a TV screen. When a decision is made to purchase a product, that decision is transmitted to a distribution center, from which the product purchased is charged and shipped to the consumer.

This method of selling would be beneficial to consumers because of convenience, since they would not have to leave home to shop; also of prime importance would be the ability of the consumer to make comparisons of competitive product benefits from information that is not available in many self-service retail situations. The advantage to retailers is that they can free expensive retailing space for high-ticket items in a dramatic presentation that not only sells expensive high-profit items but conveys the store image to the consumer and makes shopping an entertainment experience.

While the specific techniques of the system may vary, electronic retailing is on the verge of occurring. Several of America's leading retailers, including Sears, Roebuck and Co., are experimenting with systems.

A large department store chain is planning a cable TV presentation for 1982, with which it will promote expensive goods in areas where it has no retail outlets and pick up incremental business in this manner. The consumer would respond by mail or telephone to a local distribution center for fulfillment of his purchase. While the method of consumer response might be unsophisticated in this instance, it is a start toward more complex methods of communication.

The advent of electronic retailing presents opportunities not only to the retailer but also to the jobber, who may well decide to gear his operation toward working with large retailers and handling the warehousing and fulfillment aspects of distribution.

Electronic retailing could provide the manufacturer with direct access to the consumer without investment in costly real estate and retailing-personnel infrastructure. □ *David J. Freiman*

Factors Considered in Channel Selection

In competitive situations the channel commander has a choice of alternative marketing channels. In exercising his choice, the channel commander evaluates tradeoffs among channels by considering various factors. These factors can be classified as product factors, market factors, and institutional factors.

Product Factors

Four product variables must be weighed in the channel selection decision: the physical nature of the product, the technical nature of the product, the length of the product line, and the market position of the product.

Physical nature. A primary factor to be considered is the physical nature of the product. The selected channel must cope with perishability in the product—either physical deterioration or fashion perishability. If production and consumption of the product are seasonably variable, any channel used must handle the resulting inventory problem. The unit value of the product influences the channel. Generally, if the unit value is low, intensive distribution is suggested; if unit value is high, more selective distribution may be needed. Here, inventory investment and obsolescence as well as customer-service requirements are considered. Finally, if the product is such that small-lot delivery to many scattered ultimate consumers is necessary, channel selection becomes restricted.

Technical nature. The second factor of consequence is the technical nature of the product. Selection of a marketing channel depends upon whether the product is simple or complex. In addition, the ultimate consumer may need advice on product use. A complicating element for certain products, such as washing machines, is required final-seller installation. Other products, such as industrial products, and specifically computers, may require training of the buyers' personnel by the seller.

On technical products, exclusive dealers may be able to give advice; in other instances, the manufacturer will be forced to sell direct. If the product is not highly technical, intensive distribution can be selected to make the product available.

Length of product line. A product line consists of a group of products related from either a production or a marketing standpoint. The length of product line is related to channel selection. A manufacturer with a short product line is more apt to sell through middlemen than one who has a full product line. A decision must also be made with respect to using a single channel for the entire line or splitting the product and using several channels.

Market position. A final consideration is market position of the product. An established product made and promoted by a reputable manufacturer may have a high degree of market acceptance and can be sold readily through various channels. For example, a certain brand of lawn mower may have high consumer brand loyalty, in which case more channels are available to it than to a lesser-known brand. Frequently, new products sell on the reputation of established brands. This type of trading may result in larger short-term sales but have greater longer-term inherent risks.

Market Factors

The consideration of market factors also enters the channel-selection decision. These are the existing market structure, the nature of the purchase deliberation, and the availability of the channel.

Existing market structure. The channel commander may have difficulty in altering the middlemen's traditional modes of operation. The existing market may be highly concentrated geographically, or it may be widely dispersed. For example, industrial markets many times involve only large customers concentrated in a few large cities. Consumer-goods markets—breakfast cereal, for example—relate directly to population. Consumer preference is generally the critical factor in channel selection. Manufacturers of baby food, for example, changed their channels of distribution after research revealed that mothers preferred supermarkets to drug stores.

Nature of the purchase deliberation. Some products are purchased on impulse; with others the purchase is important enough for the consumer to make a rational deliberation. The consumer who purchases a set of automobile tires, for example, has a different purchase deliberation than the buyer of toothpaste. The purchase deliberation may depend on the frequency of purchase. When consumers purchase frequently, more buyer-seller contacts are needed, and middlemen are suggested.

Formal specifications and competitive bids may be used in purchasing certain products. An illustration is the government agency that buys most products, including food, by publishing detailed product specifications and then soliciting bids from sellers who have met certain financial qualifications to be on the approved bidders list. Industrial purchases are frequently characterized by a set of specifications.

Availability of the channel. Existing channels may not be interested in adding products to their assortments, and the channel commander has the task of winning cooperation from the channel. His two basic choices are pushing the product through the channel or pulling the product through the channel. In pushing the product through the channel, the commander uses normal promotional effort and rational arguments to persuade channel members to carry his product. In pulling the product through the channel, the commander uses aggressive promotion to final consumers on the theory that strong consumer demand will force middlemen to carry the product in order to satisfy customers.

Institutional Factors

Institutional factors considered by the channel commander include the financial ability of channel members, the promotional ability of channel members, and the postsales service ability of institutions making up the channel.

Financial ability of channel members. Manufacturers may find it necessary to aid their retail dealers through direct financing, either interest-free loans or liberal credit terms. Credit terms are competitive, and willingness to extend credit influences channel acceptance. Mass retailers sometimes finance suppliers, either directly or by investing in the company. Ordinarily, government agencies are barred from making payment in advance of receipt of goods, but the DOD sometimes advances working capital for the development of special products such as aircraft.

Promotional ability of channel members. Wholesalers, by their very nature, cannot be aggressive in promoting products of a particular manufacturer. Rather, wholesalers identify with the small retailers they serve. Exclusive distributors, however, are able to promote or to cooperate with the manufacturer in joint promotion. Usually, it is the channel commander who finds it necessary to promote the product; in fact, his promotional efforts often establish him as the channel commander. Manufacturers assume this function in the case of national brands. The promotion of private brands usually rests on the mass retailer or wholesaler who establishes the brand name.

Postsales service ability. In many instances a warranty is associated with a product. The question arises as to which member of the channel will make warranty adjustments. In absence of a warranty, periodic servicing may be required in order to keep the product operating. The retail distributor is the closest contact with the consumer, and the consumer may expect the retailer to service the product. In other instances the product is returned to the manufacturer for service, though in some cases services are performed by independent service organizations. In any event, the postsales service ability of various channel members affects channel selection.

Channel Strategy

The channel decision is not automatic. Channel commanders must use a combination of intuition and analysis and then exercise judgment in making channel decisions.

Suppose the channel commander compares channel A with channel B. He might find that channel B would help make his product more available, but at the same time channel B would result in a less desirable product promotion. The difference between the gain from a given course of action and the loss in opportunity through taking that action is termed a tradeoff.

The channel-decision problem is complicated by interdependencies existing among relevant factors. While it is difficult to quantify the many tradeoffs associated with channel selection, certain analytical tools (some are computer-oriented) can be applied to channel decisions.

Tools of Analysis

Cost analysis techniques will result in reasonable estimates of each channel cost. However, the channel corresponding to lowest cost may not give the intensity of distribution that is required. Or the lowest-cost channel may not be available.

Another tool of analysis is the systems approach. One definition of a "system" is an "orderly linking of separate but interdependent components in order to achieve a given objective." The systems approach views channels as dynamic operational networks through which the product and the relevant order and decision-making information flow in a synchronized, integrated way. The given objective of the channel commander is to maximize the efficiency of the entire marketing and distribution system, not merely the efficiency of each component within the system.

Systems analysis involves tradeoffs in time, service, and costs in order to maximize profits in the long run. The channel commander makes quantitative comparisons between alternative production runs, inventory-holding levels, transport modes, customer-service standards, order transmission and processing systems, and the like. Because of the number of factors that must be considered, the modeling of alternatives must involve computer-oriented OR techniques. These techniques include mathematical programming, simulation, and statistical techniques such as multiregression analysis.

Operations Research

Strategic and tactical planning are essential functions of today's channel commander. The marketing environment can be expressed in numbers and modeled for planning purposes.

Models. Operations research (OR) models have proved to be a valuable management tool by forcing the channel commander to consider all important details of the situation while eliminating those that are unimportant.

Models have been used successfully in planning and analyzing physical distribution alternatives such as warehousing, plant location and size, transport-mode selection, route configuration, and safety stock levels. Models have also been employed for selecting type and location of alternative middlemen or suppliers, for pricing strategy, and for new-product planning. In fact, valid uses for OR tools seem almost unlimited. Entire industry models exist; the brewing industry, for example, has been modeled by brewers to develop production and marketing plans.

Ideally, every problem should be analyzed separately and a tailor-made model developed to fit that situation. Success depends upon enthusiastic support by management, participation by the potential users of the models, and experienced and knowledgeable OR. The probability of success can be improved if the channel commander will (1) choose the model builder carefully, just as one would choose an architect or other specialist; (2) validate the model to show that it represents the system closely enough to be relied on for decision making; (3) clearly state and critically appraise all assumptions; and (4) check each essential item of information by an independent method.

An important consideration is the ease of getting the problem solved. Many excellent computer programs are available to help set up the data in the correct format, solve the problem, perform the computations, give side benefits, and report the results in an understandable way.

Network approach. A typical marketing problem is illustrated in Figure 6-15. The objective is to supply each middleman at lowest total cost. This, like many marketing problems, can be expressed directly as a network model and can be solved by some suitable mathematical procedure.

The advantages of the network approach are its ease of formulation and its low computational cost. The disadvantages are its lack of flexibility in terms of additional constraints and its static nature, if conditions change rapidly over time.

Linear programming. This problem can also be solved by using a linear-programming model, a technique that produces the minimum-cost solution to a rather wide range of problems. The side benefits of a linear-programming solution can be more useful than the optimum solution. The marginal profitability of adding plant, warehousing, or middleman capacity can be determined. The sensitivity of the solution to cost errors or forecasting errors can be computed. The penalty of forcing a unit of product through a nonoptimum channel is also available to the decision maker.

The disadvantage of using the linear-programming approach involves size restrictions and nonlinearity. A large problem such as 1,000 distributors and 100 products would be computationally difficult to solve. Products and distributors would have to be either dropped or aggregated, and the consequence on decision making would have to be considered. Freight rates depend in a nonlinear way upon tonnages shipped, and the assumption of linearity may cause a wrong decision.

Figure 6-15. Network representation of the plant-to-warehouse problem.

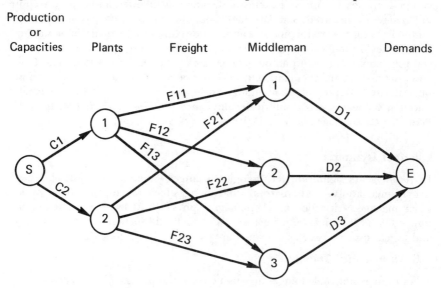

Simulation. When market-channel problems are large, complex, and nonlinear, simulation may be used. Simulation programs predict what would happen if proposed changes were put into effect. Almost any problem can be simulated, and a person with only a slight knowledge of mathematics can set up a simulation model.

Several disadvantages are associated with simulation, however. The time necessary to develop a simulation model is often underestimated. There are few computer programs to help in general simulation, so the simulator must often write his own programs. Factors that tend to make other approaches impractical can also make the results of a simulation unreliable. Finally, there is no guarantee that the solution will be close to optimum.

Legal Constraints

Section 3 of the Clayton Act is concerned with exclusive dealing. It reads, in part: "It shall be unlawful . . . to make a sale . . . on the condition that the purchaser shall not deal in the goods, wares, or merchandise of a competitor . . . where the effect may be to substantially lessen competition." While Section 2 of the Clayton Act permits a marketer in free and open competition to select his own customers in bona fide transactions and not in restraint of trade, Section 3 casts considerable doubt on the practice of exclusive dealing. Thus a company is permitted to limit the number of dealers appointed to a territory and even to go so far as to grant exclusive dealerships. However, it cannot require distributors not to sell competing products; that is, it must not practice exclusive dealing if the effect is to substantially lessen competition. The *Standard Oil Com-*

pany of California v. *United States* decision in 1949 held that substantial lessening of competition was automatic if exclusive dealing was followed and a large volume of business was involved. Standard had about one-fourth of the gasoline business on the Pacific Coast at the time and about one-sixth of the retail gasoline stations.

Other legal ramifications may exist in particular industries; for example, special regulations pertain to automobile dealers. The Dealer's Automobile Franchise Act of 1956 makes manufacturers vulnerable if franchises are canceled arbitrarily. A program of maintaining resale prices by careful and systematic selection of dealers has doubtful legality since the *Federal Trade Commission* v. *Beech-Nut Packing Company* case in 1922.

Channel Dynamics

In recent years significant technological changes—such as computer-oriented management tools—and environmental changes have taken place that have focused management action on (1) managing physical distribution as a materials-flow system; (2) business intelligence as a formalized function within marketing; and (3) customer service as a distinct area separate from sales activity.

Environmental Changes

Four environmental changes are discussed in the paragraphs that follow:

- *Trend toward a short-order economy.* With inventory holding costs generally estimated between 20 and 40 percent of the value of goods being marketed, often the best decision is to order more frequently in smaller quantities, forcing storage and related support functions on primary suppliers.

- *Rapid expansion of product lines.* In order to maintain or expand market share, the accepted strategy is the rapid expansion of product lines to secure maximum retail shelf space and thereby crowd out competitive products and minimize the ups and downs associated with the individual product life cycle. Consequently, a larger variety of models, styles, colors, packages, and price lines generates obsolescence and stock-availability problems, as well as inventory imbalance.

- *Price differentials and discounts.* According to Robinson-Patman Act requirements, price differentials and discounts must be cost-justified; therefore, a critical need exists for ascertaining actual distribution costs. Availability of reliable cost data has stimulated reappraisal of channel-structure alternatives, especially in the number of stock-location points.

- *Competitive strategies.* At one time competitive strategies centered largely around product features and price. Now added emphasis is on indirect competition such as outperforming competitors on logistical planning and customer service.

Functional Approach to Customer Service

Service provided to successive buyers in the distribution channel has great impact on distribution effectiveness and market growth. This is especially true in producer/wholesaler/distributor dealings.

Channel commanders are realizing that marketing strength and stability are more likely to be secured when all critical firms in the channel make a fair profit;

so the concept is developing to lend support and expertise not only in the analysis and solution of common problems such as materials-handling systems but in problems peculiar to the wholesaler and distributor.

Customer services fall into two distinct classifications: service analysis and technical aid. Service analysis includes transport control through computerized car control systems, analysis of in-transit loss and damage, and telecommunication-system hookup for rapid transmission of orders and inventory data. Technical aid is specialized and is given to assist customers in areas where research and successful experiences of the firm's other wholesalers/distributors can be applied. Examples include professional consultation in warehouse layout and facilities design, forecasts, inventory control, computerized truck-route analysis, fleet-management programs, equipment specification, data processing, traffic management, location of capital sources, and possibly a cooperative mass purchasing plan.

The basic concept is as follows:

▪ Although the channel commander and his suppliers and customers recognize that each of the above areas is the responsibility of each firm, these areas have potential cost-reduction opportunities where special skills are required.

▪ Specialization in these required skills, along with the one-time problem solutions, warrants that channel-commander expertise be developed and applied to dependent firms.

▪ About 90 percent of all customer complaints involve a distribution problem unrelated to sales and in areas where the sales representative has little knowledge or interest. Accordingly, a customer-service program including both service analysis and technical aid should be administered as a function separate from sales, preferably tied in with the firm's distribution department.

☐ *Kenneth U. Flood and Donald L. Shawver*

PHYSICAL DISTRIBUTION

Physical distribution has been a subject of management concern for relatively few years. In earlier times less attention was paid to practices and costs in handling materials and finished goods than was warranted by the opportunity for improvement in profits and customer service. Many managers have only recently found that an examination of the physical distribution area is the most rewarding program they have embarked upon.

Scope

In a very limited view, physical distribution may be considered to include only the activities that are involved in moving the finished product out of the plant and for which the producer pays the cost. More enlightened observation, however, shows that the physical distribution activities of concern to a company encompass inbound as well as outbound movement and storage, together with in-plant handling. Further, they include even activities for which others pay the cost, since in the long run these are paid for by the company or its customers.

Elements

The elements of physical distribution assume different importance for each company. Further, opportunities to modify the practices and influence the cost vary from one situation to another. The starting point seems to be in the recognition of what elements are involved. The following might be a partial list:

Inbound	In-Plant	Outbound
Transportation	Transportation	Transportation
Raw materials	Raw materials	Finished goods
Supplies	Work in process	Spare parts
Insurance	Finished goods	Field inventories
Receiving	Inventory	Investment
	Investment charges	Insurance
	Insurance	Loss and damage
	Loss and damage	Taxes
	Taxes	Field warehouse
	Warehouse	Labor
	Labor	Facilities
	Facilities	Inventory management
	Inventory management	Order handling
	Packaging	
	Shipping	
	Pallets	

The total cost of these elements varies widely from industry to industry and from company to company even within the same industry. For example, in the machine-manufacturing industry, physical distribution costs approximate 10 percent of sales; in the food industry, 30 percent. The transportation cost—the element frequently thought to be the only element—may be but a third of the total.

Jurisdictional Problems

Because the range of elements in physical distribution is so broad and because the elements occur in a number of company departments or divisions, it is difficult for one manager to tackle the problem and achieve the optimum solution. Shipping and receiving, for example, may be found under two separate groups. What might be best for the company and its customers is to establish a captive truck operation. The outbound trip moves finished goods, and the inbound trip hauls raw materials and supplies. Jurisdictional problems that result from the scope of physical distribution call for action by those who can bridge the gap between departments.

Historically, the traffic manager of a company has held the role of purchasing agent for transportation. Salesmen representing carriers called on him and, in one way or another, sold him on using their mode and line of transportation. Receiving and shipping departments, as well as others, expressed their preferences to him, but usually there was little economic justification for selecting one carrier over the other or even for the mode used. Keeping them all happy seemed to be the prime motive behind the traffic manager's decision. But the picture is changing; carriers are becoming more sophisticated, and the choices are becoming more numerous. Hence, the size of the problem has now far outgrown the jurisdiction of the conventional traffic manager's job.

The Changing Picture

Not only have the opportunities in physical distribution become more widely recognized in recent years; the available solutions and tools are becoming more numerous. In addition, rapid changes are occurring that affect what can and should be done. (Further discussion of the subject appears in the Manufacturing section of this handbook.)

Impact of EDP

One of the most important tools in bringing about improvements in the practice and reductions in the cost of physical distribution has been EDP. Without it, examining the masses of data necessary to reach sound conclusions on the methods to adopt would have been impossible. To react rapidly and properly in operational situations would likewise have been impossible in the absence of the hardware and systems skills of today. The computer can point out the optimum answer after considering literally hundreds of variables. A manufacturer with multiple plants and field warehouses spread across the country can examine whether costs would be lower and service levels proper with fewer facilities. Continuous decisions can be reached, taking into consideration all factors relating to which products should be produced and stocked at which plant and warehouse.

The improving picture in the data processing field, however, does not eliminate the need for fact gathering and decision making by skilled people. Simply feeding the computer with facts on what is being done today is not enough. A proper evaluation of a physical distribution system requires new methods and a variety of alternatives to be considered first by people and only second by the machine.

For the manager of a business, the increasing use of computers may be viewed with mixed emotions. It has given him a tool to be employed in the interests of his company. With it he can make decisions and operate systems that were virtually impossible before. On the other hand, it has given other managers the same tool, and the tool can be used against him. For example, through the use of computers the customer is in a better position to analyze the company services, including elements of the distribution package. The carrier is in a better position to know what to charge and with what company it is best to work. The wholesaler moving the company's products to market is in a better position to know how to shift the inventory responsibility back up the channel. The supplier is in a better position to price his products to reflect the distribution-cost elements, sometimes including costs that were previously lost in the averages.

Welcome or not, the impact of the computer will continue to be felt in the area of physical distribution. However, its maximum benefit can be experienced only if those charged with its operation and feeding are totally familiar with all aspects of the company's distribution problem.

Storage Methods

It is not unusual to see the most archaic storage methods employed at manufacturer, wholesaler, and retailer levels. The hidden costs of damage, temporarily lost inventory, and disruptions elsewhere caused by storage inefficiencies are not brought to light by the cost system; but even managers who have not adopted modern storage methods can see the rising labor costs brought by obsolete facilities and must be alarmed by them. Fortunately, storage methods for raw materials, work in process, and finished goods have undergone some dramatic changes in recent years. Entire businesses have sprung up just to serve the specialized needs of handling and stocking items most efficiently.

It is now possible to go the full route and have an automated warehouse. In such a facility maximum use is made of the building cube, and conventional labor is almost eliminated. Items can be placed in storage or retrieved by inserting a card in a computer.

Aside from the automated warehouse, great advances are being made in materials-handling equipment, pallets, racks, and warehouse design. The key seems to be in tailoring the physical storage methods and facilities exactly to the particular situation. Naturally, as this direction is pursued, flexibility is lost; hence the potential economic risks and gains must be carefully weighed.

Transportation

The transportation industry has come in for a great deal of criticism in the public press for failing to keep up with the times; it has also received exaggerated praise for some of its "far-out" ideas. However, the industry has moved a long way in recent years, perhaps in large measure because of the pressure of shippers who, in reexamining their physical distribution problems, have found unfulfilled needs. Through their individual and collective purchasing strength, new developments have been forced—container ships, integrated trains, special trucks, and giant cargo planes, for example.

Increasing interest in physical distribution has created markets for American suppliers everywhere. Almost every developing country has a government-owned airline (even if it consists of only one jet plane) equipped and sometimes manned from the United States. American carriers' equipment is to be seen at foreign airports and seaports and on foreign highways; for instance, 40-foot containers loaded in the United States are to be seen on the highways of Germany.

To the manager in U.S. industry, the proliferation of transportation types and alternatives can become confusing. It suggests that there should be some concerted thinking about the advantages to be gained from examining the company's own physical distribution picture.

Total Approach

Purchasers are giving more consideration to the total "package"—product, price, availability, and reliability of delivery. In many instances, particularly in industrial markets, the product takes on the aspects of a commodity because the specifications are well established. Thus competition is based on other elements in addition to excellence of product and ability of sales force. Managers are seeking to compete by (1) reducing the delivered cost to customer, taking into consideration even shipping costs borne by the customer; (2) providing the product in the form best suited to low-cost handling by the customer (for example, shipping on pallets or in containers); (3) combining orders into lots of economical shipping quantity; (4) developing improved ways of order handling; and (5) eliminating unnecessary steps in the distribution channel, thus improving the ability to respond to customer needs as well as reducing the cost.

The means of competing with the use of an improved physical distribution approach are numerous. What is very attractive in one industrial market may very well be of little competitive value in a consumer market.

It has been possible, in the past, for a company to use the same marketing and physical distribution approach for its entire line. This assumed that all segments of the market were alike in their needs and could be served in the same manner. Unfortunately for those who failed to recognize the growing segmentation of their market and take appropriate action, opportunities were lost to competitors that were more alert.

The best approach in an examination of a company's physical distribution activity combines it with an examination of the changing marketing patterns in each of the segments of the industry in which the company competes. It can be thought of as looking at the situation from the outside in as well as the inside out. The viewpoint of the customer is an important ingredient in making any decision. Frequently, the recognition of some modest desire or need on the part of the customer can be accommodated with little expense. In doing so, the company can find that its gain in competitive edge is far from modest.

Tradeoffs

No physical distribution plan can be both the most profitable for the supplier and the most satisfactory for the buyer. Compromises must be made.

Customer service. A 100 percent level of customer service is almost impossible to obtain. It would require investment in finished inventories and create carrying costs that could not in any way be justified.

The realistic approach is to determine what can be considered competitive. Is it the delivery of 90 percent of the orders for a certain product line within a week? If so, analysis can be made to determine what this means in terms of parts, dollars, and physical space.

Outbound-transportation cost. An absolutely minimum cost of outbound transportation from warehouse to customer could be attained only by accumulating exorbitant costs in terms of warehousing and inventory. It would require maintaining stocks next door to the receiving department of each customer—an obviously impossible situation. A much more realistic approach determines the optimum situation by considering all the cost factors.

Delivery promises. Instant delivery and 100 percent performance against promise are also beyond economic possibility. There can be no assurance that the lead time will remain constant under all conditions of peaks and valleys in terms of incoming orders. Standby costs during depressed periods would be drastic.

The need is to determine proper standards for lead time for service out of stock and provide for it in inventory and handling. Perhaps even more important to competitive success than attempting to gear for the shortest lead time is formulating promised lead times that can be met with a high level of accuracy. Customers seeking to keep their inventories and yet maintain business without interruption can be impressed by suppliers that have high ratios of performance against promise.

Creating a New Physical Distribution Plan

A three-phase, ten-step program has been used by a number of managers to examine, improve, and maintain up to date the physical distribution activities of their companies.

Development Phase

Assuming that the physical distribution activity of the company has not come under recent scrutiny, the initial phase should be the careful and objective development of a complete plan.

Step 1. Form a task force to guide the development phase. Decisions must be reached as to which divisions or departments will be represented on the task force and whether outside counsel will be employed to bring in the expertise and objectivity required. As a minimum, representatives of the marketing and production departments should be included in the team. Those chosen from within the company should have company experience long enough to know where to look for the facts and should be able to look objectively at practices that have been employed for many years. In addition to having these qualifications, the task-force leader should be organizationally and politically so positioned in the company that top-management decisions can be secured rapidly.

Step 2. Analyze the facts on distribution in the markets in which the company competes, including distribution patterns of major competitors; demand requirements of market segments; regional differences in demand; distribution policies and practices of competitors; statistics, facts, and opinions on current practices; needs and desires of major customer groups; factors influencing shifts in current practices; and opportunities to effect change.

Step 3. Determine current distribution practices and policies of the company, and compare them with those of the competition. At the beginning it might be well to accumulate all the policy statements pertaining to the physical distribution of the company's various products. It should be no surprise to find inconsistencies; this is part of the usual problem.

A starting point might be to draw up a flowchart of the marketing channels through which the company products are sold; then chart the flow of the physical movement of goods (which may not be identical to that of the marketing channels).

Step 4. Accumulate and evaluate data on current distribution practices of the company. This frequently requires the gathering of data from basic source documents—for example, bills of lading. Data should be of distribution activity over a long enough period of time to assure the elimination of isolated practices and the recognition of significant trends. As a beginning, these data might be on the following subjects: volume (units or tons) by source and destination; volume by type of carrier; costs of transportation, inventory, and warehousing; levels of service by product class, including order cycle time and back orders; and loading and unloading costs. The question to be asked in examining these and other data should be, "Can physical distribution be managed more efficiently and with greater usefulness of time and place to the customer, and all in the light of the competitive environment in which the company operates?"

Step 5. Formulate new systems. Casting aside past practice for the time being, it is useful to prepare as many alternative systems as appear feasible. Some will be only streamlined versions of the old system, while others will adopt new concepts and require more modern hardware and practices than are currently in use. Still other alternatives that will completely restructure the distribution system can be formulated.

Step 6. Cost out the alternatives. As far as practical, they should be simulated on paper, using historical or projected volumes. The simulation should include the development of investment costs of new equipment and facilities as well as of operating costs.

Step 7. Decide on the final plan. The economics of the alternatives cannot be all-powerful; certainly small possible savings cannot be permitted to influence a decision to select an alternative in conflict with marketing policy of the company. Thus, in the decision process, the task force may well consider presenting the alternatives and the recommendation to top management in a concise and written form.

Implementation Phase

So many efforts fail to attain the maximum benefit of a physical distribution review that it is useful to reflect on why this happens. Principally, it seems that the development work was acceptable but the implementation fell short. The support that comes of understanding by all parties in the organization was lacking, and thus unconsciously the plan was sabotaged. This suggests two key steps, added to the seven in the development phase.

Step 8. Communicate the plan. The necessary material must be provided and meetings must be held to do the job of educating the people concerned.

Step 9. Implement the plan. Detailed procedures and the assignment of responsibilities to capable personnel are needed. Hence an organization plan, a personnel development plan, and a systems and procedures program relating to the physical distribution program are all logical parts of the implementation.

Improvement Phase

Conditions change too rapidly for one to expect that, once a plan has been developed and implemented, it will remain sound for all time; hence a final step is required.

Step 10. Evaluate the plan on a preestablished schedule and modify it accordingly. An information system that will give a measure of the plan's performance should be put into being. Periodically (not less often than once a year), a more formal review should be made to find out what opportunities exist for improvement.

With such a ten-step program it is possible to predict the attainment of many of the rewards attributed to a physical distribution review. □ *William J. Guyton*

MULTINATIONAL MARKETING

There are three main ways in which a company may go multinational. The usual route is to start small by either exporting one or more of its products for sale in another country, sometimes through a middleman or by licensing the export of a technological process to a foreign producer, who then pays royalties to the domestic licensor. A bigger investment and a greater exposure to risk are involved in the next step—foreign production, in which the U.S. firm develops a foreign subsidiary to serve a foreign market. The biggest step of all is when a company goes truly multinational—with many subsidiaries and global strategies for creating the best possible blend of its product with worldwide markets. Then, too, there are arrangements that combine steps. A company may, for example, manufacture parts at home and have them assembled in a country where labor costs are cheaper—a case in point being the assembly of inexpensive electronic products in Hong Kong. And, of course, a company may engage in more than one of these foreign-business methods at the same time.

Whichever route a company takes, however—with the exception of licensing and middleman exporting—multinational marketing techniques and management disciplines and controls are vital if the program is to be successful. Most important among these techniques is the successful positioning of products in world markets today—a process that requires great skill. In large part, this is because consumer demands become more complex and markets more highly segmented as society becomes more sophisticated. The key to developing profitable new products in highly competitive markets lies in the identification of profitable market segments. By using an organized technique for market development, we can size, profile, and target market segments with high profit potential. In turn, this information can be used to plan a market entry and guide the development of a viable product mix.

While these techniques can be used for any product or service, in this discussion the emphasis will be on the profitable management of the multinational marketing effort of consumer products. We will discuss multimarket development techniques and methodology. For those companies that consider the United States as their foreign market, these techniques are equally applicable.

The Marketing Path

Multinational companies, and those contemplating going multinational, must stay on the lookout for foreign markets that will provide profitable business opportunities. Although the criteria for this quest vary with the characteristics and objectives of the parent company, organizational techniques such as the marketing path (a system I developed for market planning and decision making) can be used to guide the profitable selection and implementation of these business opportunities.

"Freiman's Marketing Path" consists of five basic phases—market analysis, product planning, product development, merchandising, and sales and distribution. Each of the first four phases entails a strategically placed go/no-go decision point that represents an increasing commitment of funds. By following the marketing path from phase to phase, you can get both step-by-step confirmation of the project's viability and management control over project expenditures before progressively increasing future commitments. My experience indicates that this kind of central control is vital in the proper management of multinational marketing efforts.

Obviously, the farther you follow the marketing path, the greater your financial involvement becomes. When we look at Figure 6-16 (showing relative expenditures by marketing-path phase), we see a jump in commitment as we move through successive phases. The go/no-go decision points located in each phase can be quite effective in controlling these expenditures by offering points of accountability and justification. Figure 6-16 reflects a 20–25 percent higher expenditure for expense items incurred in penetrating foreign markets over what is incurred in penetrating domestic markets. The usual reasons for this are that research connected with the former is generally more expensive, and marketing technology sometimes has to be imported. Moreover, product-design and marketing-mix skills are not always locally available in the host country, and it is expensive to learn all about a market that is foreign to you. Finally, more of a commitment is usually required in phase 3 and phase 4 (product development and merchandising) to provide a product mix for market sales test.

The least expensive way to provide a product mix for sales testing is to import the product—revised as necessary—and package it locally. Unfortunately, importation of the product is not always possible, simply because a suitable product may not exist elsewhere. In such cases, it is necessary to invest capital in production facilities that will provide the product needed for a market test. The cost of production facilities needed to produce limited quantities of a product versus a full production facility varies. As an example, if a full production facility is required, it can represent a committed investment of approximately 70 percent of the total project cost index, as reflected in Figure 6-16. A pilot-plant facility capable of producing small quantities of the market test mix can represent a committed investment in the 30–40 percent range of the total cost index. Since the profit potential of the venture and a commitment to proceed into product introduction cannot be made until after the market test, investment in manufacturing facilities should be kept to the minimum.

When we control financial expenditures relative to the marketing-path phases, we can exercise our options so as not to overcommit relative to our point of progress down the marketing path.

We will now examine each phase of the marketing path in detail and offer some practical case examples showing its application.

Figure 6-16. Marketing-path expenditures for multinational markets.

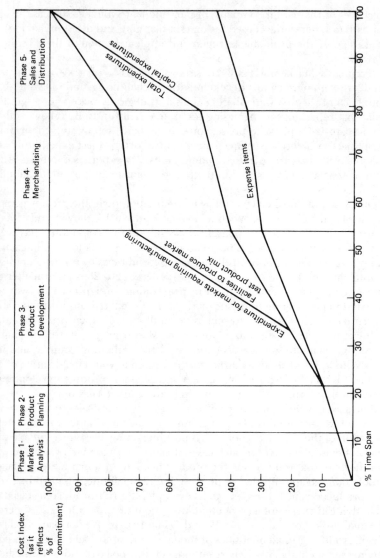

Figure 6-17. Phase 1 of the marketing path: market analysis.

Tasks: a. Preliminary market appraisal

b. Selection of tentative market segment

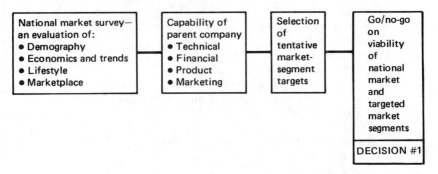

Phase 1: Market Analysis

In market analysis, or phase 1 (Figure 6-17), the objective is to conduct a preliminary market appraisal by first estimating national market potential as a viable business opportunity and then selecting tentative market segment targets. Figure 6-18 shows, as an example, a list of the needed information inputs developed in making preliminary market appraisals in the case of a consumer product. Such information, which is usually relatively easy to obtain, leads to a go/no-go decision on whether to continue on Freiman's marketing path in the particular national market being studied.

The technique of conducting the preliminary market appraisal is relatively simple. The first step in the implementation of this type of analysis is the development of the required information input list for your specific project.

Much of the needed information can be generated by contacting U.S. government agencies such as the Departments of Commerce and State, trade missions of the country being studied, banks, and business publications. Some of the required information is obtained by sending a trained observer into the subject country. When properly organized for the assignment, the observer can usually generate the required information in a relatively short time.

Marketing Opportunities in Nigeria

Sometimes a national market appraisal results in a no-go decision for market entry. For example, when we studied Nigerian business opportunities recently as a potential site for a consumer-products housewares manufacturing and marketing operation, we found that although the national market survey on Nigeria portrayed a rapidly emerging economy, illustrated by an 8 percent growth per year, this growth was largely a result of export of oil and did not necessarily reflect a large growth in industrialization manifested by the production of manufactured goods.

Figure 6-18. Market survey—sample information input.

A. Demography
  1. Population
    — Total households
    — Geographic location
    — Growth trends
  2. Economics
    — Breakdown by socioeconomic group
    — Average yearly income per household
    — Private consumption expenditure for household durables
    — Growth trends
B. Life Style
  1. Ownership of typical consumer durables
    — Motor vehicles
    — Refrigerators
    — Washing machines
    — Dishwashers
    — Cooking ranges (gas, electric, other)
    — Television sets
  2. Feeding process
    — Approximately 10 menus that are typical to the segments of the population, that make up the market being surveyed. This should include a detailed description of preparation.
    — The definition of the major sub-segments of demand, will be made from analysis of the feeding process.
  3. Culture
    — Specification of subcultures present in the national market (religion, dietary restrictions or preferences, taboos, family life, etc.).
C. Marketplace
  1. Estimated sales volume in dollars of major segments of demand, which may have interest because of your company's capabilities.
    — Tableware (domestic, commercial)
    — Tumblers (domestic, commercial)
    — Liquid and powdered detergents
    — Kitchen cutlery
  2. Total retail outlets available for previously listed consumer products by geographic area (department stores, neighborhood stores, chain stores, etc.).
  3. Percent sales by major segments of demand under C-1 above.
  4. Competitive products available in the marketplace, matched to the segments of demand as specified. This should include selling price, units sold, and material description.

The criteria for a go decision in the phase 1 market analysis will vary greatly depending on the type of product being marketed. For most consumer products, the size of the viable market and the ability to distribute the product are important factors. When we are dealing in sizable investments, such as for production facilities, majority ownership and management control are also important factors in a decision.

It was decided that the Nigerian economy, considered in terms of economically viable families with real buying power, had not emerged to the point of supporting any sort of manufacturing operation. Per-capita income at $325 per year indicated low purchasing power for the 90 million population (20 percent of the African continent). Moreover, only approximately 20 percent of the population is urban—another indication of low purchasing power, because a developing country's urban population usually represents its buying power. Using the 20 percent population estimate, we projected a figure of 2.6 million families (20 percent of 90 million equals 18 million, and 18 million divided by seven people per family equals 2.6 million). Of these families, approximately 1.5 million earn more than $7,600 per year, and they represent the major buying power in this country's economy. At the time, less than half of the 2.6 million urban families constituted a market for the products under consideration.

In addition to the small potential market for our type of products, the national market survey indicated other negative factors such as the government's indigenization decrees, which, in most industries, limit foreign ownership to 40 percent in joint ventures, with the majority ownership and control going to the Nigerian partners. Another negative factor was the lack of a viable distribution system for our type of product. Extensive distribution of product even in the key urban centers such as Lagos, Abadan, Kano, Enuga, Kaduna, Onitsha, and Wari could be a problem as a result of a lack of proper distribution infrastructure.

But even though this market was judged to be as yet immature for a manufacturing joint venture, it continues to be monitored, and presents an export opportunity; and when the economy reaches a justifiable level, action can be taken to set up a manufacturing operation there.

Termination of marketing involvement at this, the first go/no-go decision point, after some desk research and on-site inspection, is the least costly way of disengagement from a nonviable potential business opportunity. This is important, since marketing efforts in developing countries can be extremely costly.

Marketing Opportunities in Brazil

A good example of a market appraisal with a positive phase 1 go decision is a survey done in Brazil to determine the opportunity there for marketing a consumer product. Following are some highlights from this study, which indicate some of the information input and its analysis.

Brazil occupies an area almost as large as the United States but contains less than half the population. It is immensely rich in natural resources and is rapidly becoming the dominant industrial power in Latin America. In 1978, its gross domestic product was $168.2 billion. Sixty-two percent of Brazilians are under 25 years of age and 80 percent are under 40. Only 30 percent of Brazil's population is considered economically viable, however. There are about 7.5 million economically active families, approximately 80 percent of which reside in the states of Rio, São Paulo, and part of Parana. Of the national income, 85 percent is concentrated in two geographic regions: the east and the south. This fact is significant because it concentrates the market target.

When we are studying a national market relative to housewares and tableware products that involve the preparation, cooking, serving, and eating of food, we must analyze the feeding process that relates to the specifics of this basic life process (see also the discussion of phase 2 of the marketing path). As an example, we want to know the basic menu selection and the specifics of how the food is cooked (top of stove, in the oven, or, in more sophisticated markets, microwave). In Brazil, oven use is closely equated to ethnic background of the consumer and the diet, which is somewhat influenced by the climate. This information is needed to establish subsegments of demand for which products can be developed.

The Brazilian consumer seems responsive to advertising and trying new products. In order to get a feeling for how the different socioeconomic classes live, we made many in-home visits in Brazil and during each interviewed the lady of the house. Here are our impressions from four typical visits:

- Upper-income group: Ruth, ethnic Italian, age about 50, three daughters, husband comes home for lunch, large home, two maids. Five pieces of clear ovenware and some (dirty) aluminum pots. Uses metal cradle to take the dish to the table for serving. Owns one set of English china dishes (the feature she likes least is that they break). Does not like plastic dishes; says they don't seem clean. Has stemware and everyday glass tumblers. Would buy dishes in a housewares store. Owns large refrigerator, four-burner stove, silver-plated coffee server. Eats breakfast in kitchen, lunch in dining room, dinner in dining room. From the high socioeconomic level of this family and its relatively affluent life style, we can anticipate great acquisitive appetite. May be a possible customer for more sophisticated housewares and table-top products.
- Upper-income group: Erica, ethnic German, 48 years old, husband does not come home for lunch, large home, three cars, two maids. Serves food at the table in metal trays, uses aluminum pots (dirty) for cooking. Does some baking herself. Everyday dishes are Brazilian china, also has good china (Polish). Availability of replacement dishes important, break-resistance important. Drinking glasses made in France. Eats all meals in dinette except when entertaining. Owns and uses stemware when entertaining. Owns one small four-burner gas stove, two old refrigerators. Possible customer for quality products.
- Middle-income group: Eva, ethnic Portuguese, age 40 plus, husband comes home for lunch, owns one car; neither is very well educated (unusual for this socioeconomic level). Uses aluminum pots (immaculate) for cooking. Serves from pots for family meals. Has aluminum baking dishes and one set of earthenware dishes—chipped, not in very good shape. Conscious of breakage when using glass. Eats in kitchen. When a dish chips, she regards it as ruined; does not like plastic. Buys all appliances in Sears, owns refrigerator, washing machine, and excellent five-burner gas stove. Spends most of her time in the kitchen and enjoys it.
- Lower-income group: Rosa, ethnic Portuguese, age 37, husband does not come home for lunch, small apartment, very clean kitchen, no maid. Everyday

dishes (earthenware), aluminum pots (clean), double boiler, serves coffee in china pot. Does not like plastic dishes, keeps leftovers in earthenware crock. She buys her dishes from a factory outlet for seconds. She may be poor by U.S. standards, but she seems happy and well fed. Questionable customer for quality consumer products.

Housewares in the urban areas are purchased mainly in department stores, houseware specialty stores, and variety stores—though a small amount is sold through supermarkets, and indications are that this trend will increase. In general, there were good stocks in all stores visited, although buyers interviewed complained of supply problems. Housewares are usually sold directly to the larger urban retail outlets, with distributors handling the smaller and rural outlets.

The distribution system for tableware uses as the major retail outlets variety stores, department stores, hardware stores, china and glass shops, supermarkets, and mass merchandisers. The major retailers such as Sears, Roebuck, Mesbla, Mappin, Lojas Americanos, and Lojas Brazileiras usually buy directly from the manufacturer. Smaller retailers are usually handled through local distributors. In general, a wholesaler expects to make 20–30 percent on the merchandise and a retailer expects a 40–50 percent margin.

Information from the survey led us to the following conclusions about the Brazilian market: (1) Brazil has a dynamically growing, economically viable population that we estimated to be in excess of 12 million families in 1985. (2) The average economically viable consumer has a great acquisitive appetite. (3) The economically viable population is geographically clustered and relatively easy to reach from a marketing standpoint. (4) The market is also dynamic from a retailing standpoint, with a fairly well organized distribution network in the populated prime market areas. (5) The general economy is growing at a dynamic rate with a good environment for foreign business investment and involvement. All long-range future economic trends look good.

Let's assume that the parent company in this illustration has capabilities in the technology, product development, and marketing of both housewares and table-top products. If so, we can conclude the following: (1) Stainless-steel flatware, everyday dishes, and bakeware might be potential products for use in market entry. (2) Brazil seems to be a viable consumer-product market with a good future of growth.

On the basis of these conclusions, we would make a go decision to move on to the next phase.

Phase 2: Product Planning

The overall objective here is to conduct a feasibility study on the proposed product line (see Figure 6-19), which involves such tasks as defining targeted market segments, profiling consumers, clarifying the product concept, and making a preliminary profitability estimate.

When we think about product planning, we must recognize that only one out of about 55 product ideas is judged suitable for commercialization—and of these, only 60 percent are truly successful. Even under optimum conditions in

Figure 6-19. Phase 2 of the marketing path: product planning.

Objective: Feasibility study on the proposed product line

Tasks: a. Define target market segment
         b. Profile consumer
         c. Clarify product concept and develop positioning strategy
         d. Make preliminary profitability estimate
         e. Establish probability of having a winner

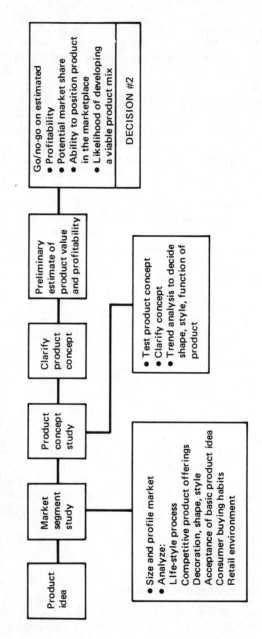

Product idea

Market segment study

Product concept study

Clarify product concept

Preliminary estimate of product value and profitability

Go/no-go on estimated
• Profitability
• Potential market share
• Ability to position product in the marketplace
• Likelihood of developing a viable product mix

DECISION #2

• Size and profile market
• Analyze:
  Life-style process
  Competitive product offerings
  Decoration, shape, style
  Acceptance of basic product idea
  Consumer buying habits
  Retail environment

• Test product concept
• Clarify concept
• Trend analysis to decide shape, style, function of product

the U.S. market, successful product development is both risky and difficult. A comprehensive knowledge of the market and its needs is vital to successful product positioning. So, to develop products that satisfy the selective needs of a foreign market, we must be thoroughly familiar with that market's individual characteristics.

Our experience indicates that the feasibility analysis is the best way to generate the information needed in the phase 2 product-planning segment of the marketing path. This analysis is used to assess a specific market segment; establish market-share potential; and provide the information needed to plan, develop, and position products before a production commitment is made. The feasibility analysis is based on the inputs of, first, a market segment study and, second, a product concept study. Division of the study into these two stages permits us to skip the expense of the second stage if analysis of the market segment study indicates that the project is no longer viable.

The Market Segment Study

Let's examine the market segment study. A segment is a specific area of demand. To illustrate: Where the general market is housewares, the specific segment of demand might be kitchen cutlery and the specific subsegment of demand might be a carving knife. For the purpose of this example, we will assume that the market segment study is for a housewares product and that the feeding process is the life-style element that defines consumer needs relative to housewares. (The critical life-style element can vary, depending on the type of product you are interested in. As an example, if you are interested in entertainment products, the recreation process should be studied.)

There are five steps in a market segment study:

Feeding-process analysis. This life-style analysis should be applied to the segments and subsegments of demand. It should include a detailed description of the specific feeding-process segment (see Figure 6-20). This process is applicable to any national market and relates to any culture. It deals with the basic process of human feeding, from the acquisition of the food, through the preparation, cooking, serving, eating, and cleaning up, to the storage of equipment used and food left over. The specifics of the process must be analyzed for each national market, since they vary greatly nationally, culturally, and geographically. The specific process must then be studied as it relates to major population segments in the market.

It is interesting to see contrasts in the feeding process in different cultures. Consider, for example, oven cooking. In Japan, only 8 percent own and bake in the traditional ovens, while in the United States, the use of such ovens is almost universal. It would seem the Japanese market would not currently be as receptive to a casserole product as the U.S. market would be. In contrast, the Japanese ownership rate of microwave ovens (25–30 percent) is probably the highest rate in the world.

By American standards, the typical Japanese kitchen is primitive. Natural or propane gas is used exclusively because of the relatively high cost of electricity. The stove is small with usually two or three burners, rarely four, and in many

Figure 6-20. Feeding-process chart.

I ACQUISITION

A. *Audit Supplies*
   Cupboards, refrigerator
   Survey store specials,
      newspapers
   "Mental menus"
   Purchase

B. *Storage*
   In and from refrigerator
   Freezer, pantry/cupboard
   Foods
   Laundry
   Cleaning supplies

II HOUSEWARES

A. *Preparation*
   Open: cans, bottles, jars,
      boxes, bags, packages
   Defrost: cans, packages, meats,
      bulk items
   Clean: wash, drain, trim, cut,
      peel, scrape, butcher, skin,
      filet, dress
   Measure: weigh liquid, dry
      bulk volume, count, grade
   Mix/Form: stir, blend, beat,
      mash, whip, grate, chop,
      dice, grind, fold, roll, cut,
      slice, shake, sprinkle

B. *Cooking*
   Range Top: Boil, blanche,
      stew, deep fry, fry on
      griddle, sautee, simmer,
      steam
   Oven (conventional, micro-
      wave): bake, roast, heat, dry,
      broil, rotisserie
   Special: coffee, toast, waffle
      iron, grill, chafing dish

C. *Serving*
   Keep warm, apportion, present,
      transport: platters, bowls,
      trays, cradles, ladles, spoons,
      pour, dispense, carve, slice

III TABLEWARE AND DRINKWARE

A. *Eating* (everyday, entertaining):
      dishes, flatware, glassware,
      napery, decorative ware
B. *Cleaning Up*
   Remove from table: food,
      glasses, utensils, plates
   Dispose of: garbage, trash
   Wash and dry: dishes, flatware,
      kitchen tools, glassware,
      cookware

C. *Storage*
   Kitchen tools, cookware
   Dishes, flatware, glassware
   Napery
   Cleaning, laundry, wrappings
   Foods: kept clean, unbroken,
      uncontaminated, "visible"
   Foods: kept dry, wet, cold,
      protected

instances, family cooking is accomplished on a one-burner appliance. In general, the Japanese bake very few traditional foods at home, but as the traditional diet gets Westernized, there will probably be more baking. Most Japanese have refrigerators. These are small by Western standards and in many instances are used primarily for beverages.

There is evidence of a great trend toward Westernization of the traditional Japanese life style. This trend is largely evidenced in style of clothing, entertainment, leisure activities, and feeding habits. It is important to understand that the Westernization retains some of the traditional Japanese characteristics. In feeding habits this is manifested in a Western breakfast consisting of bacon, eggs, toast, vegetable salad, soybean soup, and coffee. Use of a microwave oven to prepare a traditional hot towel and to dry flowers rather than primarily to prepare food is another enigma.

An evaluation of the national menu, when coupled with the feeding-process analysis, which deals mostly in how the food is handled through the process, often uncovers viable subsegments of demand that can be exploited by the proper product mix. In Germany, for example, there is heavy consumption of boiled potatoes. If a company were in the cookware business, it might find that a critical part of its product mix in Germany is pots for potato boiling.

Clarification of the market segment. Clarification involves assessing the size of the total market on the basis of pieces sold and their factory sales value. The next step for many housewares products is to break down the market by (1) materials used to fabricate product offerings and (2) the price ranges of retail selling. We need this information to make our market-share estimates and to plan our marketing strategy. Ways of gathering this information could be through (1) retail analysis, which involves conducting interviews in retail stores and with distributors; (2) consumer surveys to measure consumption patterns; (3) interviews with major manufacturers serving the market; and (4) government and trade statistical data, such as import and export data.

An example of this type of market sizing and profiling technique is found in Figure 6-21, which shows the estimated 1978 household tableware market in pieces for Brazil. In tableware, the material used and price points are very important in the market profiling. In the Brazilian market the basic tableware materials are earthenware (the least sophisticated material), glass (two grades,) china (three grades), and plastic. As Figure 6-21 shows, the average factory sales values in 1978 U.S. dollars for average tableware fabricated from the first three of these materials were 51¢, 76¢, 94¢, $1.32, and $2.09 and up.

Analysis of consumer buying habits in connection with the product being studied. This entails: (1) describing retail outlets that sell the type of product being studied; (2) breaking down the retail outlets by number, sales volume, and geographic location; (3) determining frequency of consumer purchase; (4) finding out where the product is being purchased; (5) determining the average quantity purchased and the mix (individual items or sets); and (6) determining whether purchases are planned or impulsive.

This kind of information may be obtained through the retail analysis technique mentioned above plus consumer sampling, a technique in which consumers are questioned about the purchases they make.

Figure 6-21. Estimated household tableware market—Brazil 1978 (consumption in pieces and U.S. dollars).

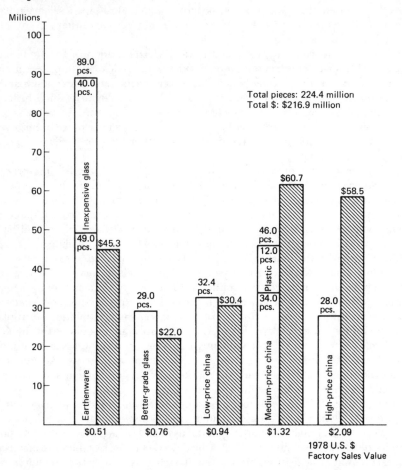

Total pieces: 224.4 million
Total $: $216.9 million

Investigation of competitive product offerings. Such an investigation starts with a list of competitive brands along with an estimate for each of market-share and factory sales value. Next, a detailed description of the products should be made and samples procured of the best-selling competitive products. Finally, trends should be forecast for decoration and shape aspects of the product under study. Here, too, interviews with retailers and consumers can be held to obtain information.

Preliminary evaluation of consumer acceptance of basic material and product idea. Again, we begin with a list—this time of characteristics of the *ideal* product offering needed to fulfill the demand subsegment under evaluation. Next, we evaluate technological capabilities (in materials, process, and design) as they relate to the characteristics of what the ideal product offering might be. Finally, we must check with potential consumers through the consumer sampling technique on how they view contemplated product benefits. Do they like the product or don't they? If they do, how enthusiastically? The inputs we get from this probe of the basic product idea is of great value as we develop the product concept.

On the basis of the foregoing information, an assessment of the market size and a preliminary evaluation of consumer acceptance (of the basic material and the basic product idea) is made. This is followed by a preliminary decision on the project's viability and a decision on whether to proceed with a product concept study.

Product Concept Study

The first step in a product concept study is to clarify the concept by testing it (in terms of function, shape, and surface decoration, for example) with consumers. Results of the consumer tests are used to modify and refine the product concept, and product prototypes are developed accordingly.

The next step is to estimate product value. First, product prototypes must be evaluated on how well they satisfy the subsegment of demand. This is followed by evaluation of product prototypes against competitive products and measurement of their perceived value by consumers.

The preliminary market-share estimate is assessed by equating your products' perceived value with the estimated market size (developed previously in the market segment study) and making a subjective decision as to the size of the market share your product can expect to achieve. On the basis of this information, a critical decision is then made on whether to proceed into phase 3—product development, the next stage of the marketing path. It must be remembered that the market-share estimate is tentative and a best guess made from information available at this point. A more reliable estimate can be made when we get further along the marketing path. The product concept study usually is conducted through individual consumer interviews and techniques such as focus-group sessions. In most developed countries, it's fairly easy to conduct consumer research, but it is extremely difficult to do in less developed markets. A solution that sometimes works is to bring in trained personnel from outside the country to conduct the research—a tactic we have successfully used.

Product Positioning Strategy

It has been said that the ability to successfully position products in domestic markets is the mark of a good marketer, and the ability to successfully position products in multinational markets is the mark of a great marketer.

Successfully positioning a product multinationally is a sophisticated process that requires awareness of and sensitivity to the needs of many national markets. One of the important ingredients in establishing a positioning strategy is the inputs from our market research; but intuition, timing, and a marketing sense also play important parts in developing this strategy.

The final activity in phase 2 of the marketing path is to develop a strategy for the successful positioning of the planned product line into the national marketplace. The product positioning strategy should be established before the product is developed, because it influences its ultimate characteristics. When we discuss positioning a product in the marketplace, we are referring to the filling of a void in a demand environment. The niche in which we position the product is a benefit separation between products available in that market. The position a product fills might be based on unique functional benefits that satisfy a need of a market segment of demand. The niche benefit can be a price point for a product that does not have any unique functional benefit but represents a favorable price/value relationship over the other products available in the market. Sometimes the niche is a styling difference. The three-dimensional product positioning matrix shown earlier as Figure 6-1 allows the visualization of a market, or market segment, with competitive products defined as to price point, product differentiation characteristics, if any (styling, product functional or service differentiation benefits), and market share. This visualization with its definition of the critical factors found in the competitive market environment is helpful in establishing the position niche for the product offering.

In forming the positioning strategy, a company usually analyzes its product benefits as they relate to the needs of the demand that it intends to satisfy, and then compares its planned product benefits to competitive products if they exist.

If there is very little difference between products, we are usually dealing with a commodity, which becomes very competitive in pricing and difficult to merchandise. This type of product is usually to be avoided.

A product developed with real benefits that are unique and demonstrable is usually easier to merchandise and normally has sufficient elasticity in its price/value relationship to permit aggressive pricing that generates maximum profits. Product pricing is a function of what the market will bear for the product benefits offered and should have no relationship to the manufacturing cost.

The positioning strategy gives management the shopping list of the required product benefits needed to fulfill the strategy. This is an important input to phase 3 of the marketing path—product development. The positioning strategy is also used throughout the marketing path as a model for the character the product develops in its ultimate presentation to the consumer.

Let's assume that we have another go decision, and we're ready to move into the product development phase.

Phase 3: Product Development

In this third phase, the overall objective is to develop a viable product mix that reflects market needs. The tasks involved are to (1) develop the final design and engineer the product, (2) determine the cost of the product mix, (3) establish consumer acceptance, and (4) conduct preliminary profitability analysis (Figure 6-22).

This product development phase of the marketing path turns abstract product benefit concepts (which came out of product planning) into a tangible form of product that has implied value. For products other than services, product development consists of two important elements: product design and product engineering. Product design is concerned with visual attractiveness; product engi-

Figure 6-22. Phase 3 of the marketing path: product development.

Objective: Develop a viable product mix that reflects market needs

Tasks: a. Finalize design, engineer product
b. Cost product mix
c. Establish consumer acceptance
d. Conduct preliminary profitability analysis

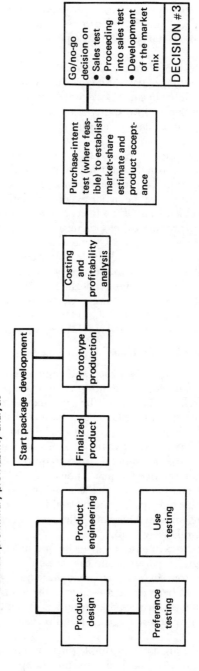

neering with function and economic manufacture of the product. Good product development is a complicated process at best—and a treacherous one when applied in national markets that lack personnel trained in product development and research.

Fortunately, it is often possible to adapt to the targeted market products that are sold in another national market. Sometimes this entails only minor revisions —such as a change in surface decoration or a change in either packaging or formulation—depending on the type of product involved. These minor revisions are normally rather easy to execute even in the most primitive marketing environment.

Access to products in various national markets is one of the advantages of the multinational company. Companies that enjoy this advantage should always consider making minor revisions in existing products to satisfy local marketing needs before they undertake the major expense and effort involved in developing a totally new product. In addition to economic benefit, this course of action cuts the time spent in product development and avoids the pitfalls posed by a lack of trained product development personnel.

Packaging is a very critical element in the marketing of most consumer products. You will note we recommend package development be started in the product development phase. While all the necessary inputs required to develop the marketing characteristics of the package are not yet available at this stage, the package construction options should be defined while local resources can be evaluated and the physical protective requirements of the product can be established.

Purchase-Intent Testing

When the product is designed and engineered and prototypes are available, it is possible—and often prudent—to conduct a purchase-intent test. The results of this theoretical indication of the consumer's intent to purchase your proposed product, when given the choice in a simulated situation, can be used to make a preliminary estimate of the product's viability in terms of both consumer acceptance and potential market share. It is necessary to have this type of information to justify the large amounts of funds required to conduct the market sales test and to develop the needed marketing mix.

There are many methods that can be used to conduct a purchase-intent test. Some of the techniques are highly sophisticated and use special computer programs for the analysis. There are other techniques using matched consumer samples that are relatively simple.

Whatever the purchase-intent technique used, it should be remembered that the test is highly theoretical and can give only a gross indication of intent to purchase. Aside from theoretical market-share numbers, the most meaningful information that can be generated is an extreme indication of either intent or lack of intent to purchase the proposed product. This information can justify a decision to proceed or cause you to go back and reevaluate your product or product concept.

We prefer using a rather simple purchase-intent test technique that measures the reactions of two matched consumer samples. We consider this technique as accurate as any.

Let's look at the use of the purchase-intent test in a national market. For our case study, let's assume the following:

◻ Product classification is tableware (dishes)
◻ Materials used for tableware in the national market are low-priced china, melamine plastic, medium-priced china, high-priced china, and glass.
◻ Estimated market shares in units and dollars for each material are:

	Market Share in Units (%)	Market Share in $ (%)
1. Low-priced china	30	12
2. Glass	25	17
3. Medium-priced china	20	30
4. Melamine plastic	15	21
5. High-priced china	10	20
	72 million units	$46 million

◻ The market base (see Figure 6-23) has been sized and profiled using the technique outlined in phase 2.
◻ Our research has indicated that the consumers for the product that we want to market are in the lower and upper middle income groups and also the higher income levels. The woman of the house usually makes the purchase decision.
◻ The product we are contemplating for this market is made from a unique material that gives the product extreme durability, tactile qualities, and other benefits that are visible and quite apparent. For the purpose of this discussion, let's call the product Kasualware, a fictitious name.
◻ Research indicates Kasualware has the product benefits that are desired by the consumer and are not available in existing products.

The objectives of the purchase-intent test are to measure consumer acceptance and intent to purchase the Kasualware product, to get an indication of the potential market share that could be expected from Kasualware, and to clarify certain aspects of the product offering.

The method used is to select two matched samples of potential consumers divided into two groups, a control group and a test group. All groups saw three low-priced china patterns, three glass patterns, three medium-priced china patterns, three melamine plastic patterns, and three high-priced china patterns. The best-selling patterns for these products were selected. The items selected also represented the price spread in each category and made up the competitive products in the market segment we wanted to penetrate. Only the test group saw three Kasualware patterns in addition to the competitive product offerings.

We took a valid statistical sampling of housewives in the socioeconomic classes that our research indicated made up our potential market: 1,200 housewives in three income groups to be interviewed in two major urban market areas. These people were asked: "If you were buying dishes for everyday family use and for entertaining friends, which, if any, of these products would you definitely buy?" One point was scored for each "definitely buy" selection.

Figure 6-23. Household tableware market (consumption in pieces and U.S. dollars).

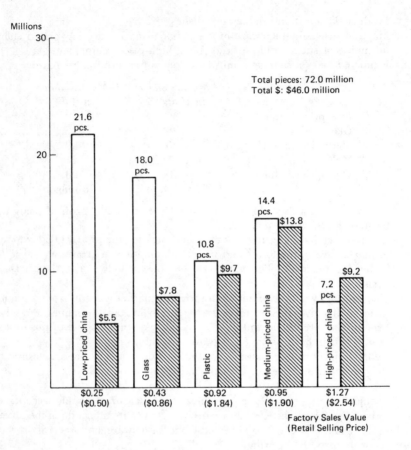

Total pieces: 72.0 million
Total $: $46.0 million

While the prime purpose of this research technique is to determine purchase intent of both the competitive tableware product offerings and the Kasualware proposal before and after price disclosure, it is also possible to use the consumer sampling to elicit information on product mix and set composition and to rate product attributes. This information is very useful in establishing the sales-test product offering and the proper marketing mix.

Let's look at the purchase-intent test results (Tables 6-4 and 6-5) and see how they are used to make our projections.

The purchase-intent test can give an indication of the validity of market sizing and profiling. The response of the first-stage control-group sample to the "definitely will buy" question in the purchase-intent test is interesting because the re-

Table 6-4. Purcase-intent test: first stage (control group only).

Retail Selling Price	Pattern Number	Control-Group Percent	Percent by Material	Test-Group Percent	Percent by Material	Shift of Market Share to Kasualware
Low-priced china
0.50	1	6	28			
0.50	2	12				
0.55	3	10				
Glass
0.85	4	10	25			
0.90	5	6				
0.95	6	9				
Medium-priced china
1.85	7	5	19			
1.85	8	6				
1.90	9	8				
Plastic
1.90	10	8	17			
1.90	11	6				
2.00	12	3				
High-priced china
2.50	13	2	11			
2.60	14	4				
2.75	15	5				
		100	100			

sults, when compared to the basic tableware-material market-share percentage, projected market shares similar to those determined in the phase 2 national market sizing and profiling exercise found in Figure 6-23. This similarity also indicated the validity of the consumer sample used.

In the second stage of the purchase-intent test we use the second part of our matched consumer sample to evaluate the 15 competitive products and the three Kasualware product offerings. The consumer sample is asked for a "definitely will buy" purchase intent with and without retail selling prices.

After factoring regression and other compensating equations into our purchase-intent test, we find that our potential share of the tableware market with Kasualware in the country we are studying could be 10.3 percent (Table 6-6). Our share of the market seems to be coming mostly from glass, plastic, and medium-priced china.

When we project the 10.3 percent potential market share for Kasualware against the estimated national market (Figure 6-23), we develop the following consumption estimate:

	Total Market Pieces (millions)	%	Shift to Kasualware (millions of pieces)
Low-priced china	21.6	10	2.160
Glass	18.0	12	2.160
Medium-priced china	14.4	11	1.580
Plastic	10.8	11	1.188
High-priced china	_7.2_	_5_	_.360_
	72.0	49	7.448

An evaluation is made factoring 7.4 million pieces of Kasualware against the retail value per piece to establish the value of the unit volume.

This potential market share is considered sufficient to indicate a go decision and the justification of the expenses that will be incurred in phase 4 of the marketing path.

Table 6-5. Purchase-intent test: second stage (test group).

Retail Selling Price	Pattern Number	Control-Group Percent	Percent by Material	Test-Group Percent	Percent by Material	Shift of Market Share to Kasualware
Low-priced china						
0.50	1	6	28	5.0	25.2	10
0.50	2	12		11.0		
0.50	3	10		9.2		
Glass						
0.85	4	10	25	9.0	22.0	12
0.90	5	6		5.0		
0.95	6	9		8.0		
Medium-priced china						
1.85	7	5	19	4.0	17.0	11
1.85	8	6		6.0		
1.90	9	8		7.0		
Plastic						
1.90	10	8	17	8.0	16.0	11
1.90	11	6		5.0		
2.00	12	3		3.0		
High-priced china						
2.50	13	2	11	1.4	10.4	5
2.60	14	4		3.5		
2.75	15	_5_		5.5		
		100	_100_			
Kasualware						
2.00	1			4.4	9.4	
2.00	2			4.0		
2.00	3			_1.0_		_—_
				100.0	100.0	49

Table 6-6. Projected market share based on purchase-intent test.

Category	Market Share	Shift to Kasualware
Low-priced china	27.0%	10%
Glass	22.0	12
Medium-priced china	17.8	11
Melamine plastic	13.4	11
High-priced china	9.5	5
Kasualware	10.3	—
	100.0	49

It should be noted that a purchase-intent test can be developed for almost any type of product. While the stimulus will change according to the product tested, the basic technique for carrying out this research procedure remains constant.

Phase 4: Merchandising

The very first action we take in phase 4 of the marketing path (see Figure 6-24) is to establish a distribution system strategy for the product. To do this, we must first thoroughly analyze the distribution system for the type of product we intend to position in the national market. (Information on the distribution system is usually obtained during the phase 2 market segment survey.)

A complete understanding of the distribution system, which we define as the process involved in moving the product from the place of manufacture to the consumer, is necessary in order to develop a viable, effective marketing mix and sales and distribution strategy. It is important to remember that your success or failure will be largely determined by the effectiveness of your distribution plan.

In general, distribution systems can be classified as two general types: (1) simple one- or two-tiered systems that involve sales either direct from manufacturer to the retailer, or from the manufacturer to wholesaler to the retailer, and (2) complex multitiered systems that use many sub-wholesalers in the distribution chain of product from the manufacturer to the retailer.

Usually, the more developed the country, the simpler the distribution system. The reasons for this are better communication, transportation, warehousing, and business infrastructure, and a more sophisticated retailing environment.

As an example, most countries in Western Europe and North America have simple one- or two-tiered systems. Countries in Africa, parts of Latin America, the Middle East, and Asia usually have the complex multi-tiered variety.

It should be noted that occasionally tradition rather than the stage of economic development dictates the type of distribution system. Japan, with its multitiered distribution system, is a prime example of this type of exception.

An example of the simple one- or two-step distribution system would be the distribution of a housewares product in France. The manufacturer would either

Figure 6-24. Phase 4 of the marketing path: merchandising.

Objective: Marketing mix and distribution system planning

Tasks: a. Establish distribution system strategy
b. Develop marketing mix and purchasing proposition
c. Confirm market share potential and viability of product offering
c. Justify manufacturing facility if required or other source of product

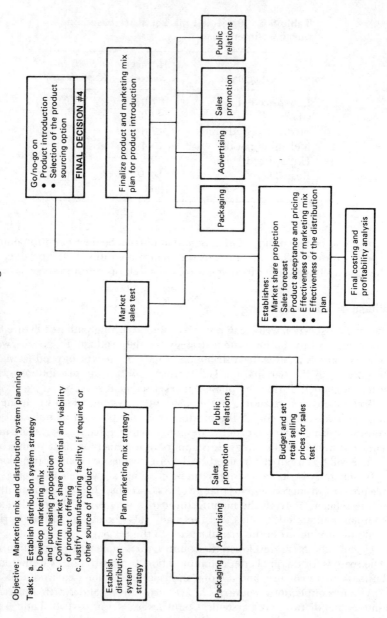

sell directly to a major retailer, such as a hypermarche chain like Carrefour, which would warehouse and deliver product to branch stores, or sell to a distributor, who would warehouse and deliver product to larger retailers, with smaller retailers working on a cash-and-carry basis.

One advantage of this system of distribution is that, with fewer people in the chain of distribution, the markups are relatively small, resulting in a favorable selling price to the consumer. Another advantage is the ability of the manufacturer to exercise some control at point of sale on how the product is merchandised.

An example of the complex multitiered distribution system typical of the Middle East and African countries is the distribution of consumer products in Iran. For many consumer products in Iran, the distribution system is a bazaar-oriented one involving many sub-wholesalers transmitting merchandise from manufacturer to retailer. The manufacturer sells to major wholesaler, who in turn sometimes sells to any number of minor wholesalers in outlying cities, who then sell to the retailers. All of them mark up the product's price. This type of distribution system operates without the benefit of credit ratings, and at certain levels, barter rather than money transactions takes place. Intimate knowledge of whom you are selling to becomes a necessity.

Let's assume for our case study that the national market we are considering has a good distribution infrastructure for consumer products and is of the simple one- or two-tiered variety. We could be dealing with a distribution system similar to what is found in Venezuela, Brazil, or Argentina.

We plan to sell Kasualware dishes directly from our factory to key retailers, who will handle their own distribution from centralized warehouses. We will give these key retailers a 50 percent discount from list retail selling price, with an 8 percent allowance on total purchases to be used for promoting the product. We will sell to the smaller retailers in the interior of the country through wholesalers. We will sell to the wholesaler at a 60 percent discount from list retail selling price. We anticipate that the wholesaler will sell the product to the retailer at a price that will permit a 35–40 percent markup on cost for the retailer. We recognize that to pay for warehousing, transportation, the cost of giving credits, and sales expense, the wholesaler needs to make at least a 20–25 percent margin on what he distributes.

The development of the marketing mix is a key task in phase 4 of the marketing path. The marketing mix, when combined with the product mix developed in phase 3 of the marketing path, gives the necessary ingredients required for the sales test, which is the major activity in this phase.

Purchasing Propositions

In order to develop an effective marketing mix we must first develop the purchasing proposition for the product. The purchasing proposition is defined as the organization of the key product benefits in a manner that, when presented to the consumers, convinces them to buy the product. The same purchasing proposition must be reflected in each of the marketing-mix elements. We must recognize that even though we are dealing with four different elements (packaging, advertising, sales promotion, and public relations), these elements must not be treated separately. They must function as a totality, with each using its own medium to convey the purchasing proposition to the consumer.

When we look at marketing on a multinational level, we find that the same purchasing proposition can be valid in many national markets. The only difference is the type of creative presentation that is appropriate for conveying the proposition to the consumer.

For our case study, we will assume that our purchasing proposition for Kasualware dishes in this national market as developed from our research in phases 1, 2, and 3 of the marketing path is as follows: Kasualware dishes are dishes that can be for either everyday family use or peer group entertaining. Kasualware dishes have high durability in that they are very strong and would not be likely to break, chip, or stain in normal use. These dishes have a surface texture and a variety of decorations that are considered very attractive by the consumer. The product is sold in assortments appealing to the way the consumer wants to purchase these types of goods at popular price points, giving a high price/value relationship.

Let's examine each marketing-mix component and see how it can relate to our purchasing proposition.

Packaging

It has been said that "a package is to a product what clothes are to man." As clothes protect our bodies during our journey through life, the package protects the product during its journey from its place of manufacturer to the consumer. As clothes convey an image of ourselves to others, a package can convey an image of the product, with its benefits, to the potential consumer.

Recognizing the importance of packaging in promoting the purchasing proposition, we must be aware that there are factors that make it necessary in many instances to develop specific packages for specific national markets. These factors may be language, cultural differences, the need to package for specific modes of transportation, and the availability of certain types of packaging material in that market.

In the more developed countries, design capability and most types of packaging materials are readily available. In the less developed countries, creating packaging that functions as a marketing tool is a real problem that requires great ingenuity to overcome.

Foreign subsidiaries are generally of two types: new enterprises, and existing operating units that have been acquired by an American company. In a newly created enterprise owned by a U.S. company, the upper echelon of management is usually trained in the parent company's methods of operation, and the organization of functions such as packaging—as far as structure, training, and packaging strategy are concerned—is usually done before operations are started out of the country.

When the U.S. product and the foreign product are similar, it is possible to develop packaging for a foreign subsidiary that is as good as or better than that used by the parent company, right from the initial introduction into the market. Until foreign packaging personnel can be trained, it is necessary to have an American packaging manager who knows the foreign market, knows the product, knows the sources of supply, and has the respect and confidence of top management of the foreign subsidiary. The engineering and design can be obtained locally, but it will take a packaging professional to find the right basic packaging concept for the product and then supervise the execution of the concept properly.

The role of the American packaging manager in a situation like this is almost the same as the role that he has in the parent company. He is responsible for the initial packaging used for his foreign subsidiary, although, as the initial packaging is developed, personnel of the foreign company can be trained to assume this development responsibility. From the corporate standpoint, use of this technique for package development for foreign subsidiaries provides immediate maximum efficiency with regard to both cost and package effectiveness.

When dealing with foreign subsidiaries that have been acquired and have previously existed as an operating unit, often one has to contend with problems that have been built up to a critical level through long-term nonmanagement of the packaging function. In such situations, it takes a long time to reverse the effects of poor packaging and reduce the funds wasted through packaging inefficiencies.

We can usually assume that the American packaging manager is not called in to consult with the foreign subsidiary until problems have come to the attention of top management at both the parent company and the foreign subsidiary. The American packaging manager is usually in a sensitive position. He must come in as a foreigner, often as a stranger who cannot speak the language, and develop a working relationship with the personnel of the subsidiary. This requires creating an atmosphere of trust, mutual respect, and understanding between the foreign subsidiary people and the American packaging manager—even though he is criticizing much of what has been done in the past. To accomplish his goal, which is to improve the packaging of the subsidiary, the American packaging manager must be not only an expert on packaging but also a diplomat.

At best, all the consultant can expect to accomplish is to outline packaging needs, suggest solutions to current problems, and show how these solutions can be implemented. The actual job of implementation must be the responsibility of the foreign subsidiary personnel. Unfortunately, trained packaging personnel are very often unavailable to follow through and execute recommendations optimally. A large part of the American packaging manager's role when dealing with foreign subsidiaries is to train their personnel to become competent in techniques of package development. This is one reason for the long time it takes to reverse the effect of long-term nonmanagement of the packaging function.

When consulting with foreign subsidiaries, these are our ten commandments of how to work with them:

1. Gain a commitment on the part of the foreign subsidiary by charging to it all expenses incurred by the visit. (This includes the option to charge the consultant's salary.)
2. Set down in writing, at the beginning, the specific objectives of the consultations, and reach an agreement with the principals involved on the validity of these objectives.

3. Establish a work schedule relative to the time allotted to the project.
4. Thoroughly study the situation before making any comments or suggestions.
5. Make no criticism without giving possible solutions to problems and ways of implementing them.
6. Give a verbal report to the principals involved before returning to the United States, and try to satisfy the objectives stated at the beginning of the project.
7. Write a formal report covering in detail all aspects of the study, including an investigation of possible alternatives that you have considered and worked on after your return to the United States.
8. Get confirmation in writing that the subsidiary accepts the recommendations covered in the report.
9. Check the subsidiary's progress in following up on the recommendations.
10. Assist the subsidiary with services, information, or guidance to enable it to carry out the recommendations.

After the initial consultation, make it a policy to continue consultation with foreign subsidiaries that accept and implement the recommendation.

Packaging: A Case Study

Our Kasualware product mix as developed in phase 3 (product development) of the marketing path is (1) 30-piece sets consisting of six five-piece place settings (nine-inch plate, six-inch plate, bowl, cup, saucer), and (2) open stock modules containing three each of the nine-inch plates, six-inch plates, bowl, cup, and saucer.

In order to provide a package with sufficient product protection to move it safely through the distribution system, we equate the product fragility to the stresses anticipated in the mode of transportation that will be used to distribute product in our national market, and then select available materials and package construction required to provide that protection.

Let's assume the mode of transportation we must package for in this national market is shipment by truck. We can anticipate a poor road system in the interior of this country causing high vibration and "G" forces to be transmitted into the load of a truck. These conditions are not uncommon and are prevalent in most Latin American, African, Middle Eastern, and Asian countries.

As for the merchandising aspects of the packaging required for Kasualware dishes, we want to convey our purchasing proposition to the consumer at point of sale, and, since we are trying to build a quality brand image in this national market, we need a quality package presentation to bolster the quality image of our product.

Our package objectives, simply stated, are as follows: (1) The package must protect the product from the abuses encountered in truck shipment. (2) The package must have graphics that effectively convey the purchasing proposition of the product. (3) The package should function dramatically in telling the product benefit story when used in mass display at point of sale. (4) The package must convey a quality image of the product. (5) The packaging materials used should be available locally. (6) The total cost of the package (material and labor) should be minimum without endangering accomplishment of the packaging objectives.

Since we are part of a multinational company, we will get assistance from our parent company's corporate staff packaging group to help us develop a package that meets our objectives.

As a result of our efforts, the packaging developed for Kasualware dishes that will be used for sales testing the product is as follows:

A 30-piece-set package of corrugated board die-cut construction featuring a carrying handle and four-color graphics depicting the product in use in a family situation, with bold copy highlighting the major product benefits (strength, will not stain or chip, and so on) that convey the purchasing proposition to the consumer. The open-stock packages use a simple folding-box construction with a window showing the product and copy depicting the product benefits. A special green color has been developed as part of the package graphics to give the line an identity that the consumer will be conditioned, through our advertising and sales promotional efforts, to identify with our brand. The use of color as a method of building brand awareness in a market, particularly if there is any degree of illiteracy in that market, should always be considered when planning the marketing-mix strategy.

Selection of an Advertising Agency

Advertising is an important component of the marketing mix, since it is used both to gain distribution of product and to aid in the selling of that product to the consumer. Our market sales test in phase 4 of the marketing path is an ideal place to test our advertising strategy and evaluate its effect on the sale of the product.

In order to develop effective advertising in a national market, it is necessary to have a competent local agency handle the account. In the more developed national markets of the world, there is a good selection of advertising agencies. The major problem in this situation is how to select from all the competing agencies the one that will do the best job.

Selection of the right advertising agency for a national market is a major commitment that should reflect the thinking of both the marketing staff and corporate top management. We have found that the formation of a selection committee, consisting of several individuals who represent top marketing and corporate management, is a great aid in getting a consensus and making the right selection.

The first step in the selection process should be the preliminary screening. In this activity you screen potential agency candidates against basic criteria such as agency size, reputation, client list, or any other criteria you want to establish. We have found that it is best to screen down to the minumum amount of potential candidates, certainly not more than four or five.

The following evaluation technique of potential candidates can be helpful in selection of the advertising agency that can best serve your needs in a national market. The technique is a scaling evaluation of a number of facts that influence the performance capability of an advertising agency. For the scaling exercise, the factors should be grouped under the following categories: important, very important, and vital. A 1–10 rating scale in order of importance can be used for the important factors, a 20–50 rating scale for the very important factors, and a 50–100 rating scale for the critical factors. An evaluation form should be produced using the factors selected with their rating scales (see Figure 6-25).

The final step in the selection of an advertising agency is to invite the candidates to make their presentations to the selection committee and to rate them, using the evaluation form. After analysis of the ratings and the application of liberal amounts of gut feeling, you select the agency that you will entrust to handle your advertising for the national market.

When operating in countries that are less developed both economically and businesswise, the infrastructure system we find usually has a great scarcity in the availability of competent local advertising agencies. This situation is prevalent in many African, Middle Eastern, Asian, and some Latin American countries. When confronted with these conditions, you must usually take what you can get and hope for the best. Fortunately, very often this type of market does not require the same advertising sophistication a more developed market does in getting the pur-

Figure 6-25. Criteria for advertising-agency evaluation.

Vital Factors—After each factor, rate on a scale of 50-100 (100 highest).
1. Competence of the people working on the account. _____
2. Compatibility of your people with agency personnel. _____
3. Creativity in the execution of the message. _____
4. Is the agency part of a multinational group that you have dealt with or might deal with in other national markets? _____

Very Important Factors—Rate each on a scale of 20-50
1. Creativity in the selection of the media. _____
2. Creativity in planning. _____
3. Compatibility of client list. _____
4. Quality of client list. _____
5. Financial arrangements. _____
6. Reputation of agency in national market and ranking in size. _____

Important Factors—Rate each on a scale of 1-10.
1. Relationship of potential size of your account to other agency clients. _____
2. Ability to perform package-design services. _____

    Grand total of all factors .... _____

    Name of Advertising Agency   Date

chasing proposition across to the consumer. In these markets the major portion of the population is often illiterate and the media of choice are often cinema, loudspeaker, and occasionally radio.

Sales Promotion and Public Relations

Development of the sales promotion and public relations strategies completes the pre-sales-test marketing mix. We shall not go into too much detail on these two components of the marketing mix except to state that the extent and nature of their use in sales testing is largely dependent on the national market, type of product being tested, and whether the sales test is a regional test or a selective national market test. As an example, such consumable products as soft drinks, foods, and tobacco can benefit from a sales promotional sampling program, whereas consumer hard goods and durables might benefit from in-store demonstration, which is another sales promotional tool.

Public relations performs a valuable function in establishing product and brand awareness. In many national markets, because of the media distribution, publicity is difficult to pinpoint into a specific test region and is completely unwieldy to use when you are dealing with a sales test in specific retail outlets in different geographic areas. In most instances, we do not make much use of public relations as part of our sales-test marketing mix but instead reserve its use for market penetration after a successful product sales test.

The Sales Test

Upon completion of the marketing mix we are ready to move into the "moment of truth," which is the confirmation of market-share potential and viability of product offering through sales test, a key task in phase 4 of the marketing path.

After our development of the sales-test marketing mix, we have sufficient data to cost our product and set the retail selling prices for a sales test that reflects our profit-margin goals. In setting retail prices, we usually use this formula: cost of packaged products plus cost of advertising or point-of-sale promotion, if required, plus profit margin equals cost of goods. We then apply the discount structure that we developed when we established our distribution strategy early in phase 4 of the marketing path, and from this we get the required retail selling prices.

Our sales test can represent a sizable investment, and a budget must be established. To develop the budget, we must ascertain the magnitude of our test and the marketing-mix components required. Usually packaged product and point-of-sale display materials are necessary. Depending on the type of product, advertising is sometimes used to measure its ability to effect product sell-through.

The first step in planning a sales test is to define the objectives of the test. From the objectives a sales-test design is developed. The sales test can define such things as market-share projections, sales forecasts, product mix, pricing, product acceptance, rate of sale in different types of retail outlets, effectiveness of the marketing mix, sensitivity to advertising, effectiveness of the distribution, consumer buying habits, and, in certain national markets, the effect of geographic variations on the sales-test data base.

The objectives, the product, its mode of distribution, and the national market will indicate the scope of the test, which can be conducted either in one or more isolated market areas or in selected retail outlets throughout the entire national market.

If it is necessary to use advertising in the sales test, a test in one or more isolated marketing areas is indicated, since it is usually not practical to apply advertising throughout an entire national market. Consumables are usually tested in an isolated market sales test, since they usually require advertising, and a valid test requires the use of many retail outlets to establish market-share potential of the brand.

In many national markets, a sales test in one or two key markets is projectable and can be used for decision making in that national market. On a number of occasions, we have found it beneficial to conduct a sales test in one typical urban market and in scattered retail outlets in the interior rural markets.

Once the test market or markets are established, retail outlets are selected that reflect the retail-outlet mix anticipated if the product is introduced into the national market. This information should have been generated in phase 2 of the marketing path when consumer buying habits were analyzed.

The product is then placed in the test retail outlets and offered for sale. The rate of sale, measured in both units and dollars per store day, is compared to the rate of sale of competitive or control items. At the end of the sale-test period, which is usually a minimum of eight to 12 weeks, the units and dollars per day generated in the test are then related to the potential targeted retail outlets in the national market, and sales-volume and market-share estimates are developed.

The mechanics of the sales test are relatively simple. There are three stages:

□ Stage 1: establishing the test mix, the packaging, and any point-of-sale material required.
□ Stage 2: selecting the retail outlets, taking the store orders, procuring and packaging product, and distributing product.
□ Stage 3: monitoring the sales test (counting stock, refilling, and so on).

A sample sales-test schedule is found in Figure 6-26.

Sales Test: A Case Study

Our case study will demonstrate the use of the sales test to indicate a go or no-go decision on product introduction as found in phase 4 of the marketing path. This is the final decision point in the marketing path. We will continue the case study on Kasualware dishes that was used for our phase 3 purchase-intent test.

Our sales-test objectives are to establish the following: (1) market-share projection as reflected in pieces and dollars (our projected market share for Kasualware dishes, as generated by our purchase-intent test, was 7.4 million pieces); (2) three-year sales forecast; (3) confirmation of product acceptance and pricing; (4) effectiveness of the marketing mix; and (5) effectiveness of the distribution plan. We will use the schedule found in Figure 6-26.

The national market being evaluated has a simple one- or two-tiered system of distribution that involves sale of product directly from the manufacturer to the

Figure 6-26. Staged sales-test schedule.

July	Aug.	Sept.	Oct.	Nov.	Dec.	Jan.	Feb.	Mar.	Apr.	May

Stage 1

- Finalize test product mix
- Develop packaging point-of-sale display, etc.

Stage 2

- Procure product*
- Select retail outlets
- Obtain store orders
- Package product
- Distribute to sales test stores.

Stage 3

Monitor sales test (Count stock, refill, etc.)

A decision on how to proceed can occur anytime during the sales test depending on results.

*Product sourced from a corporate facility in another country and packaged locally for the national market.

key retailers in the ten major urban population centers and through distributors in the interior rural areas of the country.

The type of retail outlets that would sell our Kasualware dishes in this national market and their estimated percentage share of tableware retail sales are as follows (this information was established in phase 2 of the marketing path, the market segment study):

Type of Store	Estimated Share of Tableware Retail Market
1. Department stores	40%
2. China and glass shops	30
3. Mass merchandisers	20
4. Hardware stores	5
5. Miscellaneous—specialty shops	5

The retail outlets selected for the sales test will reflect this mix.

Let us assume for our case study that we already manufacture the basic Kasualware product in another national market. In order to avoid the expense of creating a pilot production operation, we will surface-decorate the product suitably for this national market and import sufficient quantity of product for the sales test. The product will be packaged locally, with graphics and language appropriate for this market. The basic package will consist of a 30-piece set consisting of six 5-piece place settings. Due to import restrictior., we can market only 7,000 sets of 30 pieces.

Experience in similar markets indicates that sales of one or more 30-piece sets per store day are required to justify manufacturing facilities. In order to get reliable test results, it is necessary to conduct the sales test for at least 90 store days. Given product availability, we will use 40 test stores. In order to get projectable results, we will break down the type of stores used for the test to reflect our estimate of market share by type of store. The retail selling price will be $25 per set.

The test-store mix is as follows:

Number	Type of Store	Estimated Share
16	Department stores	40%
12	China and glass shops	30
8	Mass merchandisers	20
2	Hardware stores	5
2	Miscellaneous—specialty	5

Each participating sales-test store will be stocked with an initial inventory totaling 72 of the 30-piece sets (24 sets each of three different decorative patterns). Stores will be restocked as necessary.

We will test in the major urban marketing area, which is located in the eastern part of the country, and in two rural areas in the northeast and the south. The breakdown by type of sales-test store, region of the country, and percentage of national income in that region is as follows:

1. Urban Marketing Area—Eastern Region—30% of National Income

Number of Stores	Type of Store
10	Department stores
7	China and glass shops
2	Mass merchandisers
0	Hardware stores
0	Miscellaneous—specialty
19	

2. Rural Marketing Area—Northeast Region—9% of National Income

2	Department stores
2	China and glass shops
3	Mass merchandisers
1	Hardware stores
1	Miscellaneous—specialty
9	

3. Rural Marketing Area—South—14%of National Income

4	Department stores
3	China and glass shops
3	Mass merchandisers
1	Hardware stores
1	Miscellaneous—specialty
12	

Total: 40 stores

Each sales-test store will be checked once a week, and the stock counted. Sales will be tracked as to units and dollars generated per selling day.

Analysis of the sales-test results. The pertinent information gained from the test is as follows:

▪ Average units sold per day was 1.97 of the 30-piece sets (59.1 pieces), worth $49.30 in retail dollars.

▪ The 40 sales-test stores generated sales of 6,950 of the 30-piece sets, or a total of 208,500 pieces, worth $173,750 at retail in a three-month selling period. We convert the sets into pieces, since this is the unit that is meaningful when evaluating production capacity.

▪ Total units sold by type of store during the test period and average rate of sale per store day are as follows:

Department stores	52.4%	2.53 sets × 30 = 75.9 pieces
China and glass shops	27.1%	1.87 sets × 30 = 56.1 pieces
Mass merchandisers	15.5%	1.50 sets × 30 = 45.0 pieces
Hardware stores	2.5%	0.95 sets × 30 = 28.5 pieces
Specialty shops	2.5%	0.95 sets × 30 = 28.5 pieces

- Popularity of decorations sold is as follows:

Decoration A	49.8% of the mix
Decoration B	39.7% of the mix
Decoration C	10.5% of the mix

- From in-store observation and customer interviews, it was determined that the packaging and displays seemed effective in promoting the product at point of sale.
- Interviews with the salespeople in the test stores indicated good reception to our product even where the customer did not immediately buy our product.
- In most instances, we were unable to get sales data on competitive products to use as a control. In the few instances where we were able to get these data, Kasualware sales were two and three times greater than competitive brands.

Using our knowledge of the national market that was gained during the activities in the earlier phases of the marketing path, our analysis of the sales data indicates that historically, a 1.97-set average (59.1 pieces) rate of sale is considered very good. From our experience in other national markets, this rate of sale indicates high-volume demand for the product.

Volume projections can be made two ways: (1) the direct projection using average rate of sale, and (2) a projection by specific type of retail outlet. Sales volume of 208,500 pieces in the 40 different types of retail outlets in the three-month test period indicates that, with no seasonal fluctuation of demand, these 40 stores should generate yearly sales of about 803,760 pieces (1.97 times 30 pieces equals 59.1 pieces, times 40 stores equals 2,364 pieces per store day, times 340 store days equals 803,760 pieces per year). If we have 400 retail outlets reflecting the mix of our sales-test stores, we should achieve a yearly volume of 8,037,600 pieces of Kasualware.

Our retail analysis for this national market, performed earlier in the marketing path, indicates that there are 250 department stores, 225 china and glass stores, 150 mass merchandisers, 200 specialty shops, and 200 hardware stores with housewares departments.

Our first-year volume projection, based on the retail penetration our sales department estimates and the sales-test estimate of rate of sale by pieces in the different types of retail outlets, is as follows:

Type of Store	Sales-Test Rate of Sales (pcs. per store day)		Store Days		Total per Store		Quantity of Stores		Total pieces per Year
Department stores	75.9	×	340	=	25,806	×	164	=	4,232,184
China and glass shops	56.1	×	340	=	19,074	×	114	=	2,174,436
Mass merchandisers	45.0	×	340	=	15,300	×	82	=	1,254,600
Specialty stores	28.5	×	340	=	9,690	×	50	=	484,500
Hardware stores	28.5	×	340	=	9,690	×	50	=	484,500
Kasualware volume projection—total pieces								=	8,630,220

Our first-year volume or base projection for Kasualware, as generated by the purchase-intent test and the sales test, is a range from a low of 7 million pieces worth $5.8 million (at a retail value of $0.83 each piece) to a high of 9 million pieces worth $7.5 million, with a probable estimate of 8 million pieces worth $6.6 million.

Using a base of 8 million pieces and the country's inflation-rate projection of 12 percent a year, we project the following five-year volume:

Estimated Growth Rate*

Base	1980	8.0 million pieces at $0.83 per piece = $ 6.6 million
20%	1981	9.6 million pieces at $0.93 per piece = $ 8.9 million
20%	1982	11.5 million pieces at $1.04 per piece = $12.0 million
25%	1983	14.4 million pieces at $1.16 per piece = $16.7 million
30%	1984	18.7 million pieces at $1.30 per piece = $24.3 million

This volume projection is enough to support a production facility in this national market.

When we analyze the units sold by type of retail outlet, we find some variations over what we originally believed to be market share by retail outlets of tableware presently being sold in this national market.

Type of Store	Market-Share Projection	Sales-Test Market Share
Department stores	40%	52.4%
China and glass shops	30	27.1
Mass merchandisers	20	15.5
Hardware stores	5	2.5
Specialty shops	5	2.5

We judge the only significant variation to be the high market share achieved in department stores with Kasualware over conventional tableware (52.4 percent versus 40 percent). This indicates to us that Kasualware is extremely well received in the department store and generates high-volume sales. The higher-than-normal performance could also indicate a very high market-share potential for Kasualware dishes over competitive tableware. This situation could be explained by the relatively good product-display opportunities found in department stores. We feel that the variations in china and glass shops and mass merchandisers are minor and not significant. The variations in hardware stores and specialty shops are probably a result of the small sampling.

We will use this market-share information by type of retail outlet as generated in our sales test when we plan our strategy in our finalized marketing plan.

Kasualware dishes were sales-tested in three decorative patterns, which were identified as A, B, and C. Test results indicated good consumer acceptance of

* Growth rate reflects increased distribution, market growth, and market share.

pattern A (49.8 percent of mix sold) and pattern B (39.7 percent of mix sold); pattern C reflected only 10.5 percent of the mix sold. It would appear that pattern C should be replaced by a more acceptable decoration when the product line is introduced into the market.

Judging from the results of the sales test, packaging and point-of-sale display functioned very well and required no revisions for product introduction.

We have reached the final go/no-go decision point in phase 4 of the marketing path. This final marketing decision is perhaps the most crucial, because it involves the decision on whether or not to proceed with product introduction into the national market and selection of the product sourcing option. These options can include: (1) building a production facility; (2) importing finished product and distributing it; (3) importing product components, assembling the product, and packaging locally; and (4) licensing a local manufacturer to produce the product and pay a royalty.

Sometimes our strategy uses combinations of these options, such as starting with the importation of the product and, when the volume is sufficient, building a production facility. The ability to use this option depends on local import regulations. In many countries there are protective tariffs that ban the importation of certain types of products. The ability to get this type of restrictive control imposed can be very helpful when you are producing locally and want to protect your investment by keeping competition out of the market.

The volume projection generated by your sales test will indicate the best sourcing option.

The Appropriation Request

All through the marketing path, we have been making profitability estimates, based on the information available at critical points, that have justified our development expenditures. We are now ready to present our top corporate management with our final profitability analysis, which will be presented in the form of an appropriation request. This request will represent our total commitment in assets and other corporate resources needed to enter the national market.

The appropriation request should include such information as capital expenditure, manufacturing costs, pricing structure, profit margins, anticipated volume, selling expense, return on assets or return on investment, strategy to expatriate profits, and analysis of risks, both political and economic. This important element of the marketing plan should include the timetable, human-resource requirements, and any other inputs that the company deems necessary.

Let us assume that we have made the decision to make the commitment to enter the national market. We complete phase 4 of the marketing path by using the inputs from our sales test to finalize our product and marketing mix and plan for product introduction.

Phase 5: Sales and Distribution

We now move into phase 5 (see Figure 6-27), which is the final segment of the marketing path. Phase 5 involves sales and distribution. Our objectives are to

Figure 6-27. Phase 5 of the marketing path: sales and distribution.

Objective: Product introduction and full distribution

Tasks: a. Create and satisfy consumer demand
b. Position product at point of sale in marketplace

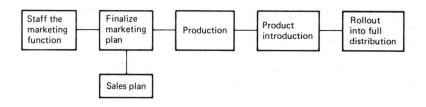

achieve product introduction and full distribution. Our tasks are to create and satisfy consumer demand and to position our product at point of sale in the marketplace.

Staffing the Marketing Function

As we enter phase 5, we are ready to staff the marketing function. Following through with our case study on Kasualware dishes, our marketing staff will consist of a director of marketing, who will have reporting to him a product manager (to coordinate all marketing activities), a manager of marketing services (to be responsible for packaging, advertising, sales promotion, and public relations), and a sales manager (to be responsible for the sales force).

The director of marketing will report directly to the general manager of the subsidiary corporation. We have elected to sell through distributors, with the distributor's salespeople making the retail calls and keeping the product in stock at point of sale. Our sales force will be limited to four salespeople. This is deemed sufficient to cover the 15 key distributors who service department stores, china and glass shops, mass merchandisers, hardware stores, and specialty shops in the national market. The salespeople will be positioned physically in the four major market regions and will be responsible for product sales in those regions.

The director of marketing will be an expatriate from the parent company. The rest of the marketing staff will be local nationals.

The Subsidiary Company

Our subsidiary company has been set up as a joint venture, with our multinational company owning 49 percent of the stock, a prominent industrial family (natives of the country in which we will operate) owning 49 percent of the stock, and a local bank holding the 2 percent balance of the stock. This type of ownership structure gives each of the principal partners equal participation on the board of directors, with the bank acting as a neutral party with enough votes to resolve any deadlocked issues.

Our parent company has management control over the subsidiary. This is an ideal situation in a joint venture, since it is always important to control the aspects of a business that make it a success or a failure. Our contribution to the business is basically marketing know-how and technology. Our local partner will furnish the financial capital and the government contacts needed to operate in the country. The ability to gain management control of a subsidiary company depends on local government regulations. In general, emerging nations that want to attract foreign investment and technology usually permit management control, since this makes investment attractive. More developed countries, for which foreign investment is not as important, often afford themselves the luxury of being nationalistic enough not to permit management control by a foreign company.

Policies of this type can be relaxed if the country vitally needs a specific technology and the only way it can get it is by giving a foreign company management control in a joint venture.

Product Introduction and Rollout

The newly established local marketing team will finalize the marketing plan for its national market. The sales plan should reflect the distribution strategy that was successfully sales-tested. Sales effort should be concentrated so as to attain the same volume of sales by channel of distribution as was achieved in the sales test.

After the product has been manufactured, the marketing team should plan for product introduction and national rollout. This final activity in the marketing path uses all the elements of the marketing mix, including national advertising. An audacious marketing team using imagination can achieve high-velocity market penetration that will quickly fill pipelines and bring product to point of sale in most of the targeted retail outlets.   □ *David J. Freiman*

MEASURING THE PERFORMANCE OF MARKETING OPERATIONS

It has been wisely said that all performance can be measured. To be able to measure, one must establish standards. As the performance of various marketing operations is examined, it is apparent that the elements are now more numerous and complex than formerly and that measurement therefore may not be as simple as it once was.

Objectives and the Company

Knowledge of performance is insufficient. For such knowledge to be truly meaningful, there must be comparisons on an equitable basis. To measure objective against actual performance is often a very effective comparison and an acceptable measurement.

All the people interested in a company, whether they are shareholders, officers, directors, or employees, look at the company's sales, net profits, growth,

ROI, book value of stock, and perhaps other financial yardsticks, usually in comparison with those of competitors.

It is necessary to establish objectives by which the degree of goal attainment can be measured. There was a time when financial status or credit rating was considered a sufficient standard in grading a company's marketing effectiveness. Another type of yardstick is the operating statement; this is helpful in measuring overall progress but not necessarily good per se for measuring the performance of marketing operations. Under today's conditions it requires more than financial status or overall progress to properly measure; the standards used must be of a concrete nature, easily measured.

The basic foundation of a marketing program is a long-range objective; it is a road map to where the company wants to go. The word "objective" is sometimes defined as "something aimed at" or "something striven for." Other versions are "a broad aim" or "a desired end." All these definitions are loose and general. Most companies have objectives of some kind, even if only stated as "to increase sales." To be useful, specific goals should be the targets: for example, improving share of market, introducing new products successfully, selling the whole line rather than items, improving product mix, or increasing profits. Without appropriate objectives there is almost certain to be considerable wasted effort in sales, which in turn tends to create waste in other areas and departments of the business.

To set a forecast, objective, goal, or quota requires much more than mathematical computations; above all, it requires intelligent and intuitive judgment. A forecast is a company's best estimate of what will happen. An objective is the optimum performance to be expected. A budget is the forecast for a year ahead. A goal may be either a forecast or an objective. A quota is generally used in connection with sales and is the same as a goal.

Most business firms, whether manufacturing, wholesale, retail, or service organizations, operate against a sales objective, to which the profit expectation is tied. Occasionally, a business has objectives other than short-term profits; for example, investment in research or market penetration for a new product. Either of these will tend to lower profits currently and for the immediate future.

Objectives and Marketing

One of marketing's many facets is advertising—and an important one it is. The effects of advertising are often very difficult to measure. Because many companies spend vast sums in advertising, and because the cost of advertising is now almost triple what it was a decade or so ago, it is important to differentiate advertising from other marketing costs. Unless the advertising campaign has specific measurable tasks to perform, there will be no knowing what was responsible for the results, good or bad: the advertising itself, the new packaging, better selling, the weather, or general economic conditions.

For many years there has been a historical relationship between advertising expenditures and sales, and between advertising expenditures and total dollar expenditures. These factors, along with projected sales volume, can be used in evaluating advertising and will be determined in differences in the reach and frequency of the advertising campaign. Advertising can also be evaluated in terms of total impact on profits.

Because marketing policies and strategies vary so greatly in industries and even in companies within an industry, no average or norm can be formulated for objectives. Company management must determine the objectives that will best suit its purpose in reaching the goals it wishes to attain.

Standards of Performance

The most usual standard is historical—last year's sales compared with this year's. The value of this comparison may be slight; it may also be misleading. If the percentage of increase in sales over a very bad year is high, the actual accomplishment may be minor if compared with an average year. However, it is better than no comparison. Standards set by engineers usually say what performance should be; marketing standards are usually set up against the performance of competition, perhaps also against industry ratios.

Profit

There are several factors that can affect profits, which makes the setting of standards more difficult. In almost any business the fluctuation of volume has strong impact. Usually, a strong increase in volume materially improves profits, since the greater part of the gross profit on the extra sales becomes net (most expenses have already been taken care of). If the pendulum swings the other way and there is a big drop in sales, profits fall off rapidly because the lowered volume cannot take care of the overhead.

Product mix often has a surprising effect on profits. If, normally, the product mix is 70 percent high-profit items and 30 percent low-profit items, the average profit might look like this:

> Volume $60,000
> 70 percent or $42,000 at 30 percent gross profit = $12,600
> 30 percent or $18,000 at 15 percent gross profit =   2,700
> $15,300
> $15,300 ÷ $60,000 = 25.5 percent average gross profit

Should the product mix change to 40 percent high-profit items and 60 percent low-profit items, the picture would change materially:

> Volume $60,000
> 40 percent or $24,000 at 30 percent gross profit = $ 7,200
> 60 percent or $36,000 at 15 percent gross profit =   5,400
> $12,600
> $12,600 ÷ $60,000 = 21 percent average gross profit

Obviously, unusual or increased expenses will adversely affect profits. A decrease in expenditures would add to profits, but this would be a rare occurrence for most business establishments. Profits can be nullified—or at least drastically reduced—by unnecessary expenses in branch offices, warehouses, or personnel.

A good profit ratio, although slightly smaller than in the previous year, on a high volume may divert attention from an existing profit lag. Perhaps on the high volume, profits should have gone up in greater proportion than sales.

For a standard of profit performance, some marketing people look with favor on the advertising cost to earnings (A/E) ratio. This relationship can be varied in the extreme, and it is hardly possible that there is a usable industry average. The A/E ratio has been known to run as high as $16.50 to $1.00, in the case of a manufacturer striving to establish a stable of new products. Infrequently, the ratio might drop down to $0.50 to $1.00. There are many people who prefer to pin their faith on net profit as a percentage of sales as an acceptable yardstick.

Cost

Surely cost can be labeled a standard of performance. Certain costs are uncontrollable, such as taxes and insurance. There remain, however, a number of expenses that are controllable in greater or lesser degree. Total costs on an operating statement are too general to be of much value. What is needed is a careful comparison, item by item, with the industry operating ratio. Public statements rarely have an item breakdown that provides the detail necessary for such comparisons. In the case of competitors who issue public statements, a fair comparison can be gained on gross profit as a percentage of sales and on net profit as a percentage of sales. The general statement can be more useful if a five- or ten-year table shows the dollar expense year by year for each item and if the same chart shows the same items year by year expressed as a percentage of sales.

Sales

Historically, the tendency has been to compare this year's net sales with last year's; if there is an increase, progress has been made. But sales as they are shown on operating statements may fail to portray the true situation. Many a company complacently looks at its sales and profits picture and accepts it at face value; but many times, when sales are broken down by territory, product, or some other category, glaring weaknesses come to light. The historical-relationship method of comparison can entirely cover up losses in the share of the market even though an increase in sales has been achieved. A far better standard to use is the potential of sales territories by some market index, such as population, buying power, per-capita income, total retail sales, or income per family.

Sales Management's annual *Survey of Buying Power* is a respected and widely used source in setting up market potential by territory, district, state, or region. The only difficulty experienced with the buying-power index occurs when the salesman's territory crosses county lines, but this too can be computed. With the buying-power index the optimum sales potential is determined, and performance can be easily and readily measured against it.

The traditional method of giving salespeople a percentage increase in quota over the previous year's sales is probably not nearly so fair a goal as the one based on potential. Territories have a way of varying from year to year. Too, a 10 percent increase per year for ten years may be unattainable.

Aside from the aforementioned *Survey of Buying Power,* information that can help in setting standards and also in measuring performance is available from government and trade sources.

One statistic, often not given the attention it deserves, is the individual salesperson's merchandise returns expressed as a percentage of sales. The problem may not always be with the salesman; sometimes a little research shows that the trouble is in distribution or production. Though returns can be a standard of performance, they should not be applied as such until a little checking is done.

Market Share

Marketing people set great store by the share of the market their product enjoys; this is, to them, a reliable standard of performance. The percentage share of a market a firm might enjoy on a given product has ranged as high as 80 percent, but currently not too many reach or hold that exalted position. The proliferation of high-consumption products, plus the "coattail riders," has long since reduced maximums by a greater split of the spoils.

One factor concerning share of the market that may be overlooked is that sales may show an increase while the share of the market has declined. A nice sales increase should not encourage the marketer until he has a knowledge of the facts.

Competition, both in products and in their promotion, is so fierce and so sustained that many changes have occurred among the leaders. For this reason some astute marketing people have preferred market segmentation to the general battle. Unfortunately, once their success is known, competition singles them out, and they are soon back in the battle.

Outside of the high-consumption, nationally advertised brands, the competition is less fierce, and a sizable share of the market is not so difficult to attain. In any case it is easier than formerly to get accurate figures, nationally or by region, on where a product stands. Firms offer their services in measuring the share of the market, the ranking of products, the evaluation of advertising, and the like.

There are also firms that, for a fee, furnish information on brand preferences, and some firms that will make periodic store inventories to tell the marketer the movement of his product in comparison with competitive items. If desired, panels of housewives will give their opinions about products, packages, and other factors. Other firms can provide product sales and distribution analyses. Occasionally, newspapers provide helpful brand surveys within their coverage areas.

Budgets

From a nonaccounting point of view, a properly prepared budget is a blueprint that guides management as management strives to reach its objective. Since practically all businesses necessarily estimate the various parts of the budget, the total budget cannot be as accurate as an architect's meticulously drawn blueprint. And because practically no entry in a budget can be considered "actual," a great deal of reliance must be put on what has transpired before. Amazingly, budgets and actual results are often close together, particularly when management is long experienced in using budgets to guide its operations.

Normally, the budget begins with the sales forecast for the ensuing fiscal year. The budget then evolves as expenses for the various departments and subdivisions are put in place. Finally, of course, an estimate is made on net profit.

The operating statement, which should be issued on a monthly basis, provides the picture of what has actually happened. When compared with the budget, which also should be broken down into months on the basis of past history, the statement quickly shows how closely actual and estimate are to each other; it readily reveals strengths and weaknesses and shows where improvement needs to be made.

For the manufacturer and perhaps for the retailer too, the most difficult element of a budget to gauge is consumer demand; here again, however, history may be helpful in developing an accurate estimate.

Budgets can be subdivided into as great detail as desired. In some businesses— especially in the manufacture of many products in different categories—the greater the breakdown of the budget, the greater the ease of measuring the effectiveness of operations.

Industry Operating Ratios

For nearly every separate type of industry in the United States, there is an association that brings its members together periodically; generally, it also provides its members with overall operating ratios of the industry that offer excellent yardsticks to measure a company's effectiveness.

The National Wholesale Druggists Association, for example, annually provides vides its members with a complete list of operating ratios on a national, regional, and sometimes state basis. The figures are highly respected, since 98 or 99 percent of the members regularly turn in their figures. The NWDA operating ratios have a historical background of many years, which increases their value as measuring devices. A great many other associations focus their members' attention on similar information at their annual conferences.

For a number of years Dun & Bradstreet has periodically issued a valuable chart of operating ratios for a sizable list of varied industries. In some industries that are government-regulated, such as the liquor industry, statistics on shipments by brand, and even by size, are easily obtainable. In such industries there is no lack of knowledge about share of the market or marketing effectiveness.

Among the operating ratios that interest top management are the following: (1) current ratio, (2) ratio of inventory to net working capital, (3) ratio of net sales to net working capital, (4) ratio of current liabilities to net worth, (5) ratio of total liabilities to net worth, (6) ratio of net sales to net worth, (7) ratio of net profit to net worth, and (8) ratio of net profit to net sales.

Obviously, when current ratios are used, the operating statement is used. It is safe to say that an accurate, detailed operating statement provides the information for current ratios of all kinds and affords the basis for many forms of comparison and measurement.

Use of Planned-Performance Data

As an additional source of measurement standards, planned-performance data can be very helpful. Usually, such data are objectives or goals of a very specific nature as opposed to the normal broad, general aspects. An objective of a company might be to increase sales, while its planned performance would be a 10 percent sales increase the coming year. Planned performances are specific as to time and place, within the overall objectives.

While the operating statement and much other available information are valuable for measuring effectiveness, planned-performance data can greatly assist by pinpointing specifics that, as yardsticks, can help answer questions of what was accomplished and whether it was profitable.

Goals

Typical planned performances are built around product mix, sales, profit, cost, or other goals in achieving marketing objectives.

Product mix. A company desiring to increase profits might devise a plan to achieve its goal by doubling sales of its most profitable product.

Sales. A sales goal for another company might be to reach 5 percent of the buying-power index in its southeastern district. Another goal might be to achieve sales of one package of a new product to 60 percent of the families within a given area.

Profit. Part of an overall plan could be a goal of a 2 percent increase in gross profit in the territories in the mountain and Pacific districts during the current fiscal year.

Cost. One worthy cost goal would be a reduction in advertising costs in relation to sales in certain selected districts where advertising costs have exceeded the company average.

Other goals. The examples cited previously are but a few of the many specifics that may be exploited for the company's benefit. Some further suggestions are the following: (1) profit contribution by products, (2) sales to certain outlets, (3) sales to specified age groups, (4) percentage goal of a share of the market, and (5) greater distribution in certain territories.

Benefits

As costs continue to rise, with no relief in sight, while profits are being squeezed by a variety of causes, planned performance can offer a partial remedy for some of industry's problems. By a careful selection of specific programs based on the individual needs of a particular business, the marketing operation can become more effective, thereby making a concrete contribution to profits. At the same time it may make an appreciable contribution toward an improved share of the market. Planned performance therefore increases in value as business conditions grow more difficult.   □ *Fred M. Truett*

Index

Italicized names indicate contributors.